ONE GAME AT A TIME

Praise for ONE GAME AT A TIME

"*One Game at a Time* is a work that should be read by everybody, not just those in the hockey world. Harnarayan takes the reader on a journey across the globe and back in time, relating his experiences of balancing his own faith and culture with Canada's favourite sport. His work ethic and commitment to be an amazing broadcaster, as well as a strong advocate for social and racial equality is truly inspiring. I'm so happy for all of his success and I urge everyone to read and learn from his story, as I have."

—Nick Bonino, NHL player

"Harnarayan has to be one of the hardest working people I know. He was given an opportunity and didn't only just take advantage of that opportunity, but he crushed it out of the park. He will always be someone I value not only as a hockey broadcaster, but as a person. I have known him a long time, well before he became this amazing broadcaster, and he is just as humble and genuine today as he was the day I first met him."

—Cassie Campbell-Pascall,
Olympian and hockey broadcaster

"Give Harnarayan Singh the Masterton. His is a story of perseverance and dedication to hockey—a small-town kid from Brooks, Alberta who wouldn't say no to any of the obstacles in his path."

—Eric Duhatschek, senior writer, The Athletic

"Being a trailblazer is never easy but with steadfast perseverance, Harnarayan Singh overcame challenges most people would have found insurmountable. Harnarayan is a true Canadian success story."

—Kelly Hrudey, analyst, *Hockey Night in Canada*
and Sportsnet, and author of *Calling the Shots*

"Whenever I hear Harnarayan call hockey I think to myself, 'He's singing the game.' It's exciting, lyrical, and beautiful. His story is one of dreams, passion, sacrifice, and dedication; his lesson is about unity and respect—all while creating a new language for hockey."

—Jeff Marek, NHL host on Sportsnet and *32 Thoughts*

"Come for the story of what Harnarayan Singh says to people who tell him to 'go back where he came from'; stay for BoninoBonino-Bonino and the hard-working kid from 'the only Sikh family in Brooks' living out his dreams on *Hockey Night in Canada*."

**—Bob McKenzie, TSN Hockey Insider
and author of *Hockey Confidential***

"*One Game at a Time* is the hockey story that Canada needs right now. Singh offers us a unique narrative, but one that is also extremely recognizable to those of us who have never quite fit into the commonly told stories about hockey in Canada. It is a beautiful story about determination and resilience in the face of discrimination, while also highlighting the power that allies have in creating space for new people and diverse perspectives."

**—Dr. Courtney Szto, Assistant Professor, School of
Kinesiology and Health Studies, Queen's University**

"Reading *One Game at a Time* was powerfully nostalgic as it reminded me of the power of hockey to connect. Harnarayan's words transported me into his living room with his family to watch *Hockey Night in Canada*; it was on nights just like those, between periods, that I would lace up and jump on our backyard rink to take shots on our net. Meanwhile, on those very same evenings, a young Harnarayan was perfecting his craft practicing goal calls, in a small town hundreds of kilometres away. Hockey unites us and I appreciate Harnarayan's remarkable ability to draw us into his gratitude for the game throughout this career, because I too know that gratitude."

**—Hayley Wickenheiser, 4-time
Olympic Gold Medalist**

"So many people told Harnarayan that his dream to be a hockey commentator was 'impossible.' The fact that he is now living his dream speaks to the opportunities and values that define our country. What a story!"

—Brian Williams, Olympic Broadcaster and O.C.

HARNARAYAN SINGH

WITH MICHAEL HINGSTON

ONE GAME AT A TIME

MY JOURNEY FROM A SMALL TOWN TO HOCKEY'S BIGGEST STAGE

McClelland & Stewart

Distributed by Penguin Random House Canada Limited, Toronto.

LIBRARY AND ARCHIVES CANADA CATALOGUING IN PUBLICATION
Title: One game at a time : my journey from small-town Alberta
to hockey's biggest stage / Harnarayan Singh.
Names: Singh, Harnarayan, author.
Identifiers: Canadiana 20200189506 | ISBN 9780771073915 (softcover)
Subjects: LCSH: Singh, Harnarayan. | LCSH: Sportscasters—Canada—
Biography. | CSH: Sikh Canadians—Biography | LCGFT: Autobiographies.
Classification: LCC GV742.42.S56 A3 2021 | DDC 070.4/49796092—dc23

Cover and book design: Andrew Roberts
Cover images: Courtesy of the author

Printed in the United States of America

McClelland & Stewart,
a division of Penguin Random House Canada Limited,
a Penguin Random House Company

www.penguinrandomhouse.ca

1 2 3 4 5   26 25 24 23 22

Penguin
Random House
McCLELLAND & STEWART

To Mom and Dad,
Surjit Kaur and Santokh Singh

Contents

Foreword
Ron MacLean

"Wherever you have friends, that's your country, and wherever you receive love, that's your home."   —Tibetan adage

During a day off while on assignment at the Calgary Stampede, I went to Harnarayan's home to enjoy a spectacular home-cooked meal. The love I received immediately made his home my own. And the thing about that home is how consistently it migrates into other areas of my life. When I am around Calgary for *Roger's Hometown Hockey* or to host *Hockey Night in Canada*, without fail, Harnarayan will send an invitation for me to swing by the house. And when that's not possible, his mom, Surjit Kaur, and dad, Santokh Singh, and the entire family will come to where I am working with *parshaadh*, a sweet pudding. As you'll discover within these pages, the idea of a Golden Temple—with nourishment for all—resides in the Singh family. It travels within Harnarayan like an iconic letter carrier for whom rain, snow, heat, or the gloom of night is no deterrent.

Harnarayan's journey to practise his faith, his hobbies, and especially his craft, are legend. With this book, you will read about him travelling across the country, paying for and arranging his own travel and sleeping on airport benches, all in the name of his goal: to broadcast NHL games. Is it any wonder he can describe a goal with such passion?

Harnarayan's boyhood love of hockey reminds me of my own love for the game. When I was a kid, we owned two televisions—a 19-inch colour TV and a 12-inch black-and-white one. In North America, it was not until the early 1970s that colour television outsold black-and-white or monochrome TVs. This became a factor in the way I followed my favourite NHL team, the Toronto Maple Leafs. In our home, the rule was, if I watched the Leafs on the colour set, they would lose, but if I viewed their game in black and white, they would win. (Now, you are likely thinking we had better bring back black-and-white television, for the sake of Leafs Nation.) It's crazy to look back on it now and realize that within a decade I would be broadcasting the Maple Leafs games.

Similarly, in Harnarayan's case, he worshipped Wayne Gretzky, and when it became apparent that the younger Mario Lemieux might supersede Gretzky as the NHL's best player, Harnarayan hatched a plan. He went to his hockey card binder and put all his Gretzky cards in the first pages, followed by any Edmonton Oilers players. Then he filled the book with the remaining NHL teams, and at the very back of the binder, he added the Pittsburgh Penguins and Super Mario. Fast forward a few years and that same Mario Lemieux and the Penguins would invite Harnarayan and his *Hockey Night in Punjabi* colleagues to lead a Stanley Cup parade. Harnarayan became a cult hero in Pittsburgh for his iconic description of a critical Stanley Cup playoff goal by the Penguins' Nick Bonino: "Bonino Bonino Bonino Bonino . . ." I couldn't help but wonder if Harnarayan was just struggling to spit out the name of one of those dreaded Penguins. That goal call may have brought Harnarayan some recognition, but it's just a part of his incredible story that he'll be remembered for.

As you'll read, for as dear a friend as Harnarayan is to me, I have also contributed to a painful chapter in his life. It had to do with ideologies: the road to multiculturalism, diversity, pluralism, inclusion. Harnarayan was the best kind of friend when he spoke to me about an error I had made on *Hockey Night in Canada*. He spoke from his heart, to the best interests of my heart. I had made a mistake. But from the wreckage came an awakening. Mistakes, like disasters, provide a window through which gifts often arrive. Harnarayan's wisdom is a gift. As the Aga Khan once wrote, what we have is not a clash of civilizations but a clash of ignorance on both sides. The pursuit of common ground is a recurring theme in this book.

Harnarayan has risked so much for what must have seemed a purely abstract goal. His daring, imaginative, even idealistic pursuit of hockey broadcasting as a bridge to the caretaking of human history conjures in me a powerful nostalgia for the dreams I had when I was starting out.

I am often asked the hypothetical question, "If you had one wish, what would it be?" I always answer, "I'd eliminate envy." It's a naive notion, of course, but it's aspirational and it makes me think of Harnarayan Singh. I feel blessed to collaborate with his talent, but more than this, I feel grateful for Harnarayan's example. His refusal to allow the appraisals of others to determine the role he saw for himself is a story in which hope is deeply rooted.

I envy that. I also know there is an antidote to this envy. This book. There is freedom and power and, most importantly, healing in these pages. I just need to take these lessons and apply them going forward, one game at a time.

Introduction
Boninoboninobonino

Here I am, standing in the middle of downtown Pittsburgh, and I can't believe my eyes. It's Wednesday, June 15, 2016, and 400,000 ecstatic hockey fans have shown up in the hot Pennsylvania sun to be a part of the Pittsburgh Penguins' Stanley Cup parade. The team, led by captain Sidney Crosby, has just beaten the San Jose Sharks in six games to win hockey's holy grail, considered one of the hardest championships to attain in all of sports. Even though the Penguins had previously won a cup with Crosby in 2009, expectations for the team had always been sky high. With the parity in the game these days, there was never any guarantee that Pittsburgh would win another championship. After a long, 82-game regular season, and four gruelling rounds of the playoffs, the Penguins' players, management, ownership, and team staff had celebrated their victory on the ice and in the dressing room. But the parade is so special, especially for the fans. They spend their hard-earned money, time, and, in some cases, their entire lives cheering for their favourite team. For them, the parade is the pinnacle.

The main stage for the celebration is in the middle of an intersection that's been blocked off, and the streets are flooded with people in every direction possible. Everyone is decked out in Penguins memorabilia—some guys even brought their lucky couch with them! The buildings along the streets are just as packed, with people watching from the windows of nearby office towers and sitting atop the walls of parkades, waiting to get a glimpse of their favourite players. Picture a huge outdoor Christmas festival that goes on for miles, but multiply it by a thousand, and, of course, with the dominant colours being gold and black.

As the buzz in the crowd grows, I'm standing on the side of the stage, alongside some of my colleagues from *Hockey Night in Canada: Punjabi Edition*. We're surrounded by security, but they're in a great mood, too. There is this amazing, positive, extremely happy vibe in the air. Every single person, no matter where you look, just has the biggest smile on his or her face. There are people everywhere—and as it turns out, many, shockingly, are there to see us. No joke. No exaggeration. Literally every couple of seconds, fans are coming up to us and shaking our hands, saying, "We love you guys. Can we get a picture?" I can't count how many selfies get taken. We have no clue what's in store for us.

Suddenly, everyone surrounding us bursts into cheers, and we see the Penguins players start arriving near the stage, standing on the beds of the trucks, with one truck carrying the Stanley Cup itself. The iconic trophy looks absolutely beautiful, gleaming in the sunlight. One by one, the players are announced and they come up onto the stage. And as soon as that's done, guess what happens? The local Penguins television play-by-play voice, Paul Steigerwald, who's emceeing the parade, goes up to the microphone and says, "I want to know if anyone can say 'Bonino Bonino Bonino Bonino' about five times really fast." He's referring to a goal call I made on a *Hockey Night in Punjabi* broadcast two weeks earlier, for Nick Bonino's game-winning goal, late in the third period, of game one of the Stanley Cup Final. My enthusiastic goal call, where I rapidly said Bonino's name, over and over again, had grabbed the attention of the entire hockey world. But I hadn't expected this.

From the stage, the emcee gets the entire crowd to yell the goal call back to him, and they do. "That's pretty good," he says. "But I'm going to bring up the guy who actually said that. He came all the way from Vancouver to be here for this event today." Just like that, my colleagues and I walk out onto the stage, and I go to take the mic. Of course, everyone wants to hear the call live. So, I take a deep breath. And: "*Boninoboninoboninoboninoboninoboninoboninobonino—Nick Boninooooooo!*"

The crowd erupts. Hundreds of thousands of people cheering . . . the sound is unbelievable.

Then I just say thank you and express how much it means for us to be part of the city's Cup run. I thank the team, the crowd, and the entire city of Pittsburgh. All four of us wave to the people gathered on the street and up in the buildings. We know the parade is really about the guys who won, but this is our special moment. Can a broadcaster ever get closer to being a part of a Stanley Cup run? The rest of the players love it, too. The Penguins goalie, Marc-Andre Fleury, is shaking our hands and enjoying the spotlight with us.

What's really crazy is, even as we were being brought to the stage, we saw so many signs referencing the Bonino goal call. A few even said, "I ♥ HOCKEY NIGHT PUNJABI." These people didn't even know we were going to be there!

So this entire time, as hundreds of thousands of strangers are yelling my goal call, and as they start cheering for me and my colleagues, I can't quite believe any of this is real. After all, we're a group of Punjabi broadcasters who work on a show thousands of miles away in Canada—our broadcasts aren't even in a language that most of the people here can understand. Plus, at heart I'm still a kid from small-town Alberta. When I was young, nobody who looked like me would ever be seen at an event like this in North America—especially in the hockey world. But now, the crowd in Pittsburgh is cheering for us as loudly as they did for Sidney Crosby, Evgeni Malkin, and the rest of the Penguins.

I'm standing there on the stage, thinking about all of this. Mostly, though, I'm thinking: *How the hell did I get here?*

Chapter 1
Lentils and Teachers Wanted

As a Sikh Canadian, I sometimes meet people who are less than receptive to my faith and culture. Sometimes those people will even say things like: "Go back to your own country!"

If only they knew the full story.

My great-grandfather, Chanda Singh, came to Canada more than a century ago. He was part of what's called a joint family, which meant that he and his older brother, plus their wives and children, shared a home together in Punjab, India. This was fairly common for Indian families back then. It was a way to share resources and to maintain a strong family bond between and across generations. But Chanda began hearing about Canada as a land of opportunity and how there were a lot of jobs available there. The idea was, Canada needed workers and Chanda could spend some time there, make some money, and eventually come back to his family in India. So in 1907, he and a couple of friends from his village decided to cross the ocean and come to Canada to look for work. During that time, in order to get from India to Vancouver, he had to cross the entire Pacific Ocean by ship. It was a tough, risky journey that lasted months, and you never knew if or when you would see your family again. There was also no guarantee that Chanda would even be allowed into Canada once he got there. At the time, India was part of the British Commonwealth, and many Indians assumed that meant they could move freely between all of the Commonwealth countries. Although this was supposed to be how it worked, it was not implemented everywhere.

Canada might have been Chanda's preferred destination, but the country wasn't without its faults. In 1907, the homes of South Asian Indians in Vancouver were attacked by a mob of white men who intended to push them out of the work-force. The mob, with help from the authorities, corralled, assaulted, and robbed the Indian workers, the majority of whom were Sikhs, ultimately forcing them out of their homes. Similar riots occurred in California and Washington, with no repercussions for the attackers.

The Canadian government also developed a bad reputation for turning people away. In 1908, Canada passed the infamous Continuous Journey legislation that required potential immi-grants to travel to Canada from their native country in one stretch, without stopping anywhere. This made it impossible for anyone travelling from India to come into Canada, and the regulation slowed down Indian immigration immensely. In 1910, the Canadian government passed the Immigration Act, which explicitly restricted "immigrants belonging to any race deemed unsuited to the climate or requirements of Canada." And a few years after that, the *Komagata Maru* incident took place, in which hundreds of Sikhs were denied entry and sent all the way back to India. This event is a stain on Canadian history that the federal government recently had to apologize for, and it probably took place at the exact same port my great-grandfather had used a few years earlier. I guess he got lucky.

Chanda found work picking apples in the interior of British Columbia, and he passed on stories about how his employers sometimes ran out of money and told workers all they had to give them was the fruit they had picked. He also worked some jobs in the logging industry and once fell into the ocean while trying to collect some logs that had been delivered near the shore. The only way anyone realized what had happened was when a co-worker in the distance noticed Chanda's hair, which as a Sikh he kept long and unshorn, drift to the surface of the water. Luckily, he survived the ordeal, but for Indian men, the difficulties didn't stop once you got into the country and found work. There was an assumption by many white Canadians, including ones with important seats in parliament, that Canada was a country meant for white people. Funny how this was a common thought, even though it was the Indigenous peoples who were here first. But that mindset was a constant reminder to people like my great-grandfather that they weren't exactly welcome here. Plus, as someone who came from Punjab, where the diet was usually vegetarian, Chanda didn't have a lot of options when it came to the food he could eat. After spending over a decade in Canada, he decided to risk his life again and go back home to Punjab. When he got there, he told the rest of his family, "I never want to eat potatoes again."

This story is a brief chapter in my family's history, but a significant one. When I was in junior high, the federal government under Prime Minister Jean Chrétien wanted to recognize the history of Sikhism in Canada, so they unveiled a list of who they believed to be the first 100 Sikhs to enter the country—and one of those names was Chanda Singh. Seeing my great-grandfather's name on that list was an incredible, revolutionary moment for me. I still get emotional thinking about it. That was when I really started to learn about my family's history, and it showed me that my identity as a Canadian goes back more than 100 years. From then on, whenever I experienced racism at school, at the store, or at a hockey game because of my turban, or even now when someone tells me to go back to my own country, I have something in my back pocket I can say in response—because, as it turns out, my family was probably here before theirs was.

———

A few decades later, my dad, Santokh Singh, had a similar idea to his grandpa. He also decided to move from his native India to Canada to build a future, but on different terms. Instead of picking fruit, he wanted to be a teacher.

Dad's always been a serious bookworm. He grew up in Dhatt, a small village outside the city of Ludhiana, in the Indian state of Punjab. When he was a kid, it wasn't common for people in villages to get a formal education. But one day my grandpa gave him a choice: either get married right away, or go to college. The family could only afford to send one kid to post-secondary school, and that child would go off and make enough money to support the others. Dad jumped at the opportunity—but getting from the villages to the city in the 1940s was much easier said than done.

From grades one to five, Dad had to walk three kilometres (about 40 minutes) to get to the nearest elementary school, and that same distance again to get back home. When he got older, he had to walk even farther: nearly seven kilometres each way. Along the way, he also had to tie his turban without a mirror, which is a skill that has basically become obsolete now. I can't even imagine tying mine without one! The good news is that when it came time to go to university, Dad wasn't concerned about how far away it was. He went to the post-secondary institution closest to his village, and became just the second person ever from Dhatt to graduate with a degree. But when he decided to get a master's degree, getting to class suddenly became a real ordeal. Every morning, he rode his bike for 45 minutes to the nearest train station, in Mullanpur, then sat on the train for an hour into the big city of Ludhiana, and then walked another two kilometres from the station to his actual classroom. On some days his classes started at 7:00 a.m., which meant he had to be on his bike by 4:00 a.m. in order to get there on time. But Dad loved it. He graduated from GHG Khalsa College in Sadhar with two undergraduate degrees and a master's in mathematics from the Government College in Ludhiana, ready to start his career.

This was the 1960s, and at that time there was a lot of demand for teachers across Canada due to a large number of immigrants coming into the country. Many people moved here from other countries for work. My dad arrived in Montreal in June 1966, with no real idea of what Canada would be like. All he'd heard was that it was cold and snowy—none of which he saw, given that it was currently the middle of summer. (The next year, he says it did snow in June, which is why you never bet against Canadian winters.) From there, Dad headed west, landing in Cold Lake, which is in northeastern Alberta, near the Saskatchewan border. Unfortunately, in some ways, things hadn't changed a lot since his grandfather's time. When he called the school board there, they took one look at his last name and said, "Oh, so you're a Sikh. You must be wearing a turban." He told them that, indeed, he was. After that, their tone completely changed. They told him he had to complete a list of requirements, including getting his teacher's certification in Edmonton, before they could consider his application. It was an indirect way of saying thanks, but no thanks.

If you ask my dad about it, he'll be nice and say that it's true: all teachers in Alberta do need to get certified before they can get a job, and at that time he wasn't. But it's interesting to me how they specifically mentioned his last name, his turban, and his religion. Let's just say I don't think it's a coincidence.

Either way, Dad got the message, and off he went to the University of Alberta to get his teacher's certificate. While he was there, he applied for jobs all around the province. One place offered him a full-time gig teaching social studies. But he was committed to math.

Another school he sent an application to was in a town called Brooks, which at the time had a population of about 3,000 people. He never heard back. But then one day, while studying at the university, he met another teacher from Brooks, who asked Dad when, exactly, he had applied. After telling him, the teacher said that all of those applications, including his, had gone straight into the garbage. Apparently, the school board in town had told the principal he wasn't allowed to hire any Asian teachers. The principal, who was Asian himself, took a stand and resigned. Meanwhile, a bunch of the teachers also quit. There was a bit of an uproar.

But for Dad, there was a silver lining. As a result of all this conflict, the entire high school in Brooks suddenly had no teachers, so he was told to apply again. This time, he got a phone call from the school right away. They had hired a new principal, and he was in panic mode. He told Dad he needed a full-time math teacher immediately, and hired him over the phone.

For my dad, life in Canada had been such a solitary experience up until that point. He had just travelled outside of India for the first time, had taken a plane for the first time, and was now living completely alone in Brooks. But now Dad had a job and a place to build a future for his family, the next step was bringing his wife and infant daughter over from India to join him.

My dad married my mom, Surjit Kaur, before he came to Canada. She was also a teacher back in India, as well as a principal at two girls' schools in different villages. When they got married, her older sister, Ajit Kaur, and her family had already been in Alberta for a couple of years, teaching in another small town there. They were the ones who sponsored

Dad to immigrate over. Mom had to stay behind to give birth to their first child while Dad looked for a job; a month after Dad landed in Montreal, Harjot Kaur, my eldest sister, was born.

Meanwhile, over in Brooks, Dad was settling in to his new life. He couldn't afford a car, so he walked everywhere, which wasn't anything new to him. And just like his grandfather decades earlier, he found the food difficult to get used to. All of the traditional spices and flavours he had grown up with were simply nowhere to be found in small-town Alberta. And of course he couldn't eat any of the beef that was on display everywhere you looked—in fact, Brooks is well known for its enormous meat-packing plant, where thousands of cattle are slaughtered every year. I heard that at one point, something like 80 per cent of McDonald's beef used to come from the Brooks plant. So for the first little while, Dad didn't have a lot of options. He told me he survived on what he called "rabbit food": carrots, potatoes, peas, and not much else.

Eventually, Mom got all of her paperwork in order, including a new passport and the documents for Harjot. They got on a plane to Toronto, and the two of them arrived in Canada exactly one year to the day after Dad.

Life was a lot different for Mom, too. There was so much to get used to. And a lot of it was different in a good way: she was impressed by the wide, paved roads throughout the province (in India there were only dirt roads between villages), and she also appreciated how clean everything was.

But other things just felt alien to her. For instance, in India it's common for part of a house's roof to be open to the elements. You would put the equivalent of lawn furniture there, with small canals down the sides of the room to take care of any rain that might fall. The idea was that you lived alongside the natural environment as much as possible. You would also sometimes sleep on the roof on a portable bed, under the sky. It was very open. The snow and the cold make that impossible in Canada. But if you aren't used to it, suddenly being indoors for so much of the time can feel a bit claustrophobic.

The biggest culture shock, though, was the people. When my parents first moved to Brooks, they were some of the only non-white folks in town. So not only did they have to adjust to a new way of life, but they also found themselves the subject of a whole lot of curiosity from basically the entire town. Most of the people were well-intentioned, but Mom would sometimes get offended when someone would ask her questions like: "In India, do you have utensils?"—as if they hadn't discovered them yet. Or: "Do you have tables?" Or: "Do you always sit on the floor?" For a lot of Canadians at that time, their image of India was the intense poverty they had seen on TV commercials for international charities. For my parents, who worked hard their entire lives, and who came from solid middle-class backgrounds, it was embarrassing to have people assume that about them.

Maybe because he was in a position of power in the school, Dad's experience was a little easier. Students would ask him questions about his turban, or how long his hair was underneath, but he isn't one of those teachers you can distract by asking about his personal life. He would just try to steer the class back to whatever math problem was next.

Mostly, everyone in town was very friendly and helpful to my parents. A retired teacher owned the first house they rented, and she would readily help take care of Harjot as if she were her own grandchild. In Indian culture, we don't call our elders by their first names, so Harjot used to call the land-lord Auntie Narum whenever she played with her or tagged along to go shopping. I know what you're thinking. That experience goes against the exclusionary, redneck reputation that small towns sometimes get—I guess stereotypes can go both ways.

But the questions my parents were asked most often were maybe a bit obvious, given that they were in Alberta: "How do you guys survive without eating meat? Where do you get your protein?" Dad still laughs about this today. It was like people had no idea that lentils existed. And who knows? Maybe they didn't. You certainly couldn't buy them anywhere in town. Mom also missed ingredients like fresh mint, which she would use in chutneys and other dishes, until one day she noticed it growing in the backyard of a neighbour's house; she quickly asked for a handful of roots from them so she could grow it herself. My parents had to figure this stuff out on their own, for the most part. Eventually, they found out about a specialty store in Calgary that carried Indian foods—including lentils. Mom and Dad started driving out there every six months and buying as much as they could fit in the trunk of their car.

It was hard to avoid meat entirely, though. The first time Mom ever really encountered it was on the plane over to Canada, when it was served as part of dinner for all of the passengers. The smell in the cabin was so intense, and so unavoidable, that she felt like she was going to be sick. In Brooks, too, it seemed like nobody could even conceive of life without meat—and that included medical professionals. One time Mom had a miscarriage and lost a lot of blood as a result. When she was in the hospital, her doctor told her that in order to recover and survive, she needed to eat liver. When she told him she couldn't, he didn't understand. The doctor kept trying to force it on her as the only possible solution. But she wouldn't budge, because her principles mattered more to her than one guy thinking she was crazy. And wouldn't you know it? Eventually another doctor of South Asian descent showed up in Brooks and came up with a plan that didn't involve eating the flesh of an animal.

I've always admired the way Mom and Dad held onto their faith and culture, even though they were in a place where people didn't understand those things a lot of the time. Even my eldest aunt, Ajit Kaur—who originally sponsored my dad—and her family decided to assimilate more to Western culture. And that's totally fine; it's their choice. Our family has assimilated to some extent—especially when it comes to things like hockey—but we've found a way to maintain our heritage, too. It wasn't an easy choice for them to make. At first, Mom didn't wear a turban around town, but when she started to, she would sometimes hear people on the street whispering or pointing at her. Covering one's head is a sign of respect in many Eastern societies. For example, at a hockey game in the Western world, people are asked to remove their hats during a national anthem, but it's the opposite in a place like India. Practising Sikh men usually wear some form of a turban, whereas women can either wear a turban or cover their head with a *chunni,* which is similar to a scarf but longer. Over the past decade or so, more women have taken to wearing turbans, but when Mom began wearing a female version, it would have been an extremely rare sight, especially in Alberta.

Mom has had a passion for spirituality and Sikhism ever since her grandfather taught her how to read from the Sri Guru Granth Sahib Ji, the Sikh scriptures, from an early age. And both my parents were inspired by a man named Bhai Jiwan Singh Ji, a gentle soul who began visiting Canada from India in the 1970s. It was my dad's younger brother, Harnek Singh, who was living in Calgary, who first called my parents in Brooks to say they had to come and meet Bhai Jiwan Singh Ji. He was travelling abroad to teach philosophy and meditation to Sikhs living in countries outside India. His humble nature and peaceful teachings emboldened my folks to drive our family out to Calgary every weekend to attend the Sikh temple (or *Gurdwara,* meaning "the Guru's door"), and participate in programs within the community.

Bhai Jiwan Singh Ji was an immensely influential figure in our family's life, helping us all connect to our faith in a much deeper way. He exemplified what Sikhs call *Charrdhi Kala*—maintaining an eternal state of optimism and undying spirit. Nothing ever fazed him. There was never a time that he didn't have a smile on his radiating face. Every aspect of him was all about helping and serving others. I can honestly say the manner in which he carried himself, with such love and humility, greatly impacted who I've become as a person today. While the traditional definition of "godfather" doesn't exactly translate in Sikhism, the relationship I had with him was similar to that. He made spirituality fun for me, and I was incredibly lucky to be able to spend so much time with him in my childhood, not only when he stayed over, but travelling together with him all over Canada and the western United States. I will never forget the blessings and love he gave me, and I remain forever indebted to him.

We were able to connect to our faith and community through Bhai Jiwan Singh Ji and the Gurdwara in Calgary, but back in Brooks, there was nobody else who looked like us. My parents don't talk very often about the difficulties and hardships they faced, but even as a little kid I understood how much bravery it took. The example they set inspired me: if I went through some tough times when I was growing up, I knew they had been through all that and more, paving the way for me and my siblings.

When Mom and Dad first arrived, Brooks was a small enough place that they weren't even sure it would survive. More and more people were moving to cities, leaving behind smaller communities. But then Brooks became known as a service hub for the oil-and-gas industry, which allowed it to not just survive but also to start to grow. And because of the promise of jobs, a few other non-white families moved into town, too, in the early 1970s. They mostly came over from the Vancouver area, and at the peak, there were about a dozen families like us. It felt like things were changing. But then the recession hit, and everyone who came over left just as quickly as they'd arrived.

Our family was protected from the ups and downs of the economy because Dad's job at the school didn't depend on the oil industry, and so the family continued to grow with the birth of my sister Prem in 1971. Most parents with two young children would choose to put aside furthering their own educational aspirations, but not mine! Part of that was because they were determined to advance themselves in the academic world. Simply getting an education was something Mom had to fight hard for back in India. She was born in 1937, when it wasn't normal for Indian women to go to school, a fact reinforced by her own grandfather. But she wanted it badly enough that she went on a hunger strike at home for days to convince her family to let her attend school. She simply wouldn't take no for an answer. Ultimately, she excelled in her education, and eventually became a principal in India before moving to Canada!

Mom had already done some subbing at the junior high school in Brooks, so she pursued a degree in education from the University of Lethbridge. Dad, meanwhile, found out that he only needed two extra courses to qualify for another bachelor of education degree from the University of Alberta. After that, he looked into doing a master's degree (his second), and the best option for that was down in Eugene, Oregon. So, beginning in 1970, the entire family took a road trip to the west coast for the summer while Dad loaded up on four math courses.

This turned into an annual vacation of sorts—a tradition that spanned more than a decade. Every summer, after school let out in Brooks, Dad would do a semester of work at the University of Oregon while the rest of the family took in the beautiful scenery. He finished his master's of education, then applied for the Ph.D. program. That degree came with a residency requirement, so the family had to stay there for 14 months in a row—not that Mom minded. The way she tells it, everything in Eugene smelled like flowers, and for a gardener like her, it was a dream come true. Both of the girls, meanwhile, went to the local public school. By that time my sister Gurdeep had also been born, in 1977, and some of her earliest memories are of picking blueberries on the coast. But then Dad graduated with his Ph.D., and my parents had a big decision to make.

When Mom and Dad first left for Canada, the plan was that they would stay there for about 10 years while Dad studied, worked, and made some money, and then they would return home with the kids to India. The whole time, they were writing letters to my grandparents, telling them that they were coming back. And in 1975, they did go back, but after nearly 10 years away, everything in India seemed different. Just like in Canada, many people were moving to cities instead of living rurally, and Dad says even his village was completely changed from what he remembered. Besides, Mom and Dad had gotten used to the lifestyle in Canada, and dealing with the corruption that goes along with even simple transactions at a bank in India was a headache they just didn't want to deal with. They weren't sure what they should do.

After completing his Ph.D. in 1983, Dad had a lot of conversations with Mom about their options. The situation in Punjab was completely different from when Dad had left in the '60s, politically and socially. In the end, they decided to stay in Brooks. Despite the cold, despite sometimes feeling isolated, and despite the fact that it was a two-hour drive just to buy a package of lentils, Canada was their home now. And so it became mine, too.

On December 21, 1984, along came a bouncing baby boy named Harnarayan. The Singh household was about to get a whole lot louder.

Chapter 2
Wayne's World

I've been a hockey fan for as long as I can remember—actually, even longer than that. The very first gift I ever received, as a newborn baby in the hospital in Wetaskiwin, Alberta, was a mini-hockey stick from one of my cousins, Swaran Sran. It was a good-looking stick, too. It had a wooden blade and a painted white shaft, and up the side, in blue capital letters, it said "Northlands Coliseum," home of the Edmonton Oilers. Even though I was an hour's drive away from the Coliseum at the time, and was about to settle even further south, that stick sealed my fate: from that day on, I was a Gretzky fan.

I also have to give some credit to my sister Gurdeep, who has played such an integral role in my life. As a child, she gave my parents little to worry about, as she was often playing alone quietly in Brooks while my mom took care of the house and read from the sacred scriptures of the Sikhs. But the house didn't stay quiet. Even though we were nearly eight years apart in age, we did a ton together. Whether it was epic seven-game mini-hockey stick battles or games on the table-top hockey set our eldest sister, Harjot, bought for me, everything seemed to revolve around hockey for the two of us. Gurdeep's own passion for hockey had a lot to do with the

Oilers, which I guess isn't that surprising given where we grew up and the timing of it all.

You have to remember the scene. It was the 1980s, and hockey was on the top of every Albertan's mind. Of course, the Battle of Alberta had existed for decades before then: some say it dates back to Edmonton being named the provincial capital despite being a smaller town, while others say it's because the first railway changed plans and ended up running through Calgary. As long as there's been an Alberta, there's been a rivalry between the two cities—but it's not an exaggeration (or not much of one) to say that the Battle of Alberta reached its fever pitch during the mid-'80s, when the Oilers and the Flames were both duking it out at the top of the NHL standings. You couldn't turn on a TV or open up a newspaper without seeing something about the rivalry. Both teams had larger-than-life players, too. But even in Brooks, which is two hours southeast of Calgary, I was obsessed with the rival team up north. As a little kid, I accumulated more mini-hockey sticks over the years, and they were all covered in the Oilers' patented orange and blue. I had a set of amazing Oilers pajamas, too—a tiny, all-cotton version of an actual NHL uniform. The first mini-stick may have set the course, but you can still blame my sister Gurdeep for which team in the rivalry I cheered for. Of all the great players that were on the Oilers in those days, there was no player she loved more than Wayne Gretzky. She loved "The Great One" so much that she even had dreams about meeting him.

As soon as I started watching him play, I was hooked, too. And then he left.

———

Gretzky was traded from the Oilers to the Los Angeles Kings in August 1988. The next month, I started kindergarten.

Even though I was young at the time, I can still picture the trade as clear as day. Gurdeep and I were in the car when the news broke, picking up our older sister Prem from her job at the Bay. The announcement came over the radio, and we drove all the way back home in silence, we were in such shock. When we got in the door, the press conference was on TV. We couldn't believe it. There was no warning. That striped shirt Gretzky wore is burned into my memory—and the way someone hands him a tissue when he tears up? That broke us even more.

Neither Gurdeep nor I could believe what was happening. How are you supposed to respond to something like that?

For us, it was simple: we became Kings fans. Because wherever Gretzky went, Gurdeep and I would follow. We loved him that much. Within a couple of weeks, black-and-silver clothes and merchandise began replacing the blue-and-orange Oilers memorabilia.

I have photographic proof of how quickly my loyalties shifted. If you look at my kindergarten class photo, which was taken early that fall, you'll see a sea of white kids smiling politely for the camera. Then, in the front row, there's one brown-skinned kid wearing a turban—and his new L.A. Kings sweater with number 99 written on the back. That's me. It's kind of funny: in a small town, in a province obsessed with hockey, it was the Sikh kid who couldn't wait to show off his new favourite team.

There was one other change in our household after Gretzky was traded. It was reported in the news that a big part of the reason Peter Pocklington, the owner of the Oilers, made the trade (which included $15 million in cash, an awful lot of money in the '80s) was that he needed money to support his other, struggling businesses—specifically, the dairy company Beatrice, which he also owned. As soon as we heard that, Gurdeep and I marched up to Mom and told her we didn't want her to buy any Beatrice products ever again.

Mom went along with it, because how hard was it to buy a different brand of milk? But for us, it was a victory against the guy who betrayed us by trading away our favourite player, number 99, the greatest of all time.

From that day forward, we were a Lucerne family.

What did I love about Gretzky? It would be easier to ask what I *didn't* love about him.

Not only was he the best hockey player I'd ever seen, but he was also so gracious. So humble. He was a great ambassador for the sport, without us even being aware of what that meant. As a Sikh, part of what we learn in scriptures is to be humble and respectful to those around you. Gretzky fit so many of those values that I was being taught at the Gurdwara—and he was a hockey player! He was clearly the best of the best, but he didn't walk around acting that way. From such a young age, Gretzky always carried himself with such grace. Whenever my classmates and I would argue about players in the league, I would always bring up Gretzky's humility as something that nobody else had.

Well, that, and the dozens of NHL records he held. And all the awards. And the four Stanley Cups. Those helped my argument, too.

Because Gurdeep and I loved it so much, hockey was on TV in my family's house a lot as we were growing up. I've always had a good imagination, so even from around the age of five, I was dreaming up all kinds of hockey-related games to play.

Whenever we all sat down to watch a game, for instance, I would turn our entire living room into my own personal hockey arena. I had the whole place mapped out. The end of the room where we had our home stereo was one of the nets; the rocking chair on the opposite end was the other net. Our couch was the benches. I even had my toy cars all lined up in rows to be the parking lot outside the arena. Once the scene was set, I would then act out every part of the game, from the players to the coach and GM, who had to stick around after the game to talk to the media (which I also played the role of). I would get so into my fantasy game, waving my little stick around in the air, that I would forget there was an actual hockey game being played on the TV. My sound effects and commentary became louder and louder until finally Gurdeep had to remind me to keep it down. My parents were good sports about it, though: whenever I shoved a mini-stick into my mom's hand and begged her to play goalie, she would always say yes.

I ran around on that carpet so intensely that in places I wore it down to the threads. So it wasn't long before the game started to creep into other rooms of the house. I turned our bathroom into the team's locker room (the tub itself was reserved for the GM to talk to reporters), and we also had this stool by our home phone that became the podium for awards night, where I did my best Ron MacLean impression.

For the players, I always made up fake names with fake stats, because that way I felt more comfortable telling everyone what to do. I was really into the Mighty Ducks movies as a kid, and you might remember that the main character in the series is named Charlie. And Wayne Gretzky's middle name is Douglas. So, naturally, one of my fictitious players was called Charlie Douglas, and he was a star! Charlie Douglas averaged over a point-per-game. But he was also very unselfish, always more interested in getting assists than goals. He was dependable, too, and had great character. Basically, Charlie Douglas was like my own personal Gretzky. It was like that with every player—not only did they all have a name, but also their own personality, based on something I was seeing in the actual hockey world.

One of my very favourite parts of the living-room game was doing my own broadcasting. Before puck drop, I always introduced each of my players one by one, and in between acting out the actual game, I would jump over and do play-by-play, plus all the hosting and analysis, all by myself.

Why broadcasting? Well, I think partly because I quickly realized I wasn't going to be a hockey player myself. For one thing, I wasn't a good skater. Nobody in my family was. Plus, I had other hobbies, like Sikh music, that took up a lot of my time. As you grow up, you start to look around and realize your situation in the world. So maybe I even gravitated towards the other roles in my little game because I knew on some level that I wasn't going to be the guy on the ice in real life. What I loved about broadcasters was that they were as close as you could get to the action without being part of the game—they were the *voice* of the game, and in some ways, for a viewer, that was just as important. I think it also fit my personality. I was a talker (I still am), and I wasn't necessarily shy. I was louder than any of my sisters, that's for sure.

I loved listening to the way the play-by-play guys called games. In Brooks, we used to get Flames games on TV, and at that time, the announcer was the legendary Ed Whalen. He had such a distinct voice, tons of energy, and he used to start every broadcast by saying "Hello, hockey fans . . ." I watched as many of those games as I could, and I always made sure to get to the TV in time to hear Ed's introduction. The seeds for what would become my own career were being planted, but of course I didn't know that yet.

One year, my parents and sisters decided to buy me this toy microphone from Radio Shack. It was yellow and black, and it really worked—it was connected to an actual speaker. That was probably my favourite toy I ever had, and in a way, it was a significant moment, because my parents were again supporting my passion, even if they personally didn't really understand it. They got me the microphone because they knew how much I loved doing play-by-play and hosting, but I also used it to broadcast my own version of the announcements I would hear each week at the Gurdwara we attended in Calgary. I was a sponge. Whatever I was seeing in my world, I was copying.

Hockey cards also shaped me as a young fan. My parents wanted to give us a sense of community, and to maintain our Sikh heritage—but there was none of that in Brooks. So every Friday after school, we would jump in my dad's red Plymouth

Caravelle and drive to Calgary for the weekend. On Sunday, after the Gurdwara service, we would drive back home. Because of that, I spent a lot of time at gas stations, waiting for my dad while he was pumping gas or wiping the windshield. So every time we stopped to refuel, I would ask, "Can I have a pack of hockey cards from inside?" That's where most of my collection came from. Sometimes you'd also get really cheap cards from inside cereal boxes or something. But they weren't even close to brands like Upper Deck. That's where the good stuff was.

Hockey cards became an obsession for me, and through them, I started memorizing all kinds of random information about players: dates of birth, hometowns, jersey numbers, you name it. I soaked it all in. Eventually I had two binders jam-packed with cards, and I was meticulous about how they were organized. The Gretzkys came first, obviously. All of my cards of number 99 went straight to the front, in order of how valuable they were, but also how important they were to me. For example, the older Gretzky cards with him in Oilers threads were considered more of a collector's item, so they were always first. Next came my favourite teams—the Oilers, the Kings, the Blues, and the Rangers. Notice a pattern? It went on like that all the way to the very back, which is where you would find my cards of the Pittsburgh Penguins. There was a reason for this, too. When I first started watching hockey, the Battle of Alberta was raging, but in the late '80s, a new rivalry formed between Gretzky and Mario Lemieux, who was putting up some amazing numbers of his own and even threatening some of 99's records. The Penguins became that new rival team—their dynasty even started right after the Oilers' run was finished. As a Gretzky fan, I couldn't have that. So it was straight to the back of the binder with Lemieux, along with Jaromir Jagr and the rest of the Penguins.

In case the hockey jerseys I wore to school all the time and the binders full of trading cards weren't big enough clues, one peek into my bedroom would have been enough for you to realize I was a sports nut. Actually, you didn't even need to look inside—just the door gave it away. It was so covered in posters and stickers that you could barely tell what colour the paint was underneath. Most of that was hockey-based, but there was a bit of basketball, too, thanks to Michael Jordan. I was also a wrestling fan—especially the Ultimate Warrior and Bret "The Hitman" Hart, the latter of whom grew up not far away, in Calgary. After all, there wasn't any hockey on TV on Saturday mornings, so wrestling was the next-best thing to watch while eating my cereal.

If you opened the door to my room, the first thing you would see was what I called my Gretzky shrine. Gurdeep and I had found this shiny silver craft material and we used it to cut out the letters of Gretzky's name and hang them in an arc along the middle of the wall. These were big letters, too. You couldn't miss them. And underneath was a special plaque I had that showed Gretzky as an L.A. King. Next to all that was a big Gretzky poster where he was in outer space, skating next to the entire planet. I had a bunch of other posters on my walls, showing other players, but the shrine was what mattered most. It was fitting that the caption at the top of my Gretzky poster read: "Wayne's World."

On either side of the Gretzky shrine were two flags, one Canadian and one American. The reason for the U.S. flag is that even though I was only four when Gretzky got traded to Los Angeles, I actually knew where that city was. My aunt, Balbir Kaur Jassal, lived in San Diego, and I'd visited L.A. when we went down to see her. In fact, when we went to the United States for the first time, I remember being fascinated by the infrastructure, from the roads to the bridges to public transit. It all seemed so much fancier compared to what we had back in Canada at the time. Also, by the early '90s, Bill Clinton was the president, and I think as a family we appreciated some of his views on multiculturalism. And, of course, Gretzky lived there now. Add all of that together, and the U.S. kind of captivated me as a kid. So even though I was a passionate Canadian, and still am, I decided to put up an American flag in my room as well.

Of all the hockey-related information I memorized over the years, one of the first was a date: January 26, 1961. Gretzky's birthday. In our family, my parents always used to celebrate one of the kids' birthdays with a prayer ceremony. Sometimes it was just us at home, and sometimes we'd do it at the temple. But no matter what, we would always make this Sikh dessert called parshaadh, a sweet pudding made of flour, butter, and sugar.

So one year on January 26, I went up to my mom with a request. "We always have parshaadh on our birthdays," I said. "Today is Gretzky's birthday. Could you make it today for him, too?" Again, Mom was such a great sport about supporting whatever passion I had, she didn't even hesitate. She just laughed and said sure. *Awesome!* As part of our faith, my family's home had a designated prayer room, and after watching over my mom's shoulder in the kitchen for a bit, I went off to our prayer room to pray for 99. That's just who I was as a kid. I kept finding ways to combine my identity as a Sikh with the game I loved. On the one hand, it was a funny juxtaposition. But on the other, what's more Canadian than a small-town kid who's obsessed with hockey?

—

The first NHL game I saw live was in the early '90s. We had some family friends, the Gills, who had tickets to a Kings-Flames game in Calgary, and they brought me along with them. I remember our seats were way up high in one of the corners of the Saddledome, which seemed so grand and humongous in person. But even at a distance, my whole world seemed to slow down a little when the Kings came onto the ice in their black-and-silver uniforms. It was such a cool experience—my first game involved my favourite player ever. Meanwhile, growing up in Brooks, the Flames were the team I had watched more than any other on TV. I was so wowed by the whole experience, I don't think I stopped talking the entire time, spouting off every fact and stat to the Gills that I could think of. The only downside was it was kind of a low-scoring game that ended in a final score of 2–1. When Gretzky is out there, you can't help but want to see lots of goals.

—

Gretzky scored a lot of goals over the years. And after leaving the Oilers, he nearly led a different team all the way to the Stanley Cup. I have such vivid memories of 1993, when he and the Kings went all the way to the finals. During the conference final that year, when L.A. played Toronto, Bhai Jiwan Singh Ji happened to be in Canada. He was visiting from Punjab, and my mom decided that our family would travel with him all the way to Regina. The trip would last a couple of days, and I knew it would be full of music, visiting people's houses, and the like. Naturally, Gurdeep and I were outraged. "But it's the playoffs!" we complained. "How are we going to watch the games?" We made such a fuss about it that Mom made us a promise: whenever a Kings-Leafs game was on, she would figure out a way for us to watch it, no matter what else was happening. That was honestly the only way she could convince us to get in the car.

The Kings were the clear underdogs in the series, and they barely forced it to game seven. But once they did, Gretzky took over. While in hostile territory, he scored a hat trick in the final game and added an assist; the Kings won 5–4. Later, Gretzky said that game was the best one he ever played, and Gurdeep and I, who had snuck away to watch and were cheering our brains out, had to agree.

It's kind of funny, because nowadays a lot of Canadians want to see Canadian teams do well in the playoffs. And being in the broadcasting industry, I know the boost in ratings has a big impact on each channel's bottom line. But these issues weren't remotely in our heads back then. The Oilers had just won so many Stanley Cups. Calgary had just won theirs, too. It wasn't much of an issue. So even in the final that year, when the Kings were up against the Habs, we felt no motivation whatsoever to cheer for Montreal. We were just rooting for Gretzky—and maybe a couple of other players we'd fallen for since the trade, like Kelly Hrudey and Luc Robitaille.

When Gretzky's team lost in the finals, I was heartbroken. I had to defend him a lot during these playoffs and afterwards. That's when he started to get this reputation as being a whiner. He took a hit that didn't get called, and he wasn't happy about it. But I always had his back, at least on the playground in Brooks. It was such a tight series, too. I was irritated at players like Eric Desjardins and Guy Carbonneau, who were able to get in Gretzky's face and shut him down. Three of the five games in the finals went to overtime, and had it not been for their goalie, there is no way Montreal would have won. I don't mind saying it: Patrick Roy single-handedly stole a Stanley Cup from Wayne Gretzky. Roy was just unbeatable. But what can you do?

———

Living in a small town, the NHL seemed far away—the kind of thing you could only see through your TV screen. But sometimes our worlds collided in small and funny ways. In 1994, when I was nine, the Lillehammer Olympics took place, and for whatever reason, Team Canada decided to get ready for the tournament by playing some exhibition games in small towns across the country. And wouldn't you know it? One of those towns turned out to be Brooks, Alberta. This was a big deal. To get the chance to see top prospects and NHL hopefuls like Paul Kariya and Corey Hirsch at our little community rink was something I couldn't miss. It had a big enough ice surface, but nothing fancy—pretty much what you would expect in a small town. I thought it was awesome that Team Canada came all the way out to us.

Mr. Budz was the principal at the high school my dad worked at and he, his wife, and their son all had tickets to the game. The son's name was Peter, and we knew each other a little bit because when I was in grade one, he was in grade six, and our school matched us up to be pen pals. We wrote to each other about how much we loved hockey, and I guess Peter remembered, because his family ended up offering me a ticket to go with them. It was so cool to sit in the stands at our local rink and see those famous red jerseys right in front of us. At one point, Mrs. Budz gave Peter and me some money to go get food from the concession. When we got back to our seats, she asked me what I'd bought to eat. Instead, I held up my new pack of hockey cards and said, with a big smile on my face, "It's okay, I'll skip the food." To them, the fact that I would choose to go hungry in order to get more cards just proved my obsession with the game. They still remind my dad about it to this day.

Another time, Dad read a story in the local newspaper that said Glenn Anderson was making an appearance at a gas station in town, and people had the chance to go meet him. It seems a bit strange looking back on it, but I guess it was a way for the gas station owner to bring in customers. Dad asked if I wanted to go, and, of course, I didn't need a lot of convincing. I ended up getting an autographed picture of him where he's standing in his full Oilers uniform, as if he's about to jump onto the ice. Instead, he's, you know, pretending to pump gas. When Anderson signed the photo, he asked me how to spell my name, but I don't think he knew what he was getting into—if you look at it now, you can see he wrote out H-A-R in big letters, but then the printing gets smaller and smaller, and eventually it's just a scribble of blue Sharpie, so that my whole name would somehow fit. Still, I treasured that photo. And when I got back home, guess where I put it? Straight onto my bedroom door. Even though every square inch was already covered, I somehow always found room for one more piece.

As I grew older, so did my obsession with hockey. In addition to my hockey card collection and my bedroom-filling mural, I used to keep scrapbooks filled with every hockey-related newspaper clipping I could find. These scrapbooks would fill up over the course of a season, but it was a way for me to keep tabs on the entire league. Well, one of the ways.

I wanted to watch every single game I possibly could. When I was young, we didn't get a lot of them on TV in Brooks. But as time went on, we were able to watch more and more games, especially during the playoffs. When playoff hockey was on, our family organized everything—prayers, supper, you name it—around the game so that we wouldn't miss a minute. But there was one rule that couldn't be broken. On school nights, my dad was always adamant that we go to bed on time. We weren't allowed to stay up and watch every game to the end, like I wanted.

Now, I already had a 13-inch monitor in my room for my Super Nintendo. (I only had three games, and they were all sports games: *NBA Jam*, a Ken Griffey Jr. baseball game, and my all-time favourite, *NHL '94*.) But that little TV also had a cable connection on the back. I knew how to work tape recorders and set-up TVs as a kid, and somehow I'd come across a really long cable wire. If other people in my family were awake, I could just sit and watch hockey with them in the living room. But on those nights when everyone had gone to sleep before the game was over, I would sneak out and run my cable wire from the main connection all the way across the living room, past the stairs, and down the hallway to the very back of the house, where my bedroom was. It was the exact opposite corner of the house from the living room. I hooked up the cable to the back of my little TV, and presto! Now I could watch games all the way into the night. Then, when everything was over, I would coil the wire back up and put it away, and nobody was the wiser.

This worked great for a while. I remember sitting on my bed one school night in 1996, watching the Capitals play the Penguins in the playoffs. These weren't even Canadian teams, but there was no way I was going to miss it—but this particular game would not end. It ended up going to quadruple overtime, and the whole time my eyes were shutting. Still, I wouldn't let myself go to sleep until it was over. I'm sure I dreamed about Peter Bondra's blazing speed, Jaromir Jagr with his long flowing hair, and Olaf Kolzig stopping the puck endlessly that night.

I continued doing this trick so often that, eventually, I must have become lazy about putting the cable away properly. At some point, my dad figured out what I was doing. I didn't realize he knew until one day he made an offhand comment about it: "Well, I know you're staying up watching hockey with your little cable . . ." In my mind, I was like, *Oh shit, he knows?* But he didn't tell me to stop. He just wanted me to know that *he* knew. Maybe he was somewhat amused that I would go to such lengths just to watch the last few minutes of a game.

So I stayed up, and kept watching.

———

The trade from Edmonton to Los Angeles set the pattern: wherever Gretzky went, my and Gurdeep's allegiances would follow. We spent eight years cheering for him and the Kings, but in 1996, news broke that Gretzky was going to be traded out of L.A. The owner who had brought him in, Bruce McNall, had sold the team a few years earlier, and the Kings were looking to rebuild. So that February, he was sent to the St. Louis Blues. To me and my sister, this was huge. *He's going to play with Brett Hull!*

St. Louis was really going for it that year. The team was stacked. Not only did they have Hull and Shayne Corson up front, but also Al MacInnis and a young Chris Pronger on defence, plus a bunch of guys from the '80s Oilers. You add Gretzky to that lineup, and automatically you had a chance for a Stanley Cup. All of a sudden, Gurdeep and I had a new favourite team, and new jerseys to buy!

The most exciting thing about that Blues team was the possibility of seeing Gretzky and Hull playing together on the same line. We'd already watched them have so much success together at the all-star game: Gretzky was the elite playmaker,

Hull the elite goal scorer. It seemed like an obvious recipe for success. The Blues even brought in Gretzky's former Oilers teammate, goaltender Grant Fuhr. That year, Fuhr set an NHL record starting in 79 regular-season games, 76 of them consecutively, another record in itself. But in the first round matchup against the Toronto Maple Leafs, Fuhr tore ligaments in his knee after a collision with Nick Kypreos and was out for the rest of the playoffs. And then the Blues met the Detroit Red Wings.

At the time, Steve Yzerman was their captain, and the team hadn't yet had the postseason success that people were expecting. Everyone was waiting for it. The series against Gretzky and the Blues went to game seven, and I remember it was a beautiful spring day in Brooks. Our patio door was wide open. My dad was out back, mowing the lawn. (I love that whole spring playoff vibe, by the way. It's so positive. It's the best time of the year in hockey, and the weather is finally getting better, too.) I remember going back and forth between the back deck, to see what my dad was doing, and watching this incredibly stressful game inside. And the game is scoreless. Nobody can get anything going. It ends up going to double overtime. Then, a couple of minutes into the period, Yzerman scores the series-winning goal—using the exact type of slapshot that Gretzky had once scored with over popular Flames goaltender Mike Vernon's shoulder, back in one of the epic Battles of Alberta.

That's it? It's over already?

Pure heartbreak. I was so stunned that I just sat there on the couch. *How could this have happened?* There was so much hype when Gretzky went to St. Louis to make this super-team, and then they didn't even make the final.

But we were able to recover quickly, because before we knew it, Gretzky was off again, this time to the New York Rangers. Gurdeep and I heard the news that summer, and boom: Rangers flags went up all over our house. We were over St. Louis so fast, it was like it never happened.

To be honest, we already had a soft spot for the Rangers, because a bunch of our favourite players had already ended up there and won the Cup in 1994. Mark Messier, Kevin Lowe, Jeff Beukeboom, Esa Tikkanen, Craig MacTavish, Glenn Anderson—thanks to former Oilers general manager Glen Sather being at the helm of the Rangers, it was like they were trying to recreate the Oilers on the east coast. So Gurdeep and I had watched the team with a keen interest. We slowly became fans of some of the other players, too. For instance, Brian Leetch had the same birthday as Gurdeep. So he was automatically good in our books.

The Rangers hadn't won a championship in more than 50 years, and they had to beat Vancouver to get there, too— another Canadian team. But, again, I didn't have any notion of supporting the Canucks. On my personal hierarchy of who to root for, "former Oilers" came way above "other Canadian teams." So we rooted for Messier's team, and when he gave his famous guarantee that the Rangers would win game six of the semifinal against the New Jersey Devils, we believed him. By this point, our VCR was getting a real workout. I used it to tape every all-star game, as well as all of the important playoff games. I watched Messier's guaranteed win over and over again.

Gretzky played well for the Rangers, but we could tell his career was slowly coming to an end. When it started coming out in the media that he was thinking about retiring, I wasn't surprised. It was 1999. Gretzky wore number 99. It just made sense, you know?

In those final few years, people started questioning whether he was still any good. That included some kids at my school, most of whom cheered for the Flames. But I still defended him. I remember one game against the Panthers; Gretzky scored a hat trick, and the next day at school I walked into my classroom, triumphant: "See? He's still got it!" Even at the tail end of his career, Gretzky still had a lot of value. People said he was washed up, but he was nearly a point-per-game player right up until the end. And this was in the "dead puck era," when scoring was near an all-time low.

Gurdeep and I decided that we had to go see him in his last ever game against the Flames. The game was mid-week, so we had to get permission from our parents for me to skip school and drive up to Calgary. Puck drop didn't happen until evening, but we had other plans that would take us all day.

We got into town bright and early. The first order of business was trying to get a glimpse of the team as they left their hotel. We started looking up all of the high-end hotels in Calgary, and calling them on the phone to ask whether the Rangers were staying there. Most of them said no. But then we called up the Westin, and the receptionist there said, "Sorry, we're not allowed to say." *Jackpot!* We went straight over to that hotel, and sure enough, we spotted one of the Brewster buses that players used to take to get to the Saddledome. We followed the bus all the way to the rink, then hung around waiting for a chance to get autographs after practice. But it turns out some other people had the same idea; there were about a hundred people waiting there along with us, all standing in the cold behind this little metal security fence.

Finally, after practice, the players started filing out, and I recognized all of them. It was a cold day in February, but none of the players were getting on the bus. We weren't sure what they were waiting for. Eventually we realized they were waiting for Gretzky. Finally he came out, and he looked so different from the rest of the team. He was wearing this long, luxurious, light-brown coat that went down past his knees. It was majestic. All of us fans waiting erupted into cheers as soon as we saw him.

Gretzky told his teammates, "Guys, it's cold out. Don't worry. Get on the bus." Then he walked over to us fans, said hello, and started signing autographs. At one point there was this lull, where nobody was saying anything. But I'm the type of guy where things don't stay quiet for too long, so I blurted out, "We love you so much!" He looked right at me and said thank you. Gurdeep and I were both wearing our Gretzky jerseys—one Kings, one Rangers—and we had also brought along that big plaque from my bedroom shrine. But as time went on, I realized he wasn't going to stand there forever. It was now or never. I reached through the crowd and shoved the plaque right at Gretzky's hand. He saw it right away, and even said, "Oh, this is nice." Then he signed it with a blue Sharpie.

A few minutes later, Gretzky got onto the bus to leave, and right away, the crowd dissipated. But Gurdeep and I were still standing there, holding this huge poster-board sign we'd made that said "#99, GREATEST OF ALL TIME." The bus started to drive away, then had to stop for a second. And just at that moment, we had a perfect view into the window where Gretzky was sitting. He saw us, pointed at our sign, and gave us a thumbs-up. We were on cloud nine. *Gretzky acknowledged us!* It was just the two of us standing there— everyone else had left. Nobody saw the exchange but us. It was our special moment with the Great One.

From there, it was on to the game. We got to the arena early so that we could watch the pre-game skate. Our seats were only a handful of rows up from the ice, between the blue line and the end boards. There was such an energy in the building that night. Everyone knew it was the last time they would ever see the world's best player in action. Gretzky does this thing during warm-ups where he stops at one spot along the boards to do a stretch. And this time, it just so happened that the spot he chose was directly across from where Gurdeep and I were sitting. Keep in mind, we're wearing the same jerseys and holding the same sign that he saw a few hours earlier, crossing our fingers that he might notice us for a second time. So he's bent over, with his weight on his knees, having a breather, and then all of a sudden he looks up—and guess who's directly in his line of vision? The kid with the turban, from earlier that morning. Again, there weren't many people in their seats yet. He was looking right at us, and gave another big smile and a wave.

To be honest, I don't remember anything about the game itself. But I do remember one thing distinctly. We were in the heart of Calgary, a city that had hated Gretzky and the Oilers for so many years. But with two and a half minutes left in the game, the entire sold-out Saddledome crowd got to their feet and gave him a standing ovation that didn't stop until time ran out. They were chanting his name the whole time: "*Gretz-ky! Gretz-ky! Gretz-ky!*" I thought it was so cool of Flames fans. How classy is that? You have to respect it.

They named Gretzky as the first star of the game. And, again, the crowd cheered so loudly that he couldn't leave the ice. This wasn't Edmonton, or New York, or L.A. This was Calgary. Enemy territory. The site of such a heated rivalry. And yet he's got his helmet off, skating around the entire rink again and again, waving to the crowd. In the middle of it, Gurdeep and I turned to look at each other, and we realized we were both crying.

———

Life without Gretzky felt a bit weird, but it wasn't like hockey came to a halt or anything. There were always new games to watch, new players to root for, and new stats for me to memorize. Plus, by the late '90s, my first favourite team was starting to make noise again. After some lean post-dynasty years, the Oilers had a wave of new young players and were again in the mix for a playoff spot. There was just one problem: the freaking Dallas Stars. For a while, it seemed like the two teams met in the playoffs every single year, and the Oilers kept getting clobbered.

My sister and I developed this hatred of the entire Stars team: Mike Modano, Derian Hatcher, Jere Lehtinen, everyone. Dallas was this bigger, meaner, more expensive team, and for once the Oilers were the underdog. It got so bad that I used to pray for them to win. Literally.

Each night my family would go to our prayer room before eating supper and give thanks to the Creator and to our Gurus for their blessings. Eventually I was old enough to be able to do the prayer on my own. My mom would send me with a plate of food into the room, and I would stand there and say thanks—but because I was by myself, I would also sneak in a prayer for the Oilers, or for whatever team I was rooting for in the playoffs that year. Sometimes I would even do a prayer for my team in *NHL '94* if I was having trouble beating the computer. Whenever the Oilers were up against the Stars, I would pray for my team to come out on top. My parents had no idea I was doing this, but as a kid, you don't really know what you're doing. You're so innocent.

That being said, in some of those Oilers–Stars series, Edmonton's goalie was Curtis Joseph, my favourite netminder at the time, and he would make these impossible diving saves to keep the puck out of the net at the last second. Nobody could believe what he was doing out there. And whenever I watched these miraculous saves, there was a part of me that thought: *Hey, my prayers are working!*

As it turned out, despite retiring, Gretzky wasn't out of my life for long. A couple of years after hanging up his skates, the Great One started a charity golf tournament, where he and a bunch of other former players and hockey people would play a couple of rounds and raise money for a good cause. The first one was held in Edmonton, in the summer of 2002, and Gurdeep was adamant: "We have to go." She's always been very organized, and somehow she got us a pair of tickets and figured out a way for us to get up there. I had just finished high school and was trying to figure out where I wanted to go to post-secondary school. This was as good a way as any to pass the time.

We arrived at the tournament, and it was obvious right away how different the vibe was than at a hockey game. Fans at a golf tournament still have to stand behind a security rope. But there's no glass separating you from the players, like there is at a hockey rink. Plus, the players have way more downtime in between shots, so they aren't focused on the game every second. As Gurdeep and I were walking from hole to hole, I was amazed at how accessible everyone was. I brought along my autograph book, and before I knew it, I had signatures from and pictures with players like Cassie Campbell and Kelly Hrudey. I had the chance to chit-chat with Kevin Lowe, who at the time was the general manager of the Edmonton Oilers. I was also able to meet a couple of CBC broadcasters, which was a thrill for me—in my mind, those guys were celebrities as much as the players were.

The big draw, though, was number 99. By the time Gurdeep and I caught up to where he was playing, we decided we'd just follow him around for the rest of the course. He had the biggest crowd around him by far. Before Gretzky teed off, he would always chat a bit with people in the crowd. At one point, he spotted a guy wearing a vintage Gretzky Oilers jersey and complimented it. They kept talking, and it was suggested that maybe Gretzky should try it on. At that point he hadn't worn an Edmonton jersey since being traded, nearly 15 years ago. But now he was retired, so he could do whatever he wanted. Gretzky took the jersey from the guy and put it on, and the crowd went wild. It must've been one of the first times he'd worn Oilers colours since 1988. As an

Albertan, that was really cool to see in person. Gretzky teed off, hit a clean drive straight down the fairway, and then gave the guy his jersey back. *Holy smokes.* I bet that jersey hasn't ever been washed since.

Later in the afternoon, Gretzky was sitting in his golf cart, waiting to go on to the next hole. Again, it's a quiet moment, which for me is an opportunity. I yelled out, "Gretzky, we love you so much. We're from Brooks, Alberta!" Nobody else said anything, so I kept going, and proceeded to tell him the whole story of my mom making the parshaadh for his birthday, and how we used to say a prayer for him. Everyone in the crowd was listening to me, and some of the security guards seemed a little on edge that I was all of a sudden directly talking to Gretzky so much. And as I was talking, I got so caught up in the story that I lifted up the security wire and started walking closer to his golf cart. Bad idea. Right away, security guards headed straight for me with the intent to stop me in my tracks. But then, incredibly, Gretzky waved them off. He said it was okay, and that security should let Gurdeep and me through.

Now the two of us were standing a foot away from Gretzky as he sat in his golf cart. It was starting to dawn on me how ridiculous this moment was. But then Gretzky noticed I was wearing a Team Canada jersey with number 99 on the back. He said, "Nice jersey. Want me to sign it for you?" He leaned over and signed it without hesitating. Then he said, "Why don't we get a picture together?" The entire time, he was so relaxed and casual about the whole thing, and it ended with Gretzky saying, "Put in a good word to your parents for me." We ran back to our spot in the crowd feeling over the moon about how nice he'd been to us.

Fast-forward to the next year. Gretzky was having another golf tournament, this time in Calgary, so it was a no-brainer that Gurdeep and I were going to be there. It was just as fun as the first time. We were able to meet a bunch of former players and talk to them for a bit as they went by. We also met Walter Gretzky, Wayne's dad, and he was just as kind as everyone always says he is.

Eventually, we found Gretzky himself, and started following him around again from hole to hole. As soon as the moment arose, we struck up another conversation with him from afar. I yelled out the story of meeting him the year before, and he called back, "Oh yeah, I remember you guys." *What?* At that point he was sitting in a chair, and he called us over to him—just like last year. Gurdeep was smart enough to have brought along the picture we took with him the previous summer. She pulled it out of her purse and showed it to him, and Gretzky just laughed. "That's awesome!" he said. We asked him to sign it, and of course he did so right away.

So we now have what I think is pretty rare: a picture of us with Gretzky, signed by Gretzky. How cool is that?

———

Both of my parents have always supported my love of hockey, but Dad was a bit worried, too. He was always the grounded one in the family. When I would scream and run around the living room after our team scored a big goal, he would just shake his head and say, "What are you getting so worked up about? It's just a game."

He used to watch me poring over my hockey cards, memorizing every last bit of information I could, and he would ask me, "What are you going to do with this information?" Again, he's a math teacher, and a very logical person in general. To him, sports statistics seemed completely useless. He was worried that I was turning my brain into, in his words, "an encyclopedia of hockey," with no room left over for anything else.

Whenever he would ask me that, I didn't have a response. In a way, knowing where, say, Owen Nolan was born *was* useless. It didn't serve any practical purpose in my life. But at the same time, these facts added up to a larger story that meant a whole lot to not just me, but to people all around North America. (By the way: Nolan was born in Belfast, Northern Ireland, in case you were wondering.) I knew it had value, even if I couldn't explain why.

I also found myself daydreaming about how I could turn my love of hockey into an actual career. One path seemed clearer than the others. Back in grade six, our class had to write little autobiographies about our lives so far and our plans for the future. In my booklet, under "What I Want to Be When I Grow Up," I wrote: "I want to be a hockey commentator."

But was that even possible when you wore a turban?

Chapter 3
The Only Sikh Family in Brooks

In many ways, my childhood was typical for a kid in small-town Alberta. Brooks was a quiet and friendly community, with lots of opportunities for me to follow my interests, meet people, and learn more about the wider world.

But in other ways, it was fairly obvious that our family was not like any of the others.

My parents had known this for years, ever since Dad had to jump through those extra hoops when he first became a teacher in Canada, all because of his Sikh last name. Personally, the first time I remember feeling different from the rest of the town was on my first day of kindergarten. The night before, my parents, Gurdeep, and I sat around our living room with an important decision to make: What was I going to wear on my head?

Let me back up a bit. As Sikhs, we believe in keeping our hair long and unshorn. The idea is that we're remaining in the natural state the Creator created us in. Your head is one of the most sacred parts of your body, because without your mind, everything else is useless. And this belief has health benefits, too, because then our bodies don't need to spend energy regrowing hair that's been cut or trimmed. Some people think that if you don't cut your hair, it will grow forever, but it doesn't really work like that. We all have a genetic limit on how long our hair can grow, and once you reach that point, it stops. My beard and hair are fairly long now, but they've been that same length for years.

Keeping your hair long comes with some practical concerns, however. You have to keep it neat and tidy. The usual way that most practising Sikh men and women do this is by wearing a turban, known in Punjabi as a *dhasthaar* or a *pagrree*, which is a long piece of cloth tied around our head in many particular styles that can vary based on region, size, or the look you're going for. History has also played a role, but nowadays it's all about personal preference and what you might be doing on a particular day.

But wearing a full-sized turban just isn't practical for toddlers and young kids. For one thing, youngsters can't tie their own turbans, and they can't really take care of it once it's tied, either—because children are always moving around so much, their turbans can come off much more easily. There are several stages of hair-covering that Sikh children go through. The first is to have your hair tied in a bun, which is called a *joorra*, also known as a Rishi knot, and then cover it with a small cloth. Later you might wear a *patka*, which is a bigger piece of cloth that ties around the joorra and the entire head, keeping the hair more neat and stable. After that comes a smaller version of the turban called a *keski*, and then, typically around high school, a Sikh child will usually switch over to a full-sized turban that he or she will wear for the rest of his or her life. Even then, the style can change. I know my own turban style has changed slightly over time—from an almost slanted football shape to more symmetrical nowadays.

Before I started kindergarten, I wore the joorra with a small piece of cloth to cover the top of the bun, like most boys my age would have. I was only four years old, but I already knew I wanted a change. Earlier that summer, I had been out shopping with my family at the Bay in Calgary. I was already so obsessed with hockey that when the television play-by-play announcer for the Flames TV broadcasts walked in, I recognized him immediately. "That's Ed Whalen!" I said to my parents, and, before they could stop me, I ran over to say hello. Ed was very gracious. He could tell I was ecstatic to meet him, and when my parents and sister caught up to me, he chatted with them for a bit, too. Then, at one point, he referred to me as a "she."

What? Why is he saying that?

It took me a second to realize it was because of my hair. Like always, I was wearing my joorra, and I guess because my hair was longer than most Western boys', it must have confused him. I now understand this was an honest mistake on Ed's part, but it was a significant moment for me. My gut reaction was that I didn't want to be called a girl, even by mistake. But it also made me realize that, to a lot of other people, I looked different than what they were used to seeing. They didn't understand my family's culture, or our faith. I was upset, and I decided I didn't want to leave the house with my hair looking like that anymore. It altogether changed the way in which I decided to present myself in public as a Sikh boy. If my parents told me to take out the garbage or adjust the sprinkler, I would refuse if I were only wearing my joorra.

The night before my first day of kindergarten, my parents asked each other, "What is Harnarayan going to wear to school, if not the joorra?" Mom and Dad had worries of their own. On the one hand, they thought that if my hair was that visible, then maybe other kids would be more likely to touch it, or pull it, or just ask a bunch of questions that I wouldn't be able to answer. On the other hand, if my hair was kept under a turban, then it would be more hidden and private— but also difficult to adjust or retie if it came undone. I started kindergarten young, because I'm a December baby, and for most four-year-olds, that was just too much responsibility.

I remember hearing my family talking in the living room, going back and forth about it. I also remember being very adamant, saying to them, "I only want to wear what Dad's wearing!"

Remember my kindergarten class photo, where I'm wearing my beloved Gretzky sweater? To people of the Sikh faith, that photo is completely startling for another reason: they see a tiny kid wearing a full-sized turban, and they aren't sure why. Again, it's totally abnormal for a four-year-old to be wearing a formal-style turban. Most people of course won't notice it, but if you understand the context, it does look a little strange.

It was an unusual choice, but I didn't know that. There were no other practising Sikh families in town. The only example I had to turn to was my dad—and he wore a full turban. So I was insistent: that's what I was going to wear, too.

As I mentioned, graduating to a full turban is a big deal in a Sikh child's life. And it goes beyond the fact that a turban is different from the other, simpler types of head coverings that lead up to it. First and foremost, when you have a turban on your head, you stick out in a crowd. This is actually intentional: back in the day, the Sikh Gurus wanted their disciples to be easily visible, so that anyone who needed help—whether it be food, shelter, or even security—could quickly find a Sikh.

But a turban doesn't just represent your faith; it also expresses your personality. To start with, there are many different ways to tie it. The turban I usually wear these days is a piece of cloth that's about seven metres long, which is then cut in half and sewn together. I like this style because it makes the layers look more defined; at that length, I can get five solid layers in. When the turban is freshly washed, it's a two-person job for me to get it tied. I'll stand at one end with someone else, like my wife, at the other end, and we'll roll it up together into what looks almost like a rope. (If I'm on my own, there are little shortcuts I can take, like tying one end to a doorknob.) I mentioned before that my dad used to tie his turban as he walked to school—but that was common for a generation of people who weren't as concerned about their appearance as we are today. These days, tying the turban is a more refined process. It takes me about five minutes, all told, but I consider it more than just a hat I throw on as I head out the door. It's closer to an art form.

The style of Sikh turbans has changed over history, too. From the mid-1400s to the 1700s, turbans tended to be sportier and aerodynamic. And people travelled on horseback, so the turban—which they called a *dumalla*—had to be sturdy enough to not fall apart in tough conditions. But that style changed in the 1800s, with the first Sikh ruler, Maharaja Ranjit Singh. Up until that point, Sikhs had always been the minority in eastern Asia, with limited political power. But after Maharaja Ranjit Singh came into power, our style of turban changed accordingly. The newer styles became more regal and were seen as a symbol of royalty.

This formal style was the norm all the way until the 1980s, when I was growing up. But now we're starting to see things change again. Sikh youth today want to wear the more sporty, casual style. There's also a new hybrid look that combines both styles. There's no right or wrong way, so everyone makes their turban their own, whether it's how many layers they like, or how high it sits on their head. If you put a hundred Sikhs in a lineup, you'd be hard pressed to find two turbans tied the exact same way.

The other big choice is colour. The Sikh faith has three traditional colours: blue, white, and orange—which is kind of funny, because those also happen to be the colours of the Edmonton Oilers. So, as a Gretzky fanatic growing up in southern Alberta, I always had an excuse as to why I was wearing those colours in my turban. *It's not just because of hockey, guys. It's my religion!*

But here, too, there aren't any strict limits. No one's going to judge you for wearing a turban that's a non-traditional colour. In fact, lately there's been a renaissance of really unconventional choices, like peach and pistachio, especially in the summertime. The important thing is that your turban matches the rest of your outfit. I also wear a small bandana under my turban that helps keep things in place, and because part of that is visible, I make sure it matches as well.

My personal turban style is influenced by a couple different things. I started out copying my dad as a youngster, but over the years I've made tweaks to the way he taught me, based on things I have learned from some of the Sikh friends I've made throughout my life. Growing up, my favourite colour was navy blue, and so I've mostly stuck with that in my turban as well. Even at a young age, it always seemed strange to me that other Sikh boys wore only black turbans. It was so boring! I'm still more drawn to blues and greys, and I like to experiment with different shades, even if the variation of colours has sometimes gotten me into trouble at work. Once, I tried wearing a teal turban on a *Hockey Night in Punjabi* broadcast, and later got accused by a couple of viewers of bias in favour of the San Jose Sharks. You have to laugh about it: Who could have known that the colour of my turban would become an occupational hazard?

———

On the morning of my first day of kindergarten, Dad tied a turban for me for the very first time. I felt proud to be wearing something that looked so grown-up, not to mention exactly like my dad's, but when I got to school, which was only a few blocks away from our house, some new feelings crept in. I didn't go to preschool, so kindergarten was my first time in a classroom. I was worried about how the other kids would perceive my appearance, especially given my recent experience with Ed Whalen earlier that year, but I was also worried about food. My family was strictly vegetarian, and suddenly here I was, out in the real world, faced with something called *snack time*. What was I going to do there? I was too timid to take any chances, so whenever I saw something unfamiliar, I just refused to eat it. Mom says that she had to be around quite a bit that first week, because I was nervous about the whole experience.

As it turned out, I had reason to be. On one of the first days of school, I was playing outside on the merry-go-round, and I noticed this kid next to me, looking at me, presumably curious about my turban. Then, he reached over, and without thinking twice, he grabbed it. The force of the merry-go-round yanked the turban off my head.

I was distraught, and I couldn't get off the ride immediately, either, because it was still spinning. Once I finally jumped off and was able to see what had happened, I realized that my turban hadn't come fully off: it was just unravelled. But that wasn't any better, because I didn't know how to retie it, and I knew that nobody else at the school did, either. Embarrassment started to creep in, and I thought of the months of school I still had ahead of me. I remember thinking: *Is this what school is going to be like?*

I was incredibly proud of my turban, but I was also stubborn about it, insisting on copying my dad in other ways. When I got back home from kindergarten, for instance, I could've taken my turban off, or put on a simpler, more casual version. Many Sikhs do that when they get home at the end of the day. But not Dad. For whatever reason, he likes to keep his full, formal turban on until he goes to bed at night. So that's what I did, too. It was this funny routine in our family. Every night Mom would ask me to get ready for bed, and every night I wouldn't budge until I knew Dad was, too.

That year, Bhai Jiwan Singh Ji was visiting Calgary, so my mom and I drove up together to host him and his wife, Bibi Joginder Kaur, at our house there and spend some quality time with them. We accompanied him to several religious gatherings where he sang Sikh hymns, and on visits to many people's houses, teaching them about meditation and humility. But my turban became an issue. That entire week, I never took it off. Not once. My dad had tied it for me before I left, and I refused to let anyone else do it. I didn't like anyone else's style, and I was worried how it would turn out if someone else tied it on me. So I wore my turban in the bathtub, to bed— everywhere. Nobody could convince me otherwise!

Once I finished kindergarten, it was on to grade one, and the challenges of fitting in continued. I'm grateful for how supportive my teachers were, because I really did stick out. It helped that by the time I was going through school, Mom and Dad had long since established themselves in the town. Plus, all three of my sisters had already gone through the same school. So the teachers and the staff were familiar with our family. But I still couldn't relate to many of the things that the majority of people in Brooks use as common ground. The music my family listened to, the language we spoke at home, the food we ate, the way we looked—it was all completely different from the rest of Brooks. And when you're a kid, you feel those differences even more strongly.

As a result, I had to answer a *lot* of questions—not just about my turban, but other aspects of my faith, too. For instance, as Sikhs, we wear a steel or cast iron bangle, known as a *karra,* on one of our arms. The circle represents the fact that we all come from one Creator, and the weight of the steel reminds us that the Creator is always with us, guiding us in our decision-making. I can explain this now, but when I was a little kid and everyone was asking me, "Hey, why are you wearing that?" it was hard to know how to respond. As I was the only one wearing a karra in my school, the questions made me self-conscious, so I needed some coaching. All of my differences had me feeling a sense of pressure, especially as a child, which lasted until I became more comfortable in my own skin. My parents did their best to prepare me. Every afternoon, I would come home and tell them what had happened at school, and they would tell me what to say next time. When it came to questions about our faith, they always said, "Try not to be confrontational about it. Look at it as a chance to explain to your friends who we are." But I found out early on that some classmates were more ready to hear the answers than others, and some kids didn't care at all. I would start answering their questions, and they'd just run away. So it wasn't necessarily easy. I had to pick and choose who I was going to talk to about this stuff: who was truly interested, and who was just trying to get a rise out of me.

One person whose interest was genuine was my grade-one teacher, Mrs. Lacey Pfahl. At our parent-teacher interviews, she told Mom and Dad that I was doing pretty well. But she had a question. She said, "Harnarayan's hands are constantly moving in class. He's always tapping out this . . . rhythm on the side of his desk." Our desks had metal sides, and when you tapped them, they made a kind of echoing sound. It took my parents a minute to realize that I was doing this because the desk sounded like a *tabla*, an Indian percussion instrument we had at home. My mom had to tell her that I played the tabla at home (on the actual drums but also on the dinner table) too, and it wasn't anything to worry about.

But Mrs. Pfahl wasn't trying to discipline me. In fact, when she found out this habit of mine was related to a musical instrument, she got excited. She asked if I would be willing to bring in our tabla from home and play it for the rest of the class.

I remember being surprised, even then, that a non-Sikh person could be interested in the tabla. As a kid, I sometimes felt like I was living two different lives. At home, our family had our own culture and traditions, and every weekend we'd leave town to attend Gurdwara in Calgary; the rest of the time, I'd go to school, where everyone was oblivious to all of that. I pretended to be like all of the other kids in my class. So when Mrs. Pfahl showed an actual interest in my other life, it meant a lot to me.

Even though I was nervous about it, a few days later my dad helped me bring in our tabla and I played it for my classmates. It went really well, and I guess Mrs. Pfahl told the school principal, Mr. Clive Joseph, about it. He was an awesome guy, with a bald head and a big beard, and he approached me in the hallway to say he'd heard about the class performance, and asked: Would I be interested in doing the same thing for the whole school? That was around 500 or 600 kids—a way bigger deal! I went home and told my parents, and they encouraged me to do it. I remember standing in my bedroom the night before, looking in my T-shirt drawer, trying to figure out what I should wear for the big day. (I ended up picking my red shirt with Goofy on it.)

The next day, Mr. Joseph and I stood on the stage in front of the entire elementary student body. He introduced me as Harnarayan Zing! (My sisters later told me that he used to pronounce our last name "Zing" for them, too.) He then asked me questions on a microphone: "So what is this called? Where is it from?" I answered his questions as best I could, and then played different patterns on the tabla to show how it worked. That assembly turned out to be another big moment. For any classmates who were apprehensive about the kid in a turban, this was a way for us to find a connection. That's the power that music can have, just like sports: everyone can relate to it, no matter where you're from. After the performance, my social standing probably improved, too. Once someone has connected with you over a song, they're a lot less likely to give you trouble in the hallway.

From a young age, I've had two main interests in my life. One is hockey, obviously. But Sikh music, which in Punjabi is called *Kirtan*, played an equally important role—and it still does. Kirtan is part of the foundation of the faith, and inextricable from Sikh practice.

I trace my interest in music back directly to my mom, who has always had an affinity for singing. When I was a kid, I used to hear her singing away in the kitchen as she cooked,

and she passed her love of music on to her kids in an interesting way. Before I was born, she used to tell Bhai Jiwan Singh
Ji that she wished she had become a better musician. She sang
often at the Gurdwara in Calgary and taught countless other
kids how to sing hymns there as well, but she never reached
the level she had aspired to. Bhai Jiwan Singh Ji said to her:
"Don't worry. Your passion for music will come through
your children." Through the Creator's blessing, that was his
blessing to us. And sure enough, when I was born, I took to
music right away.

Several instruments can be used when singing Kirtan, but
the two more common ones are the tabla and the harmonium. The tabla, as I mentioned, is a set of drums, one for
the bass and the other for a higher-pitched tone that can match
the singer's voice. You play it with your hands, not with sticks,
and it's very intricate, because each finger does something
different. The sounds and rhythms you can get out of it are
almost endless. The harmonium, meanwhile, is a hand-
pumped organ with keys, like a piano or an accordion, and
as you use the pump, you play notes on the keys and sing
along with the melody.

I started playing the tabla when I was two years old. My
dad plays a simple form of it, so he showed me the basics,
and soon afterwards, I was sitting on his lap at temple, completely transfixed by the musicians onstage. I would sit there
each week, studying their moves and trying with my little
fingers to copy what they were doing. We also had videotapes of Sikh musicians that I would watch over and over
again. Very quickly, and without any kind of formal lessons,
I was able to pick it up.

I've played the tabla and the harmonium ever since, and to this day, when someone asks me how I learned to play, I feel like I can't even take credit for it. I know it all goes back to the prayers of Bhai Jiwan Singh Ji, all those years ago. He was the first musician who ever asked me to accompany him on the tabla in front of a congregation. We still have videotapes of this. And, because I was only four years old at the time, I was so small that a family friend, Balbir Singh Kalyanee, went to arrange pillows for me to sit on. It really is my mom's passion coming through, which has been passed down to me as her son.

———

In school, I got used to answering questions about my appearance, my turban, and the other things that made me stand out. But I always appreciated those friends and classmates who didn't seem to care about our differences—people who simply accepted me for who I was.

One of the main ways I was able to bridge that gap was with hockey. Early on, I wore NHL-themed clothes to school, and that helped other kids warm up to me. Some of them were in the cooler social groups (which I definitely was not a part of!), while others played hockey themselves. I would never have fit in with these kids otherwise. But because I was wearing a Gretzky sweater or talking about the game last night, it became common ground between us, and we were able to develop at least a mutual respect. One boy in particular was a big, strong hockey player, and we didn't have much else in common. But when he noticed someone bugging me on the playground, he came up to me and said, "If they keep doing that, tell them they'll have to go through me first." He wanted me to know he had my back if I ever needed it.

I also used hockey as a way of relating to my teachers. Whenever I could, I would force hockey into my essays and school projects. Later, in junior high, I would make bets with my teachers over the outcome of that night's game, especially during the playoffs—for something small from the vending machine, like a can of pop or a bag of chips. I even helped Dad out with *his* colleagues. The staff at his school had a long-standing hockey pool, and because he didn't choose to follow the sport as much, I secretly made his picks for him. I remember him coming home from work some days, laughing about how surprised other teachers at work were that Doc Singh, of all people, was cleaning up in the hockey pool.

At the same time, I had other friendships that had nothing to do with hockey. There was one girl named Shannon Lacoste who was in the same class as me from kindergarten all the way to grade six. Not just that, but we were always placed next to each other, and I didn't realize why until recently, when my wife, who's an elementary-school teacher, told me how classes are chosen. When you're a kid, you don't have any say in the matter, so you don't think about it too much. But now it makes sense to me: someone at the school must have decided that we were good influences on each other.

My friendship with Shannon was based on a friendly but ongoing competition over marks. One year, our class had a challenge to see who could do a set of math worksheets the fastest and the most accurately. We did this every week, and there was a chart on the wall showing who had won most often. I don't think teachers would do that kind of thing nowadays—it's a little in your face about who's good at math and who isn't. But whenever the chart was updated, it was always Shannon and me rushing to the front of the room to see who was ahead. We weren't even worried, really, about being at the top of the class. It was just about beating the other person.

Math worksheets weren't the only thing we were competitive about. People sometimes ask me why my writing is so neat, and I never tell them the real answer, because it's kind of embarrassing. But it's because of Shannon. She always used to critique my handwriting. She showed me how she thought a *Y* or an *A* should be written, and I wanted to impress her, so over time my writing got neater and neater and neater. Long story short, I now have what some people call the neatest writing in the world. Since joining *Hockey Night in Canada*, I have the privilege of signing autographs for kids—and to this day, my signature still has the letters the way Shannon taught me to write them, all those years ago.

Even though I started wearing a turban in kindergarten, it was years until I was able to tie it myself. Before that, I relied on Dad to do it for me, and that dependence had a ripple effect on other parts of my childhood. Wearing my turban in that particular way became a part of my identity. Even if my mom and I went up to Calgary for the weekend to see my sisters, who by then were in university, the number-one question on my mind was always: *Who's going to tie my turban?* My mom does tie a female version of the turban, but she doesn't tie the male version—or at least not the way I liked it—so that was a non-starter for me. We also knew plenty of Sikh men in Calgary, including my dad's younger brother, Harnek Singh, but I refused to let any of them tie it, either, because I only wanted one specific style, which was my dad's.

Part of it was feeling comfortable in a routine, but part of it was aesthetic, too. As I mentioned, there are so many ways of tying a turban. It's not the kind of thing anyone can just pick up and do, and all of the other styles people suggested felt weird to me. Of course, lots of kids have habits like this. The same way a kid might only like a peanut butter sandwich the way his mom makes it, I only wanted the type of turban my dad could tie.

Most of the time, it was easy enough to keep my turban looking good, but there were exceptions. Once, our school had an outdoor fun day, and I was in a relay where I had to run to a pylon, take off one T-shirt, put on a different one, and run back. The T-shirts I normally wear have a looser neckline, so they don't disturb my turban when I'm changing—but I didn't realize that the T-shirts in this event weren't turban-friendly. In my rush to switch shirts, my turban came clean off, and in that exact moment, out on the huge grass field of Eastbrook Elementary, I decided the easiest thing to do was run all the way home. Which I did.

I also used to dread field trips where my class went swimming. My family had never been into swimming, so I wasn't very good at it to begin with. But more importantly, what was I going to do about my turban? These trips weren't optional; our whole class had to go. I simply wasn't going to take my turban off to get in the pool, but what if it got wet? I had never taken my turban off in front of my classmates or my teacher before. There were other things running through my mind, like my turban tan, which was significant, especially in the summertime. You may not have heard of a turban tan before, but no joke, it's not something you share with the public. All of these things weighed on me. I was already drawing enough unwanted attention to myself as it was.

In the end, I decided I had no choice but to get into the water with my turban on, exactly as I normally wore it. When I got back to school, the turban was soaking wet. The way Brooks is laid out, my elementary school and Dad's high school shared a grass field, and we'd planned ahead of time to meet up in the middle of two parking lots, halfway between our schools. He gave me a new, dry turban and quickly tied it for me. This continued every day that I went swimming throughout my elementary-school years. I'm grateful that my parents always accommodated me, because boy, I could be stubborn about this stuff. We definitely could've come up with a different plan, but at the time I felt strongly that this was what I needed to do to get through the day.

———

In 1994, when I was nine years old, I went to India for the first time. I was such a late addition to my family that I never had a chance to meet most of my grandparents, but my grandmother on my mom's side was still alive, and my parents wanted me to meet her. Plus, my parents had done such a great job teaching me about the history of our faith and our culture, and this was a chance to see that history up close. My two older sisters were away at school, but Mom, Dad, Gurdeep, and I headed off to Delhi.

We landed late at night, but it was July, so it was *hot*. My uncle, the late Bhag Singh Jassal, met us at the airport, after making the seven-hour drive from the state of Punjab (and that's not counting traffic!). We picked up our luggage and headed out to the parking lot of Delhi's international airport, where I found myself staring at an ocean of identical cars. At that time, in a lot of South Asian countries, owning a car was a luxury, and if you did have one, it was usually the same as everyone else's: the same brand, same model, even the same colour—white. I remember thinking: *This is nuts. How are we ever going to find our car and get out of here?*

It was dark out, but everything I could see was very different than back home. I'm pretty sure the term *organized chaos* was invented to describe the traffic in India. One second there's a rickshaw darting out in front of you, the next a motorcycle is cutting you off. Most roads back then didn't have official lane markers, so everyone was swerving around however they wanted, but it still somehow worked. Even the way they load up cars over there is wild—they just stack as much stuff on top as they can, then rope it all down. They don't care if they can see out their windows. They just do it. It's impressive!

And sure enough, on the drive back from the airport, we hit something. At that point, I knew that cows were sacred to the Hindu faith. But I didn't realize they were so sacred that they're allowed to roam basically wherever they want:

onto the road, in front of buildings and houses, wherever. For a Canadian kid from Brooks, Alberta, it seemed so bizarre. I had this formal vision of India in my head, based on the history I had been told by my parents, but hitting a cow with our car was not part of it. To my uncle, however, it was no big deal. And over the rest of the trip, I saw cars routinely bump into each other. They all seemed to have scratches and scrapes, and nobody seemed to mind too much.

That night, we stayed with some family friends in Delhi. The next morning, when we got up and walked out the main gate of the house, another huge group of white cattle was standing right in front of the house. I've never really been an animal person, even though I lived in a town with a massive cattle-processing plant, but even so, it was shocking to find myself so close to these seemingly wild cows. The whole drive up to Punjab, I kept asking Dad questions: *What were those cows doing there? Are they missing from a farm? Who's responsible for them?*

Back in Canada, I'd been raised to believe that every citizen has a voice. Once, as a school assignment, my class had even written letters to our local politicians, and some students were chosen to be a part of town council for a day. I was one of them and loved the entire experience. Well, seeing all that chaos in India bothered me so much that I decided to write a letter to the mayor of Delhi. I informed him that I was visiting from Canada, and that I felt there needed to be more organization in his city. I suggested that letting cows roam around was dangerous, not just for vehicles, but also to the animals themselves.

I signed my name at the bottom and, feeling quite proud of myself, gave the letter to my dad to put in the mail. He looked at it and just started laughing.

"This is not going to make a difference," he said.

"Why not?"

He replied, "That just isn't how it works here."

India had plenty of other issues, as it turned out, and seeing them in person made me really understand the reality of the world, and also appreciate my life back in Canada. I saw lots of people who were happy and doing well for themselves, but the poverty was impossible to ignore. Right next to the roads you would see all these makeshift homes—not just for single people, but entire families, trying to get by on the street. It was a real culture shock.

That shock continued when we met our cousins in Punjab. My whole life, I had been told so many stories about the Sikh faith, and all of the things that the Gurus taught us. Now I was there, in the land of the Gurus! But I was surprised to learn that most of my first cousins didn't seem to really care about the Sikh faith. They were more interested in the Western culture that I was growing up within—it was a big deal for them, for instance, when the first McDonald's opened in their city.

At first I was quiet and polite, because I was getting to know them, but by the end of the trip, we got into it. At one point I said to my cousin, "It's so hard for our family to keep our faith in Canada, and you don't even try to do it here? You guys live where the history comes from!" It was a classic case of the grass always being greener on the other side of the fence. We both wanted what the other person had.

But I loved being surrounded by the history and faith. One of the most sacred places in Sikh culture is in Amritsar—it's called Harimandir Sahib but is popularly referred to as the Golden Temple. It's an amazingly beautiful, serene place that reminds you of heaven on earth. Almost every Sikh family has a picture or a painting of the Golden Temple in their home, but nothing compares to seeing it in person.

One thing that particularly stood out to me was the free kitchen, which in Punjabi is known as *langar*. Having a community meal available for everyone is one of the teachings of the Gurus, and every Sikh temple has one. India has such a dominant caste system, and the Sikh Gurus wanted to break that. They wanted kings and beggars to be able to sit and eat together to symbolize equality across all of humanity. Langar is entirely run by volunteers, too, from the cooks to the servers to the dishwashers, as part of a Sikh concept called *seva*, which means selfless service. North American Gurdwaras also have langar for the public, but on a smaller scale. Sikhs in Amritsar, meanwhile, feed thousands and thousands of people every single day. It's a beautiful concept, and seeing it in person connected me to my faith in a way that just wasn't possible back in Canada.

—

I mentioned that my friend Shannon never bugged me about my turban, which is true. But that doesn't mean it never came up. All throughout elementary school, she kept asking me for one big favour: Would I take off my turban for her, and show her how long my hair was? She was interested, but it wasn't in an accusing or insulting way. With her, it was more about curiosity and openness. And by the time I was in grade six, I was fairly comfortable with everyone at school. I ended up making a promise that on the last day of classes—our very last day of elementary school—I would take off my turban in class and show her and my classmates my hair.

When the day came, I went up to the front of Mrs. Schafer's class and slowly took off my turban first, and then the bun underneath. When those were off, my hair spilled all the way down to my lower back, and the class gasped and crowded around me. It was a hit! I knew Shannon was pushing for me to do it, but I wasn't sure how the rest of the class would react. But everyone was so interested, and even though we'd been in school together for years, lots of them peppered me with a new round of questions: *So you've never cut your hair? Ever?* They wanted to touch my hair, too, and I let them. Then I showed everyone how I comb it, and then I retied the bun and the turban on top. Thankfully, I had been tying my own turban since grade five, which helped my confidence, too— I knew that if it came off, I could retie it.

My classmates were fascinated, and it was also such a positive experience for me. Like when I played the tabla in the school assembly, that afternoon showed me that maybe my Sikh faith was something people in my small town might be able to not just tolerate but appreciate. It gave me confidence that it was okay to be a little different. Maybe people would be fine with it after all.

Then I went to junior high.

———

In elementary school, any difficult situations I went through usually came from a place of curiosity. Even if I felt uncomfortable, at least the kids were well-intentioned. But Brooks Junior High was different. That's the first time I experienced outright bullying because of how I looked.

One of the big reasons was because there were a lot more kids to contend with. In elementary school, my one class grew up together. In junior high, however, suddenly there were all these new kids from the *other* elementary schools in Brooks. Just when I thought the hard work of integrating myself was over, now I was going to have to do it all over again.

Of course, school itself changes a lot between elementary and junior high. Grade seven was the first time, for instance, that we had to change into separate clothes for gym class. One day I was in the boys' change room, getting ready to go outside, and I noticed this one kid looking at me. Without having ever talked to him before, I was already afraid of him. He had been held back a grade, so he was much bigger than I was. Plus, he gave off a dangerous vibe that made you want to keep your distance. He looked at me with this sort of conniving smirk on his face—typical of a bully sending a message to someone he or she feels is inferior. It took me a bit longer than everyone else to change because of my turban, and this kid waited around until it was just the two of us. Then he came up to me, grabbed my gym bag, and emptied it out, throwing the contents all over the room, onto the floor, and even into the showers.

I just stood there, too stunned to move. It was obvious that out of all the kids in our class, he had chosen me because of what I looked like. Again, I was one of the only non-white kids in the class. I was scared he was going to do something else to me, but luckily, once my clothes were on the floor, he left. As I gathered my belongings, I knew I couldn't end up alone with this kid again. I didn't even tell anyone what happened, because I was worried that if he found out, it would be worse the next time.

Fast-forward to biology class a few weeks later. The bell rang, and everyone left. I looked up from gathering my books and realized I wasn't entirely alone: that same kid from gym class was still there, too. We were on totally different sides of the classroom, but I knew nothing good was going to happen, so I rushed as quickly as I could to pack up. But when you rush too fast, you're only more likely to drop things, and that's exactly what happened. When I glanced over at him again, he started laughing, then opened up his backpack and pulled out a couple of large knives. I froze. Then he started making a cutting motion with one of them. I don't know—maybe they were legitimate hunting knives or something, but when you're carrying something like that around in your backpack at school, alongside your textbooks and your pencil case, then something strange is going on. Either way, I got the message and booked it out of the classroom. Fearing the safety of my classmates, I told a teacher as soon as possible, leaving out the fact that I was being targeted.

A few months later, I was walking home from school by myself. All of a sudden, I heard someone yelling at me from behind. I looked back, and it was him. I started picking up the pace, trying not to be obvious about it. Then instinct kicked in, and I started running. But he caught up to me on a grassy area and tackled me to the ground, ripping my turban right off of my head in the process. This time was scarier, because I was away from school property, and if he wanted to keep going, there was nothing I could do to stop him. He managed to get whatever satisfaction he wanted, and left me lying there.

I wish I could say I solved my bullying problem by finally standing up to this kid and showing him the errors of his ways. Unfortunately, it didn't work out like that. One day, I was walking through the parking lot of my former elementary school and saw my old principal, Mr. Joseph. Someone had smashed the windshield of his car, and it turned out that it was the same kid who had been bullying me. That got him expelled from school, and thankfully, I never saw him again.

There were some other unpleasant incidents at junior high and high school, but they were typical things that a lot of kids deal with. I need to give credit to the teachers in Brooks for that. They handled things well and always did their best to make sure I felt welcome and supported in the classroom.

But there was nothing anyone could do to prepare for September 11, 2001.

I was just starting grade 12 on the morning the World Trade Center buildings collapsed. It was instantly the top news story around the world, and even in my little town in Alberta, teachers wheeled in TVs on carts so we could follow the news coverage live. It was shocking. Once I saw the images of the towers falling, I knew they'd stay in my mind forever.

At one point, I left the classroom and was walking down the hallway. All of a sudden, someone grabbed my neck from behind and threw me up against the painted cement wall. He was so strong that he actually held me up off the ground. I was scared, and then, once I saw who it was, confused: this guy wasn't a bully. I knew him. We'd gone to school together for years. In fact, he was the same guy who had stuck up for me when I was younger—the one who told me to tell him if anyone was picking on me, so he could take care of it. But now here he was, grabbing me by the throat and screaming in my face.

"You motherfuckers should go back to where you came from!"

It was hard to speak, but I tried to respond. "What are you talking about?"

His eyes were lit up with anger. "You come into our country, and this is what you do to us? Get the fuck out of here!"

"Buddy, I've known you since kindergarten!" I said. "Our families know each other." Finally I was able to push him off me. "What's wrong with you? This is ridiculous."

After the initial shock wore off as I stood there trying to compose myself, I went straight to the office, because I was still confused about what was happening. It was only then that I realized that in the photos the news was showing of Osama bin Laden, the man allegedly behind the 9/11 attacks, he was wearing a cloth on his head that somewhat resembled a turban.

Later, I did some research, and learned that a very small percentage of Muslim people wear head coverings. But it's such a low number that I'd never heard of it happening. And, really, what bin Laden was wearing wasn't even tied like a turban. He also had a long beard, which, again, is not as common in the Muslim world. But the average North American didn't understand that level of nuance. And sure enough, when you put those two things together, bin Laden kind of resembled a Sikh.

We in the Sikh community were worried right away. We knew that CNN showing those images non-stop were going to affect us. And it did, immediately, as my incident in the hallway showed. Here I was, in this small town in Canada, thousands of miles away from New York, and the panic was in my high school literally before the buildings had fallen.

In the aftermath of 9/11, hate crimes against people of colour spiked across North America. Because of the confusion around bin Laden's appearance, the Sikh community was lumped right into it. Within a week of the attacks, a Sikh gas station owner in Arizona was shot and killed because of his appearance. There were countless incidents, like attacks, harassments, and vandalism. I've tried to keep a record of the hate crimes on Sikhs in North America, but the number is staggering, and you can never really keep up.

In response, the Sikh community tried to go above and beyond. We all knew 9/11 had nothing to do with us, but we also knew the media was lumping us into it anyway, alongside the billions of similarly innocent Muslims worldwide. We decided to hold public candlelight vigils, and to offer prayers for the victims of 9/11, as a show of solidarity. We wanted to demonstrate that we weren't with the attackers. We were with humanity. Hate crimes against any religious or minority group are not okay.

The hostility that many white people suddenly developed towards people of colour affected me and my family on a personal level. Not long after the attacks, I went to a Calgary Flames game along with another Sikh friend of mine, Tejinder Singh Sidhu, who is now my brother-in-law. I'm not sure at what point the word *Taliban* started to be used, but several people yelled it at us while we were walking through the crowd to our car—it didn't matter that Tejinder was wearing a Flames jersey just like they were. Another time, I was in a Walmart parking lot with my sister Gurdeep, and someone called me a "raghead" and told me to go back to my own country. These things started happening more and more, and it put me on high alert. Anytime I went out in public, around people I didn't know, I knew that I was automatically going to be targeted. One of the biggest impacts out of all of this was noticing that people around me seemed to be more uncomfortable whenever I wore a white turban, specifically a white casual turban, because to them it resembled what bin Laden was wearing. This was particularly evident when I was at an airport or on a plane. It's something that has stuck with me since those years after 9/11: no matter how long the flight, I always make sure to have on my full formal turban—especially if I'm flying into or within the United States. To this day, I try not to ever wear a white turban to any airport—the visual can quickly lead to negative assumptions.

It was difficult to deal with, especially as a teenager. My parents' mentality has always been to stay quiet and ignore people who are being ignorant, but I'm not like that. I would get angry. When some tow truck driver yelled at me, I'd yell right back. Why not? I knew I was just as Canadian as he was, if not more so. He needed to know. And I was going to tell him.

Around this time, there was a knock at our door. I answered it, and it was an alarm-system sales representative. I knew right away that Dad was not going to go for this. He isn't an easy guy to sell anything to, and besides, this was a small town: we didn't even lock our front door most of the time, let alone worry about being robbed. I listened to the whole spiel, and at the end politely told him thanks, but no thanks.

"Thanks anyway," he said. "Oh, and I just wanted to say— welcome to Canada!" And he walked off.

I stood there in the doorway, stunned. It hurt to hear him say that, and it took me a minute to process why. At that time, the Salt Lake City Olympics were about to begin, so my bedroom—which already had multiple Canadian flags hanging in it, even one from the bedroom window that was visible to passersby—now had a bunch of Team Canada jerseys and paraphernalia all over the place, too. When I got back upstairs, and saw all of those maple leaves, it clicked in my head: *That guy only thought I was a newcomer because of how I looked.* He clearly didn't know the long, rich history Sikhs have of being in this country, and contributing to it. The more I thought about this one ignorant comment, the more angry I grew. *I* am *Canadian,* I thought. So I did what I had been raised to do (and what had definitely *not* worked back when I was on vacation in Delhi): I wrote a letter.

This time, I wrote to the editor of our local paper, the *Brooks Bulletin*. I explained what had happened with the salesperson, and I said to remember that just because some-one is a visible minority, that doesn't mean they're new to Canada. I also mentioned that my family had been in Brooks since the 1960s, and my ancestors had first come to Canada a century ago. Writing it all down in one place made me feel better, but I wasn't sure if anything would come of it.

The next week, my letter ran in the newspaper. I remem-ber standing with my dad in the cereal aisle of my local Safeway when a woman I didn't know came up to me and said, "I read your letter, and I'm so sorry this happened to you." What's funny is that she didn't even have to ask if it was me who wrote the letter—it was obvious, because we were the only family in town with turbans! That was very kind of her, and typical of my childhood: whenever I experienced moments of bullying, or feeling like an outcast because of what I looked like, it was always followed by another moment of warmth from someone else, who wanted me to know that that sort of thing was not okay. All things considered, I felt like Brooks always had my back.

A few days later, I went home from school for lunch, and when I got there, Mom was frantic. She has this funny habit of getting way ahead of herself when she's telling a story, so sometimes you have to ask who she is talking about. When I walked in the door she said, "You need to call them right now! He's going to get fired!"

"Who are you talking about?"

"The alarm-system company! They called, and they said they're going to fire him. You have to call them back right away!" Mom was really worried. In her mind, it wasn't right that the salesman was about to get fired because of my letter to the editor, and for her it was the worst thing that could happen to someone who had come to our door.

I called the number she'd written down, and some high-up executive within the alarm company answered. He told me he wanted to apologize for what had happened, and that the company was going to fire the person who came to our door. He also asked if he could take me out to lunch sometime. I think he was in damage-control mode, worried that I would keep causing problems, because I had specifically named his company in my letter, and it was the kind of story that could easily spread beyond our town.

I wasn't interested in eating lunch with him, and more importantly, I asked him not to fire the salesperson. Instead, I asked him to tell the employee to remember this the next time he met someone of a different ethnicity—that he shouldn't assume that anyone is new to Canada, no matter what the colour of their skin is.

As soon as I said that, I could hear Mom breathing a sigh of relief behind me.

This experience really showed me the power of the media. My little letter to the editor of a small-town newspaper had led to a conversation with a company executive, and could have led to someone losing their job. Part of me wondered how this guy had even gotten our phone number in the first place, but then I figured it out: if you looked up Singh in the Brooks phone book, we were the only ones.

Chapter 4
"You Have to Start with the Dream"

The drive from Brooks to Calgary is about two hours each way, along a prairie-flanked stretch of the Trans-Canada Highway. They say beauty is in the eye of the beholder, and while the vast prairie landscape isn't for everyone, I absolutely love it. My family and I would drive up to the big city every single weekend without fail, as we would attend Gurdwara services there, and my folks also taught classes to youth in the local Sikh community. Over the course of my childhood, I must've spent hundreds of hours on that stretch of Alberta highway, staring out the window. For most of the drive, we'd listen to music from some of my favourite Sikh musicians. But as soon as we got close to either Brooks or Calgary, Dad would switch over to his all-time favourite radio station: CBC Radio 1.

This was before podcasts, so we listened to whatever was on: big national shows like *The World at Six* and *As It Happens*, all the way down to local news and weather broadcasts. Most Sundays, on our way back home, we'd catch some of the call-in show *Cross Country Checkup*, with Rex Murphy, to hear what our fellow Canadians were talking about. My parents were interested in pretty much everything. When Dad was growing up in India, they used to get most of their news from the radio; later, when he arrived here in Canada, the CBC and CKUA in Edmonton would keep him company, especially the science shows. My mom, too, has memories of learning about all kinds of world events via the radio in Punjab, whether it was World War II, the nuclear arms race between the U.S. and Russia, or JFK's assassination. So they've always had an interest in news and media, and all of that carried over to me from a young age—without my even realizing it. My parents say that I predicted Brian Mulroney would win the 1988 election, based only on how he performed during the debate, which we all watched together on TV. I was three years old.

As I got a little older, that interest in current events went up a notch. The high school Dad taught at was just across a field from my elementary school, so a lot of times, I would walk over to have lunch with him in his classroom. Sometimes I would also go after school, and I would hang out there while Dad was catching up on marking or doing other prep work. It was always cool for me to see him there (later, in high school, I actually had to take his math class as a student) because he acted differently than he did at home. At our house, he was always the rational, serious one. But in his classroom, he would tell these incredibly corny jokes to try to connect with his students, comparing *pairs* in math to *pears* the fruit, or doing voices from *Sesame Street* to encourage kids who were having trouble with what he felt was a simple problem. He also decorated his classroom walls with these big posters of Albert Einstein and other famous mathematicians and scientists. This decorating style was not unlike a certain son's bedroom back at home, come to think of it . . .

I loved the giant chalkboards, and later the whiteboards, that ran along the walls of Dad's classroom. While he was marking, I would try to fill every last inch of the boards with as much information as possible. Sometimes it was about hockey. But sometimes it was about politics, or whatever else I had been hearing about on CBC lately. One day I decided to fill the whiteboard with a list of all the levels of government, the different political parties (and where they fell on the political spectrum), the ministers of each portfolio, and as many MPs and MLAs as I could think of. Just as I'd finished, a social studies teacher named Grant Jensen walked in and saw what I'd written. He paused as he took it all in, then said to my dad, "Did your son write all this? He *has* to go into politics." Mr. Jensen pointed at the board. "Just look at it!" I was just amusing myself, and had no idea anyone else would walk into the room, let alone care about what I was writing, but that still felt pretty good.

Social studies was my favourite subject in school. I was always very interested in how society works at different levels of governments, and one of my go-to video games was *SimCity*, where you were able to build an entire city from scratch. (Some kids I knew preferred the sillier parts of the game, where you had to do things like fight off Godzilla, but I always thought all that destruction was just counterproductive.) I also really enjoyed school projects like when I was able to spend time at town council. In junior high, one of our social studies teachers, Mr. Cameron Brown, was enthusiastic about current events, and if something important was happening in the world, he would bring it up in class. One day he mentioned the PLO, and, without thinking, I blurted out, "Oh yeah, the Palestine Liberation Organization." He gave me this look of total surprise, and that's when I realized I knew more about this stuff than some of the other kids did, just because I'd watched and listened to so much news from being around Mom and Dad. Names of world leaders, even capital cities—I soaked it all in without really trying or meaning to.

Mr. Jensen wasn't the last person to suggest that I go into politics. I knew early on that I had it in me. I was very devoted to the idea of public service and making my community a better place. But honestly, I'm glad I didn't. As a kid, I had no idea how much a life in politics affects your family, and how tough it is to go out there every day and try to keep soliciting votes. Over the past decade, I've had several people ask me if I was going to run for something, but I know it isn't right for me, or for my family. We're just not built for that kind of thing.

———

At the same time that I was developing an interest in the news media, I was also applying that interest to the world of sports. From a young age I read the sports section of our local newspaper, which was a good start. But things really got serious when Dad got me a subscription to *The Hockey News*. An entire magazine dedicated to my favourite sport? It was almost too good to be true. Whenever the new issue showed up in our mailbox, I would stop everything to read the entire thing cover to cover. I couldn't put it down. I also couldn't get myself to throw the old issues away, because there was just so much cool stuff in them. For years, I kept boxes and boxes full of those magazines, until I realized they were turning my whole room into a fire hazard. I still have a few boxes left with some issues that I just couldn't get rid of.

By the time I reached grade four, I still had that old microphone my parents gave me, which I used for my live play-by-play in the living room. I also had an all-in-one boom box with a radio, cassette player, and recorder built in. One day, while listening to music in my bedroom, I got the idea to make a show of my own. It was called the *HSTS: The Harnarayan Singh Talk Show*. And it was all about hockey. I also had a keyboard in my room, which I used to create and play my own theme music for the show. Then I would introduce myself to my listeners, and from there it was off to the races. The first few times I recorded everything on my own, then listened back afterwards and had a good laugh. But eventually I realized I needed a co-host.

Luckily, Matt Schneider was as obsessed with hockey as I was. Matt was a friend of mine from school, and a really funny kid, too. (He also shares his name with Stanley Cup–winning defenceman Mathieu Schneider!) One day after school I showed Matt my keyboard and recorder, and right away he wanted to be part of the show. My initials are HS, and his are MS, so we rebranded it as *The HS and MS Show*. The format was the same: We would talk hockey, throw to (pretend) commercials, then come back on air with our theme music. It was so much fun.

The other thing I used my microphone for was recording pretend award shows. I've already mentioned the stool in my kitchen, which I would drag into my room and then set up with the mic for my own version of the NHL awards, but I would also do award shows for Sikh music. I'll admit I wasn't the most objective juror: whoever I was listening to the most that month was a shoo-in to win an award, which I based on North American music awards like the Grammys. I had Best Solo Vocal Performance, and Best New Artist, but also Sikh-specific categories like Best New Tabla Performance. It's funny, because up until very recently, there weren't any awards for Kirtan. The idea was that the music is very spiritual, and our hymns talk a lot about leaving your ego behind. Awards almost go against what the hymns are saying. It wasn't until recently that a TV channel in India started giving out an award for best album of the year. Little did they know I was doing the same thing in my bedroom, 20 years earlier.

For years, broadcasting was a dream of mine, but I wasn't sure how to go about making it a reality. But when I got to high school, a new opportunity came along that put me onto the right track.

Because my dad taught at my high school, I became friends with another kid whose father was also a teacher there. His name was Mark Scholz, and his dad, Bert, was my biology teacher. The two of us weren't really friends before that, because we'd gone to different elementary and junior high schools, but once we got acquainted as teenagers, we really hit it off. Not just that, but I became more brave because of Mark. For example, the school staff room, which is normally off-limits to students, became our second home. If either of us wanted a cup of tea or coffee, we would just walk in there and make some. If we needed to photocopy something or use a desktop computer, we'd go use the teachers' machines. Sometimes we'd go in just to hang out on the couches for a bit. We felt that nobody could really say anything to us, because our dads were on staff. And thankfully, no other teachers did.

Maybe because Dad was one of them, some of my other teachers felt more like friends than authority figures, and I felt comfortable enough to joke around with them, too. Mr. Brown, who taught me in junior high, transferred over and taught at my high school, too, so I had known him for quite a while. One day, he walked into class, put a can of Five Alive on his desk, and then had to leave the room again. The period had started, and the whole class was just waiting around for him to come back. And I was feeling thirsty. I went up to his desk, opened the can, and chugged the whole thing. Then I put the empty can down exactly where it was before and went back to my desk.

When Mr. Brown returned to class, he didn't notice right away. He started his usual lesson by writing on the whiteboard and then gave us some work to do. The whole class was trying to hold in their laughter. Finally, halfway through the period, sitting back at his desk, he picked up the can, and realized it was totally empty. He muttered to himself, "*What?*" Then he looked up and scanned the classroom. Everybody was trying not to make eye contact. Then he just said, "Harnarayan!" Right away, I played the race card. "What?! Just because I'm the only brown kid in class, that means I drank your juice?"

By that point, this was part of our dynamic. Making my differences humorous was a good way to break the ice for me. Mr. Brown laughed, but he kicked me out of the class anyway. That used to happen a fair bit, to be honest. But it wasn't ever too serious.

I was standing outside the classroom, waiting to see if he was going to come out and talk to me. Then I realized: *Wait a minute. This is the same hallway as Dad's classroom.* I started getting nervous, but I also knew Dad didn't ever leave his class during a lesson. Plus I thought, *He doesn't even drink coffee. There's no way he's out of his room right now.* Of course, right as I finished that thought, he came walking by.

"What are you doing out here?" he said.

"Uh . . . just taking a break."

Dad wasn't an idiot. He knew what was happening. But all he said was, "Do you realize I know your marks even before you know them? You better straighten up." Then he walked away. That was the thing with Dad: He always had these perfect one-liners that you couldn't really respond to.

Anyway, back to Mark and me. We were a team. Like me, Mark was very interested in politics, and he also had a great sense of humour. In class we would sit next to each other and draw pictures of this future empire that together we'd own one day. Because my community has a monopoly on the taxi industry, I joked that I would be the head of the taxi world. Mark was in charge of other territories. And we'd join forces to rule the empire as a duo. We'd fill pages of our notebooks with these drawings and laugh our heads off the whole time.

Over time, Mark learned about my passion for sports broadcasting. One day in class, near the end of the day, he leaned over and told me that he did a weekly segment about high-school news and sports at Q13, the local AM radio station in Brooks, and that if I wanted to come along that week and record his report with him, I could. This was a total shock. I knew that Mark was interested in radio, because at our school they let kids do the morning announcements over the PA system, and even though I occasionally got to do them, mostly it was Mark's terrain. But an actual radio station? I didn't realize he would be so open to sharing that role with me.

"You'd be okay with that?" I asked him. "What would the station say?"

"We can just ask them," Mark said. "I'm sure it would be fine."

I couldn't believe it was that easy to get onto the radio. I went with him to the station, and Mark walked in the door like he'd been there 100 times—probably because he had. He was so comfortable and confident. He introduced me to one of the other hosts, as well as the station manager, John Petrie. John was the type of person who volunteers all around town just because he cares about helping the community. From the first moment I met him, John was so welcoming, and I was a little surprised. I remember thinking: *Are they not even going to ask me for my resumé? I mean, this is the* radio*!* For me, after listening to so much radio during those drives to and from Calgary, this was a thrilling opportunity, and they were so laid back about it.

Mark showed me how he put his segments together, laid out what he wanted to talk about that day, and asked if I wanted to read out half of it. Just like that, I was on the air, and after the first segment went well, Mark decided we'd be a duo from there on in.

Our segments aired on Q13 twice each week. They were short, one- or two-minute hits about whatever was going on at the high school, and we would record them in the afternoons, after class, so the station could air them the next day as part of their morning show. Mark and I had so much fun with it. Sometimes we would throw in a random clip of music, like the *Rocky* theme or a song from *Inspector Gadget*, to introduce us. Making the segments was enjoyable, but so was hearing the reaction around Brooks. People would come up to Mark and me in public and say, "Are you those boys from the radio? Oh, you guys are great." For me, the whole thing was surreal. I'd been dreaming about having a radio show since elementary school, and all of a sudden, it was happening for real.

Being on the radio was everything I dreamed it would be. You could have fun. You could be creative. And, most importantly, you could be yourself. The morning our segments aired, I would keep the radio on the whole time as I got ready for school, eating breakfast, brushing my teeth, and then— there it was! My own voice, talking to what felt like the entire town of Brooks at once. And based on how many people came up to us at school, or at the grocery store, it really did feel like everyone was listening. I enjoyed the technical parts of the job, too, whether it was finding music clips or using the faders in the studio to cut the segment just right. I took a lot of pride in sounding as professional as possible.

As time went on, our segments became more popular, and new opportunities presented themselves. We started getting sponsors, like Meyers Norris Penny, an accounting company that has its head office in Calgary. John increased our airtime by giving us another sponsored segment called the A&W Student of the Day; teachers in town would nominate the students, and we would find out information about them to talk about on the air. The best moment, though, was during Brooks's annual rodeo and parade, when Q13 chose Mark and me to sit on top of their van and wave to everyone in the crowd. That was such a great feeling.

Once school let out, John asked the two of us to continue to record segments for him over the summer. This took a bit more coordination, because my family and I were still spending a lot of time in Calgary. Sometimes we would record our segments over the phone, and I would have to call in, like I was a foreign correspondent. But there was also less news to discuss over the summer, so a lot of times Mark and I would end up talking about the most random stuff. ("Can you believe how many mosquitoes there are this year?") As long as we hit our time mark, John would let us do more or less whatever we wanted.

Even though we were having a lot of fun, the job at Q13 was something I cherished. To this day, I don't think either Mark or John quite realized what it meant to me. I'd always wanted to get into broadcasting, but I had doubts in the back of my mind: whether I was good enough, and whether someone who looked like me could even get an opportunity to prove it. But for them, it wasn't even a question. Mark didn't have to share his airtime with me. He could've kept it all for himself. And John was always so welcoming. Looking back, being on the air that first day in Brooks was one of the key moments in my career. That's what encouraged me to seriously think about broadcasting as a job, and what convinced me to apply to a post-secondary program in the field. My thinking was: If Q13 Radio, in small-town southern Alberta, is willing to give me a chance, then maybe other doors can open for me, too. I'm forever grateful—had it not been for them, I probably would've taken the safer route and become a chiropractor or something.

There were other people I had to convince besides myself that broadcasting was an option. All three of my sisters had taken more traditional career paths, not to mention more financially stable. Harjot was an MD, and the first Sikh woman in Canada to graduate from med school while wearing a turban; Prem had her own successful consulting firm in the energy sector; and Gurdeep used her degree in commerce and business management to become a general manager in the car-rental industry overseeing hundreds of employees. If you asked my dad, there was no better path to a meaningful job than through math. But I was more of a social studies and English guy. My marks for those subjects were always above the 90 per cent range, and then it went downhill from there. Math was the hardest one for me. I did alright, but it took a lot of work. And there was added pressure, because I knew it was the mark Dad would scrutinize the hardest. I wanted him to be proud of me, or at the very least, not horribly disappointed.

By the time I was in grade 12, you could take the regular math classes, one of which was called Math 30, but you could also take an additional calculus course, which in Alberta at the time was called Math 31. Dad taught the majority of the higher-level math classes, and he knew them like the back of his hand. In fact, he was such an old-school math nut that he didn't even believe in calculators. He felt that because he grew up without them, my generation shouldn't need them, either. He used to joke to his students that calculators made our brains weak. Looking back on it, there might have been something to that idea: I'm in my mid-30s now, and my mental math is so bad, whereas he's always so quick. And he's always right. (That's why he's always the scorekeeper during Scrabble game nights!)

One night, I was getting ready for the new school year, trying to figure out my schedule for grade 12, and there was a big issue for me that needed to be resolved. Was I going to take Math 31, or just Math 30? Of course, I personally had no desire to do calculus whatsoever. It's not like I was getting by so easily in the regular class. But I knew Dad wanted me to. I was reluctant to even bring up the topic.

That evening, Dad was marking papers at the dinner table, so I went up to him and tried to broach the subject gently. "So I've been looking at my math options," I said, "and I'm just not sure . . ." There was a pause. And then Dad said, "Well, you're never going to take the derivative of a hockey score, so just leave it." He didn't even look up. He just kept marking.

It took me a moment to understand what he meant. *Did he just say I don't have to take it?* But when the news sank in, I was ecstatic. It was another of Dad's perfect one-liners—and maybe some backhanded words of encouragement, too. On the one hand, he was giving his blessing for me to follow my passions. But on the other, it's not like he was thrilled that I was trying to get out of taking a class that he felt was important. He understood my thinking, but he also made sure to let me know what he truly felt about me giving up on math. Which—as long as it meant I didn't have to take calculus—was just fine by me.

The funny thing is that a lot of my friends ended up taking Math 31, and the class happened to fall during the same time that I had a spare. So after worrying for weeks about how to get out of calculus, sometimes I ended up sneaking into the classroom anyway, and sitting at an empty desk in the back until the teacher, Mr. Walton, noticed. It was all in good fun. But he used to shake his head and say, "How are you Dr. Singh's son?"

He wasn't the only one to notice the different personalities in my family, either. My biology teacher, Mr. Scholz (Mark's dad), used to joke that he couldn't believe I was related to my sister, Gurdeep, whom he'd taught before me. Keep in mind that all three of my sisters were high-school valedictorians. All of them! And then along comes me, a rowdy, talkative little troublemaker. One day in class, Mr. Scholz said to me, "Harnarayan, you've officially done it."

"What?" I said.

"You've broken the record for the amount of times I've had to move one student in a semester," he said. "I've tried to put you next to people I don't think you'll get along with, or talk to, but you just can't seem to stop."

I must have had a big smile on my face, because then Mr. Scholz asked me what I was so happy about.

I replied, "You just told me I broke a record!"

Once it was established that I was allowed to follow my own interests, the next step was applying for a post-secondary program. Still, I was nervous. My family was well educated, so I knew I had to make my degree count. Should I study communications, and learn about media from a more academic perspective? Or should I look for an actual broadcasting program, which would be more hands on? The biggest draw in the industry was Ryerson University, in Toronto. But as a 17-year-old who'd spent most of his life in a small prairie town, it seemed so far away from home. How would that even work? I never really imagined moving away to go to school, and we'd never talked about it as a family; all three of my sisters had attended post-secondary in Calgary. Leaving home for school wasn't something I had really considered. Closer to home was the University of Calgary, which had a four-year communications degree, but that seemed a bit too theoretical for me. Whereas programs at places like Mount Royal University, or SAIT (the Southern Alberta Institute of Technology), were much more hands-on, which I liked. Then, when I was reading through their brochures, I saw that a couple of Mount Royal students had received an internship to The Sports Network, a.k.a. TSN, and that's all I needed to know. I thought: *If there's a path into the sports-broadcasting world, then that's the school for me.*

Thousands of people apply to get into Mount Royal every year, and back then, they only chose 80 for their broadcasting program. The application process was different than other programs in that I had to create an entire profile about myself, similar to creating a portfolio to land a media job. Luckily, I had Gurdeep to help me put my application together, and, even luckier, I got in.

Mount Royal was such a great experience. I'd hoped the program would show me the tools of the broadcasting trade, and I was not disappointed. Right away, we were learning things that actual, working journalists did every day. One day we'd be practising how to write a lede in a news story, and the next we'd be learning how different kinds of microphones worked. I was going out into the field to interview people in the morning, and trying out audio- and video-editing programs in the afternoon. One semester, my class voted me Most Likely to Become a Weatherman, based on my expert work in front of the green screen (which I chalk up to years and years watching the news with my parents). We made everything from mini-radio documentaries to infomercials. There was an entire class called Speech, where they taught you how to address a room, how to project your voice—everything that could help you talk with confidence on the air. It was exactly what I was looking for.

Whatever we did at Mount Royal was geared towards our future careers. For instance, the university had a radio station, run entirely by students from the broadcasting program, that ran 24/7. We used to run it in shifts. Of course, I had a show all about hockey, which I called *Power Play*. I would talk about how teams were performing and share stories from the hockey world, and I also brought in guests to add new voices to the conversation, which was a blast.

After that first year, it came time for the TSN internship. The school had told us early on that it was coming, and that we should start preparing. But I hadn't really realized until then how many people in my class also wanted to do sports broadcasting. There were people of all ages in the class, but it turned out a lot of us had the exact same goal in mind. I'm not a very competitive guy, so this was bad news. If there was so much competition even within our little group, how was I ever going to make it once the entire country was involved?

To make things more difficult, I felt my background was becoming an extra factor—one that didn't necessarily work in my favour. Out of the whole broadcasting program, I was the only Sikh person, which I was used to, by now. But naturally, I started to wonder if a lack of diversity in the industry might affect my chances of becoming part of it.

One day, one of the teachers in our program heard I was thinking about the TSN internship, and he came to me with a word of caution. This teacher also worked as a producer at CBC Radio, and I respected him. To this day, I don't hold what he said against him. But he came over and said, "Look, sports is a different world. If you're going to have success, I think you'll have a better chance in news. You know a lot about it, and you're good at it. Forget about sports and focus on where you have a shot at being successful." He wasn't blunt or mean about it, but he was saying the same thing I had heard from people back in Brooks (I even heard it from my family doctor!): the sports world didn't have a lot of room for people like me. And he wasn't wrong! The sports landscape was a lot less diverse in 2003 than it is today. Plus, I *was* good at news. So I had his voice in my head as well.

The more I thought about it, the more discouraged I grew. I was shocked at how many people in my program were going to apply for the internship. And I knew that Mount Royal's program was, at the time, smaller in numbers than some of the ones in British Columbia and especially in comparison to similar programs in Ontario. I'm kind of a worst-case-scenario thinker, and I was like that back then, too. Given the sheer numbers, I figured there was no way I'd get through.

When I got home that Friday night, Gurdeep asked how school was going, and I blurted out the whole story: that the internship was coming up, and it sounded amazing, but I wasn't going to apply, because I knew I wouldn't get in.

"What do you mean?" she said. "That's the whole reason you went to Mount Royal! You have to apply for it!"

"It's too late," I said. "Applications are due on Monday."

"*What?*" Gurdeep could not believe I was going to let this pass by. She was actually upset about it. So she just took over. She said, "You have to do this. And I'm going to help you."

"I don't even know where to begin," I told her. "They want this whole portfolio full of stuff. I can't get it all done in time."

But Gurdeep wouldn't take no for an answer. She cancelled all of her plans for that weekend, and instead made me hunker down with her at the dinner table along with a print-out of the internship details, a big yellow folder, and a blank piece of paper to write our plan on.

I said, "So where do we start?"

"You have to start with the dream: the kid from Brooks who wants to be a broadcaster." That was Gurdeep's idea, and

I didn't have a better one, so we went with it. When I noticed that you weren't allowed to send in a video, she read over the entire application and said, "It doesn't say we can't send pictures." We hunted around the house and put together all these pictures of me as a kid, decked out in my Gretzky gear, or putting on a show in front of my little microphone. Then together we wrote this whole essay about my life up to that point—how I'd wanted to be in broadcasting starting when I was a tiny kid, yelling made-up play-by-play on the carpet in my living room. Gurdeep and I filled out all the forms and put the whole package together in 48 hours. We finished it late on Sunday night, and I sent it in the next morning, fingers crossed the whole way.

It was exciting to put the application together, but I was still unsure whether it was worth it, because I didn't think I'd get chosen. That wasn't me just being a pessimist, either: the teachers at Mount Royal had told us that 1,000 people applied for this thing, and TSN only chose eight people each year. Even if I hadn't waited until the last minute to get my act together, it would still have been a long shot.

Then I got the call.

Not that I'd been accepted, but that I was through to the second round. The people at TSN had whittled down the 1,000 people who'd applied to just 50 finalists—and I was one of them. I couldn't believe it. The next step, they said, was that I would receive another phone call on a certain day and time, in which I would have to answer a 50-question quiz about the sports world. I asked for examples, and they said the questions could be about anything. *Who was last year's Wimbledon champion? Who won the most recent Kentucky Derby?*

Name four players on the Minnesota Wild. Or the Minnesota Vikings. Or the Minnesota Twins. I did pay attention to other sports, not just hockey. But it still sounded super intimidating. "Be prepared," the person said, and hung up.

Right away, I went back to Gurdeep and asked for more help. And together we started preparing for this, too. She would create mock tests over the phone to get me used to what it would feel like during the real thing. I'm a visual learner, so I also printed off rosters of every team I could think of, the previous 10 winners of all these different sports tournaments, and that kind of thing, so I could memorize them. In our basement in Calgary, Gurdeep and I came up with this whole system for where I would stand during the actual phone call. All around me, we put categories of notes with "HOCKEY," "FOOTBALL," and so on, written at the top, so if I blanked on a question during the phone call, I would have something I could quickly look at for reference.

The studying went well, but right before the call was supposed to come, I started to get really nervous. At one point I even said to Gurdeep, "Could you get me a bucket?" She said, "Why, are you going to throw up?" I wasn't sure, but my stomach was tied up in knots. I knew there was so much riding on doing well on this quiz. I couldn't blow it.

When the call came, it was exactly what I'd prepared for. The questions came one after another, so there wasn't much time to think. The ones about hockey and basketball were the easiest, and I did okay in sports like tennis, too. But when they asked about horse racing, for instance, I'll admit I needed some help from my notes. Then it was over, just as quickly as it had started, and the voice on the other line said, "Okay! We'll let you know."

In the meantime, I had to act like everything was normal and go ahead with my usual school schedule. At this point I was in my second full year of broadcasting school. The first year was all radio, and the second year was TV. I was just a few weeks into learning all of the TV stuff when TSN called me back. On the line were Ken Volden, an executive with the channel, and Gwen Doucet, the woman who ran the program on a day-to-day basis. She said, "Harnarayan Singh, you've been chosen as one of eight people across Canada for the TSN Broadcast Education and Skills Training"—or BEST, for short—"Program." My jaw dropped. After all the work Gurdeep and I had done to get ready, I still hadn't believed I had a shot at getting the internship. And then I did.

It was amazing news. But there wasn't a lot of time to take it in. By the time I got the phone call, it was already October, and my semester at TSN started at the beginning of the new year, in January 2004. I only had about six weeks to figure everything out about my new life in Ontario. The internship was so highly coveted, and the people at TSN didn't tell me a lot: just the address of the building and when to show up, essentially. Everything else I had to figure out on my own— well, with a bit of familiar help.

Once again, Gurdeep took the bull by the horns. I was still a teenager, with almost no experience fending for myself in the real world, and she helped me figure out a lot of significant details, most importantly, where I was going to live. I knew that the TSN building was in Scarborough. And eventually we found some family friends in Calgary who had relatives that lived within driving distance of the building. And it turned out they were willing to let me stay with them. That winter break, before the semester started, Gurdeep and I flew out there and we all went out to dinner together, to make sure it was a good fit. They were surprisingly Canucks fans, but I could live with that.

Another hurdle to deal with was driving. Because I was under 21, I wasn't allowed to rent a car from any of the major rental companies. Gurdeep, being in the car-rental industry, knew that some of the smaller companies don't have that same age policy. She approached a bunch of them in and around Toronto and ended up negotiating a deal on my behalf, where I was able to rent a car on a monthly basis for a set fee, paid in cash. To get insurance coverage on the car, Gurdeep got a new fancy credit card under her name and then made me the secondary card holder so the coverage would transfer to me, too. Also, my mom was paranoid about me, as a teenager, driving on the 401 in intense Toronto traffic, so as a test, Gurdeep drove with me from Etobicoke, where I would be staying, to the TSN building and back, just to make sure I knew the route. (This was before phones all had GPS. Back in 2004, getting lost was a very real problem for a guy like me.) Every step of the way, Gurdeep went above and beyond to help me out—as she always does. It's certainly not wrong to say that she helped mould me into the person I am today. I'm not sure I could've asked for a better sister, and you'd be hard pressed to find a more selfless, loyal, and helpful person out there. I'll never forget the lengths she went to on my behalf.

As for TSN, the whole experience was overwhelming. I was even impressed by the building. Where I was working, there weren't any windows to the outside world, and the walls were all black, covered with high-end TV and computer screens, lighting rigs, and the station logo spelled out in huge red letters. It was its own little world. Once you stepped inside, it was like you lost all connection to the rest of the planet— the only thing left was sports. For me, I couldn't have asked for anything better.

On my very first day, I was trying to find a place to hang up my coat, and when I turned around, there was a woman standing in front of me who was so tall that I couldn't see her face. I had to physically crane my head up, and that's when I realized it was Jennifer Hedger, one of the TSN hosts. It was my first time meeting an on-air personality at the station, and she made sure to introduce herself and make me feel welcome in the building. From there I met a few of the other hosts, like Darren Dutchyshen, James Duthie, Jay Onrait, Dan O'Toole, and Gino Reda. Of course, they didn't need introducing to *me*. They were all people I had watched on my TV at home for years. But it was a thrill to shake their hands and say hello, face to face, as co-workers—because that's what we were, if only for a few short months.

My official job title at TSN was editorial assistant, and there were a number of us there, from broadcasting schools all over the country. Each day, we would be assigned a certain game, whether it was hockey, basketball, tennis, or something else, and we would make a shot list for the whole thing. If there was an isolated shot of a player doing something interesting (in the industry, this is called an "ISO"), we'd write it down. Each time someone scored a goal or made a basket, we marked down who scored and who assisted. We also noted the different kinds of replays that were shown on a play, and even fan reactions and celebrations. At the same time we were doing that, we had to create the highlight pack that SportsCentre showed later that night. As I was watching a game, I was noting things like: *Curtis Joseph's save here was amazing. We need to show Joe Sakic's goal for sure. Steve Nash's three-pointer was a pivotal moment in the game.* And as you're assembling the highlights, you have to also be aware of the time limit the producer has given you. There might only be time to show a 30-second clip from a certain basketball game, for instance. That's all I had to tell the story of an entire game. We also wrote the scripts that the anchors would read out on TV later that night—with their changes added in, of course, to alter the wording to match their own style.

After we finished all of this—made the shot list, selected the highlights, and wrote the script—we would sit down with an editor and put everything together. If you were working on an early game, you had a bit of time until the show. But sometimes SportsCentre would go on the air only a few minutes after your game had ended. Sometimes the game was still in progress! But they still needed an update to use on the show. It was a very fast-moving environment. I used to look up and see people sprinting across the room with fresh scripts in their hands, or rushing over to an editor to tell them about a last-minute change that needed to be made.

Everything I did at TSN was a learning experience. I took notes from interviews that had been done, or I sat with a producer to find content for an upcoming top-10 list. In those cases, I'd have to wander off to the archives to find the appropriate video clips, and that, too, was a lot different than it is today. At that time, the archive was full of these big-ass Betamax video tapes. They were higher quality than VHS tapes and had more memory on them. But they were huge, and I would have to physically rewind and fast-forward each one to find the time code for every single clip that we wanted to use. To someone coming up in media nowadays, when everything's digital, this probably all sounds out of the Stone Age.

My internship lasted from January to April, at which point TSN hired four of us interns to stay on with the company full-time. Luckily, I was one of them, and I accepted an entry-level job on the production side. I couldn't believe my luck: I'd somehow been able to make a perfect transition from broadcasting school right into the industry, and, even better, I was covering the thing I cared about more than anything.

But in a cruel twist of fate, the spring that I was in Toronto was the same year the Flames went on their first Cup run since the '80s. The Flames had done okay that year, finishing in sixth place in the Western Conference, but they weren't expected to do much damage in the playoffs. Then they upset Vancouver in the first round, and then they did it again against the first-place Detroit Red Wings in the second round, and before you knew it, they were in the finals, with Jarome Iginla and Miikka Kiprusoff squaring up against Vincent Lecavalier, Marty St. Louis, and the rest of the Tampa Bay Lightning, who were the top seed in the east.

It was a strange experience. I had just lived in Calgary and followed the team closely while I was there, but now I was watching the whole city come alive through my TV screen, as I stayed up late into the night, two time zones away, watching the games by myself. I vividly remember Chris Cuthbert's call on the Flames' overtime goal against San Jose in the conference finals: "Montador . . . scores! Steve Montador is your hero in game one!" Most of all, I remember watching the Red Mile. After every game, thousands of people showed up to party along 17 Avenue SW. It looked so different on the broadcast compared to the street that I knew. I tried to absorb as much of the festivities from afar as I could, but I knew it just couldn't compare to seeing it in person.

By that fall, I realized that living my dream life in Toronto wasn't quite as straightforward as it had first looked. After nearly a year living in the Greater Toronto Area, I was getting more and more homesick. For some of that time, I lived with the host family, and after that, I moved into a friend's basement suite in Toronto. But I missed Alberta. I missed my family. Plus, I realized that if I kept going on the path I was on, I would end up fully on the production side—and I still dreamed about being on camera, even if some people around me thought it was a long shot. So, near the end of 2004, I decided to leave.

Before my last day at TSN, I put together some material for a video resumé. I recorded news segments where I was the anchor: talking about real sports stories and sitting at the actual anchors' desks, but of course the pieces weren't aired. The point was that I could use them on my resumé as samples later on. Then I cleared out my desk, packed my bags, and got on a flight back home to Calgary.

Chapter 5
Hockey Night in Punjabi

Leaving TSN was an incredibly difficult decision. I'd spent years dreaming of making it in the national sports media, and now that I was on the brink, part of me felt like I was throwing it all away. What if I was making a serious mistake? But I just couldn't get over the feeling that I was being led down the wrong path. People seemed to think that I could make a career for myself in broadcasting if I stayed behind the scenes. My next job was convincing them I could make it in front of the cameras, too.

Plus, I did have a bit of a plan. A year earlier, in 2003, after my first year at Mount Royal University, I had worked over the summer at the CBC in Calgary. It all started with a phone call from an unfamiliar number. I was on vacation with Gurdeep in California, visiting my aunt and her family, when I noticed I had a new voicemail from back home. The man in the message introduced himself as Mike Spear, a station manager at CBC Radio in Calgary, and I called him back right away—even though, back in the day, roaming charges on cellphones were ridiculous. I guess I had a hunch it might be important. When I got Mike on the line, he said, "We've had a position open up. Would you be able to come in sometime to chat?" I was a little confused, because I hadn't applied for a job, at the CBC or otherwise. But I told him I'd be there as soon as I got back to Canada.

Immediately after Gurdeep and I landed in Calgary, I ran straight to my computer, updated my resumé, got all suited and booted, and went down to the CBC offices. I put my brand-new resumé on Mike's desk, but he kind of waved it away. "Oh, I don't need to see that," he said.

Now I was really confused. "I thought this was a job interview."

"No," Mike said. "You already have the job." I hate to sound boastful, but he told me I came so highly recommended from my professors at Mount Royal—some of whom also worked at CBC—that he decided to skip the interview process. If I wanted it, the job was mine.

My next question: "Okay . . . what *is* the job?"

The position, it turned out, was the summer festival reporter. Each summer, tons of festivals happen around Calgary and the rest of southern Alberta: music, food, sports, culture, you name it. My job was to cover these events for CBC Radio, reporting live about what was happening, and running a promotional tent on behalf of the station. It sounded like a blast. A chance to represent the same radio station I'd grown up listening to as a kid? I wasn't going to say no to that. Sign me up!

The job was very exciting, and also very hands-on. Of course, I started out by looking at how previous reporters had done their stories, and what sorts of events they had attended. But I was able to decide for myself which ones I wanted to cover, which was a lot of freedom for a young reporter. The CBC provided me with a branded van, which

I filled with whatever merchandise I thought would be fun to have on hand at the events; I had my pick of everything from a giant prize wheel down to pins and pens with the CBC logo on them. I also made sure to have my Mini Disc recorder on me at all times, which is what we used at the time to record interviews.

My first assignment was that June: a Greek festival in a far corner of Calgary. I was supposed to go there, walk around, take it all in, set up my booth, and then do a live radio hit on a show called *The Homestretch*, where the host would ask me some basic questions about what was going on at the festival.

It was a pretty far drive to get there from the studio, and my company van was decked out in CBC logos on all sides. The first thing I noticed was how many people would wave at me whenever I was stopped at a red light, or as I drove past them on the street. I thought: *Wow, I didn't realize people loved the CBC so much.* After a while, I noticed a bit of a weird smell in the van. It was my first time driving it, and it was getting on in years. It also couldn't accelerate very quickly, so I didn't think too much of it. As I got closer to the event, I started noticing more and more people were waving to me— almost as if they were trying to get my attention. I thought: *Man, this is great!* Finally, I arrived at the Greek festival and pulled up onto a large grassy area near the front entrance. Meanwhile, the smell was just getting worse and worse. As I parked the van, I saw a bunch of people, from far away, running towards me and waving their arms from side to side. *What's going on?* I opened the door to get out, and all of a sudden this wave of black smoke hit me. It was billowing out from underneath the van. That's when I was able to hear the people yelling: "Get away from the van! Get away from the van!" They thought the whole thing was going to explode. Finally, after I'd shut off the ignition and the smoke cleared, I realized what had happened. I'd driven all the way across the city, including on highways at high speeds, with the emergency brake on, waving and smiling to people like an absolute idiot. That was embarrassing!

There wasn't a lot of time to think, because I had my radio hit to prepare for. I ran around the festival as quickly as I could, trying to get a sense of what was going on there, and then I ran back to set up my booth. The producer called me for my first-ever live radio hit, and it's funny: I don't think the CBC realized I was still just 18 years old at the time, still in school at Mount Royal. I could think on my feet, and I did well in my classes and all, but I was still limited in my life experience. I didn't know a lot about other cultures—including Greece's. My reference points at that time were some basic facts about the Olympics, and maybe a line or two from the movie, *My Big Fat Greek Wedding*. During the radio segment, the *Homestretch* host asked me about the foods at the festival. I said, "Well, I'm vegetarian, but I did try this thing called a spanakopita." The problem was, I had only read the name on the sign. I had never said the word *spanakopita* out loud before. Needless to say, I butchered it. That was rough already, but then the host, who was white, started laughing at me, and said live on the air, "You've never had spanakopita before?" In my head I thought: *Why are you so astonished? You've probably never had any of the foods I have at my house!* She made such a big deal out of it. I was slightly embarrassed, but it also made me realize that in the future, I needed to be quick on my feet and ready for anything that might happen on live radio or TV.

After I got off the phone and finished up at the event, I still had a damaged, possibly explosive van to deal with. I called Mike Spear back at the office and said, "Uh, I'm not sure I can drive the van back." I confessed to him about the mishap with the parking brake, and he said to pack up the van, lock everything up, and then just take a cab home. The next day, I came into the CBC office, and Mike set me straight. "I've never seen anybody cause so much damage to company property on their very first day on the job," he said, laughing.

After an intense first day, I ended up having lots of fun that summer. I attended all kinds of events that I never would have gone to otherwise, from rowing regattas to festivals at Head-Smashed-In Buffalo Jump, a UNESCO World Heritage Site in the south of the province. I even went to a *Star Trek* convention in Vulcan, which isn't technically named after Spock's home planet but has all kinds of buildings and statues dedicated to the TV show anyway. That summer was also the summer of the Mad Cow crisis in Alberta, and because Brooks is such a strong cattle town, CBC ended up doing a bunch of live broadcasting from there. Naturally, I was involved in that coverage, and Mom even invited a bunch of CBC staff over to my parents' home for a big Indian lunch. To this day, the staff still talk about how good the homemade appetizers were. They even remember the names: *pakoras* (vegetables coated in seasoned batter and deep-fried) and *gulaab jumans* (deep-fried Punjabi-style Timbits made of dried milk that are dipped in a rose cardamom sugar syrup).

———

Fast-forward to fall 2004. After nearly a year away in Toronto working at TSN, my plan was to go back to the CBC in Calgary and see if I could get a full-time job. My bosses there had positive memories of my time as the summer festival reporter, and because I had been on the air regularly in that position, they were comfortable having me come on as a reporter. In the CBC world, the job I took is called "casual," which is almost like freelance work: whenever there are shifts available, you can put your name in to cover them. I started getting work that way, covering for a vacation here or a maternity leave there, until soon I was in the office every single day.

The duties varied, depending on where I was stationed. Sometimes I'd be covering a shift for a reporter doing local news. Other times I'd be filling in as an associate producer on the big shows in the morning, over the lunch hour, or in the afternoon. I gravitated towards local news. Every morning, the news reporters would show up to a story meeting, where we had to bring ideas for potential stories that could be covered that day. I was always trying to push stories about the Flames. The assignment desk noticed how passionate I was, and started assigning me stories about hockey whenever they came up. Slowly but surely, I was moving back into the sports world, just like I'd planned.

I was there, for instance, the first time Sidney Crosby came to Calgary to play against the Flames, in 2007. He was still fairly new in the league, so it was a big deal when he first got to the Saddledome. Normally when I go talk to a player, there's just a media scrum in the dressing room, where all of the reporters, photographers, and camera operators gather around as the player talks for a couple of minutes. But with Crosby, an official press conference had been set up in the media room. When I got there, he was sitting at a table with a bunch of mics that had been set up ahead of time, and all of us reporters were sitting in a row of folding chairs in front of him. Even at such a young age, Crosby was very accommodating and personable, and made a point of answering everyone's questions as politely as he could.

If there was another superstar who was as personable as Crosby, it would have to be Jarome Iginla. I first knew him through his on-ice persona as the NHL's ultimate power forward. He was one of the league's best goal scorers, and he also played with a ton of grit. The most iconic moment from Calgary's Cup run in 2004 has to be Iginla fighting Vincent Lecavalier, star against star. But I'd always heard Iginla was a very gracious individual off the ice. You could get a sense of that from his interviews.

I met Iginla during one of my first visits to the Saddledome as a reporter. This was in the Darryl Sutter era. The Flames GM and former coach was a no-bullshit style of manager. From what I heard, his players weren't allowed to celebrate much or display too much emotion. Loud music was banned from the dressing room. Sutter ran a tight ship. I'm sure some of the players—and other team employees, for that matter—were scared of him. It was a weird vibe to walk into as a new reporter.

The CBC was already in an odd place within the local sports media, because we didn't cover hockey full-time. We only showed up for the bigger stories, so when we were there at an event, we stuck out. I arrived that day carrying my big CBC microphone, nervous about what to expect—as if Darryl Sutter himself was going to bark at me with that amazingly deep voice of his. Plus I was, once again, the only person in the room wearing a turban. That's something I can't help but notice.

Anyway, the first person to come out of the dressing room to talk to us that day was Iginla. He was standing in the spot where the coaches always did their media availabilities, and we all gathered around him. There were probably a dozen other reporters there. I don't know if he noticed that I looked nervous, or maybe he does this to every new reporter he sees. But he put out his hand to me and he said, "Welcome. Everything good?" Right away, I was taken aback by his humility. I did not expect him to do that. It was a small gesture, but it made me feel so much more comfortable, and it gave me the confidence that I belonged there with the other media in the arena. There was the Iginla I knew from watching interviews on TV. Such a class act.

———

Being a visible minority in an industry dominated by white people wasn't all bad, though. Sometimes, it even had its advantages. For instance, I don't think I would have ever come across the most important story I broke at the CBC if I weren't a Sikh Canadian.

One of the challenges of being a reporter was that I constantly had to come up with new story ideas. I found this part of the job really difficult, in part because I wasn't a seasoned reporter yet and hadn't learned the tricks of the trade. But I was learning. For example, I figured out early on that you had to pay attention to absolutely everything around you, because you never knew where a story could pop up. I might find an idea while shopping for groceries, or driving to work. You just never knew. That's advice I would pass on to all up-and-coming reporters out there: it all comes down to what you notice.

One day I was sitting at my desk, looking around for story ideas, and for whatever reason my mind drifted back to something my dad had mentioned a couple of times around the house. In Sikh culture, Singh and Kaur are names that were given to us in 1699 by our tenth Guru, Sri Guru Gobind Singh Ji, when he created the *Khalsa*, a code of conduct for a righteous way of living. Every Sikh boy is given the name Singh, which means fearless lion and represents bravery. And every Sikh girl is given the name Kaur, which means warrior princess and represents nobility. These names are tied very strongly to our faith. When Dad and Mom came to Canada, they used Singh and Kaur as their last names, which was the norm at the time. But lately, Dad seemed to think that was changing. I remembered him saying to me, "These days, you never see anyone come to Canada with the last name Singh or Kaur. Now, those are always used as people's middle names, and there's a different last name added on." He had a hunch that there was a reason for the change that we didn't know about.

When I remembered this conversation sitting at my desk, I decided to look into it, to see if there was maybe a story there. I made a cold call to Citizenship and Immigration

Canada. I said I was looking to apply for Canadian citizenship, and I made sure to mention my last name was Singh. The person on the phone told me that there was, in fact, an official rule from the department: they didn't allow people to immigrate to Canada if their last name was Singh or Kaur. If you wanted to apply, you were required to list a different last name. I couldn't believe it.

"Well, there are other common last names out there," I said to the person on the phone. "Asian names like Chung, or Caucasian names like Smith. Does the same rule apply for last names associated with other ethnicities?" But it didn't. The rule was specifically for Sikh names.

Okay, now I could tell I was onto something big.

I went and told my superiors what I had learned, and they were blown away, too. They told me that to report this story, I needed to find someone who was currently applying for citizenship with those last names and who had been told by the government to change them. It didn't take me very long. I called around a bit, and lo and behold, there was a woman in Calgary whose husband was originally from India, and they were in the process of applying for his citizenship. They had actual documents from the government that said, "The names Kaur and Singh do not qualify for the purpose of immigration to Canada." Boom! Now we were really in business.

Now, had this been a policy that included lots of common last names, maybe it wouldn't have been such a big deal, but the fact that it specifically targeted one community— one faith, one ethnicity—was what made the story so important. I went off and put together a first draft, then sent it to my superiors.

Within the CBC, whenever a story has potential, it quickly moves up the ranks. That's what happened with mine. My bosses decided that it wasn't just a Calgary story: it was a national story, with national ramifications. Before I knew it, *The National* itself decided they wanted to include it on their nightly broadcast. From there, everything happened so quickly. The story aired on Monday, and by Tuesday, every other major media organization in the country was following it up. Then it made international headlines: "Canadian Government Bans Sikh Names." All that week I was inundated with interview requests as the person who broke the news. And we had to keep furthering the story, too, so all the while I was constantly reaching out to Immigration Canada, trying to get them to comment. At first they didn't want to. But by the end of that week, the Harper government felt it had to respond, and announced it was repealing the policy, which turned out to have been in place for more than a decade.

Once again, I was reminded of the power of the media. A little story I wrote on a Monday was able to change an entire government policy by Friday—and all based on a stray observation made by my dad.

When I told him everything that was happening, he just said, "See? I knew something was going on."

So smart, that guy.

In the spring of 2008, I started to hear rumblings that people high up at the CBC were thinking about expanding *Hockey Night in Canada* to reach new audiences. For decades, *Hockey*

Night had been the flagship hockey broadcast in the country, airing to millions of people in English and French, from coast to coast to coast. To this day, if you ask any Canadian about their childhood memories of Saturday night, chances are they'll tell you about sitting around the TV with their friends or family, watching two of their favourite teams go at it. I personally must have logged thousands of hours doing exactly that. It was my favourite thing in the world. After so much success in that format, the CBC was interested in trying something new. The idea came from a long-time producer with CBC Sports, David Masse: Why not expand the coverage so that multilingual Canadians can fall in love with hockey in their own language?

The CBC first tested the concept in 2007, when they aired a regular-season game in Italian on a specialty cable channel called Telelatino. I guess that experiment went well enough that they decided to go one step further. The next year, for a special *Hockey Day in Canada* episode, they decided to broadcast that day's three games on the CBC website in three different languages: Mandarin, Cantonese, and Hindi. They later had another game called in the Inuit language Inuktitut. But it was in 2008 that an executive producer at CBC Sports named Joel Darling decided to have the entire Stanley Cup Final broadcast online in Punjabi. This was a game-changer.

There were already some advocates within the CBC for calling games in Punjabi. At the beginning of that season, Marc Crawford was doing colour commentary for *Hockey Night in Canada*, and he told his bosses, "If you guys are trying other languages, you have to try Punjabi." Marc was coming off of seven years as the head coach of the Vancouver Canucks, and he told them how large and devoted the Punjabi fan base was in and around the Lower Mainland. I've since talked to Marc about this, and he told me some cool stories: how whenever he was pumping gas, or standing in line at the grocery store, he'd meet all these Punjabi kids and adults who wanted to come over and introduce themselves. Other times, when he'd drive through Surrey, a city in the Greater Vancouver Area with a particularly large Sikh population, he would see kids in turbans and mini-turbans playing ball hockey on the street. Marc's own kids were really into track and field, and they competed at a rec centre in Surrey. Every time he walked in the door, he was bombarded by Punjabi families. And not just little kids and their families, either. Grandparents, too. Lots of them. And they knew their hockey. Marc told me he was always impressed by how closely the Punjabi community followed the Canucks.

It turned out Marc wasn't the only one who brought this up. Joel told me there were a lot of people who suggested Punjabi as a language to highlight on the show, including a young broadcaster from the Greater Toronto Area named Parminder Singh, who was the host of a Sikh specialty show on Omni Television called *Chardi Kalaa*, where he would attend and talk about local events, show live music performances, and interview people from around the community. Also, the numbers backed Punjabi as a viable option. At the time, it was the fourth-most-spoken language in Canada. First was English, obviously. Second was French, and third was Chinese—but what the census called "Chinese" was really a combination of several different languages and dialects that originated from China. So, really, Punjabi was third. When they realized that, the bosses at CBC decided that a Punjabi-language version of *Hockey Night in Canada* might actually work. The next question was: Who should do it?

It might sound like an easy decision to make, but it was a lot more complicated than it seems. Joel, who became the show's executive producer, had to find broadcasters who fit multiple criteria: who could read, write, and speak the Punjabi language fluently, accurately, and effortlessly; who had previous broadcast experience in radio or television; and—most importantly—who really understood hockey.

From what I've been told, because I was already working at the CBC in Calgary, my name came up quite early in the process. Also, I already knew Kelly Hrudey a little by then. The legendary former goalie and Gretzky teammate in L.A., was now a broadcaster and lived in Calgary. Whenever he came into the CBC building to record something, I would immediately get up from my desk and run over to say hello. I had first met him years earlier, when I was a teenager, at Gretzky's charity golf tournaments, and he was really kind to me—I told him I was thinking about going into sports broadcasting, and he encouraged me to go for it. Once we became co-workers, I did my best to stay friendly and keep in touch with him, because he was approachable and always gave me time to talk. (Okay, the fact that he used to play on a team with my hero didn't hurt, either.) Anyway, Kelly and Joel used to work closely on a number of things, and when Kelly heard about the idea for *Hockey Night in Punjabi*, he spoke very highly of me, and said I would be a great fit for the show.

I can remember exactly where I was when I got the call. I can picture the desk I was sitting at in the old CBC Calgary building. I can even picture the phone itself. It had a beige case and grey numbers, and it was so old that it didn't even have call display. When it rang, I had no idea who was on the other end.

"Hello," I said, as I did so many times during an average workday. "Harnarayan Singh, CBC Radio."

The voice said, "This is Joel Darling from *Hockey Night in Canada*."

Just those words froze me in my seat. I knew Joel's name already, because when you're in the industry, you're always aware of who the important people above you are. But we'd never spoken before, and I had no reason to think he knew who I was.

Before I could overthink things any further, he said, "We're thinking of doing a *Hockey Night in Canada* show in Punjabi, and your name has come up."

At this point, I remember looking at the phone and thinking to myself, *Is this real?* I had always wanted to be on *Hockey Night in Canada*—it was my ultimate dream, even as a kid. But part of me still thought I might have left that opportunity behind the day I left Toronto and came home to Calgary. When I got that phone call, I was sitting in a chair thousands of kilometres away from the centre of Canadian sports media. And now, not only was I hearing my name in the same sentence as *Hockey Night in Canada*, but I was also hearing another key word: *Punjabi*.

"We're trying to piece together a team," Joel was saying. "We already have Parminder Singh on board."

Then he said: "Would you be interested in joining us?"

No time to hesitate now. "Of course!" I said. I quickly filled Joel in about my love of hockey, and my past experience at TSN, and he said they would send along more information soon.

Next thing I knew, I was sitting in Toronto at the CBC *Hockey Night in Canada* headquarters, in a tiny booth next to Parminder, calling the Stanley Cup Final.

If it sounds like a blur, that's because it felt that way to me, too. Once the project had been approved, the CBC didn't waste any time getting Parminder and me on the air. The final that year featured the Detroit Red Wings and the Pittsburgh Penguins, and it had a great storyline built in: this was the first year that a young Penguins team, led by Crosby and Evgeni Malkin, had made it to the final. It was a showdown between the young guns, on one end, and the super-experienced Red Wings team, who had won three Cups in the last 11 years, on the other. In that first series, Parminder was the one doing the play-by-play, and my role was colour commentator. That meant I needed a steady stream of interesting facts and stories to tell, so I spent a lot of time at my parents' house beforehand, making pages and pages of notes. Having never called an NHL game before, I had no idea how much material I would need, or what would come up over the course of the game. But I figured it was better to have *too much* information in the booth, instead of too little. Better safe than sorry.

The other issue was the actual words I had to say. Of course, I was fluent in Punjabi, and I knew about a million hockey terms—in English. So there, too, I had to fill sheets and sheets with new verbiage, because, in a way, Parminder and I had to create a new hybrid language for hockey. For instance, what were we going to call the penalty box? How should you say *cross-checking* in Punjabi? There wasn't a term for it. We had to invent the terminology, being creative as we went along.

Our studio for those first games was a tiny little sound-proofed room in the CBC building in downtown Toronto. We were a four-person operation: Parminder and I on the air, plus one producer and another person to run the audio board. The room had space for a chair for each of us, the two TV screens we watched the games on, our audio gear, and that's about it. I also had to bring in my rosters, which I taped underneath the screens, and of course my pages and pages of game notes. It was snug, but we made it work. Luckily, it was a great series that went back and forth between both teams, including a triple-overtime win by the Penguins in game five to keep the series going, but the Red Wings ended up winning the Stanley Cup in six, on a game-winning goal from Henrik Zetterberg.

The games were broadcast on the CBC Sports website, and even before the series was over, it was clear that the *Hockey Night in Punjabi* experiment was an immediate, astounding success. After every game, I was shocked by the amount of feedback we got, whether through social media, texts and emails from family and friends, and especially the press. Once word got out about what we were doing—this multicultural twist we were putting on a classic Canadian sport—it seemed like every publication you can think of wanted to talk to both Parminder and me about it. We counted each time one of us did an interview, and before we knew it we'd hit 40. Given that our show was under the CBC umbrella, it made sense that we were invited onto other CBC programs, including *The National* and *The Hour* with George Stroumboulopoulos. But every major newspaper in the country also wrote about us. We even appeared on shows produced by other TV networks, like CTV's *Canada AM*. The amount of attention we received was just crazy.

Still, I went home to Calgary that summer, not knowing what to expect in the future. The show had been so fun to make, and it seemed like we had reached a whole community of new hockey fans, not to mention generating a ton of positive media attention that made the entire CBC look smart and progressive. Joel Darling remembers this time fondly, too, and he told me he was so proud of what we had done together. Sure enough, he and the other *Hockey Night* producers decided they wanted to do the show again on a more regular basis. The next time I talked to Joel on the phone, he was asking if I wanted to call the Saturday night double-headers—which are also the standard *Hockey Night in Canada* games—for the entire 2008–09 NHL season.

Even though our little trial run had been a success, turning that success into a regular, ongoing show was going to be much harder. It's one thing to get people to try something once but something totally different to get them to tune in every single week. Still, Joel and the other CBC executives were confident that people would tune in, and that all of the positive media attention had built up some goodwill from the larger hockey community. The big question mark, though, was money.

If the show was going to survive long-term, we needed a sponsor. No matter how much the CBC loved *Hockey Night in Punjabi*, if the show couldn't pay for its own keep, we knew we weren't going to be there for long. I have to give a ton of credit here to Scott Moore, who was the director of CBC Sports at the time. He took a leap of faith to get the show off the ground, and without his support, it never would have had a chance to survive. Scott is the one who decided that, at first, they would pay for our show—which was extremely low-budget, by network standards—by taking some money out of the regular *Hockey Night in Canada* budget. That was huge for us. When you are trying something new, it takes time to get it right. You have to be willing to experiment, and to tinker. We didn't have time to line up a sponsor for our first regular season, but the CBC bosses like Scott were confident they could find us one eventually. In the meantime, we got by, using money "borrowed" from the regular English broadcast. (Thanks Ron!)

Before any of that could happen, however, I had to decide whether I could even accept the job in the first place. When Joel called and said they wanted to do *Hockey Night in Punjabi* for the entire regular season, I told him I was in. But he also told me they didn't have a budget to pay for my travel to and from Toronto, where the show's studio would be located each week. For the second time in five years, I had to decide whether it was worth it to uproot my entire life and move to Ontario. My family and I had a discussion about it that lasted several days. "The show is in Toronto," I would say, talking to myself as much as to them. "But I live out here. And I'm still young. Does it make sense to move out there for a show that only airs once per week?" I remembered how homesick I had been during my time at TSN, and I didn't expect that to change this time around. Plus, the money wasn't really enough to live in Toronto. I would probably have to find some other kind of work while I was there. And what would that look like? Then again, this was *Hockey Night in Canada* we were talking about! I would have been nuts to just give up on the opportunity. This was everything I had ever wanted—and I would be doing it in a new and groundbreaking format, in a language that is very important to me.

My parents, who are pretty cautious people, surprised me in their response to all this. At the end of all my talking, going back and forth over every aspect of the situation, they said to me, "You've always wanted to do this, and we're always here to help you. If they say they can't pay for your travel, then just tell them you'll be there, and we'll figure out the details later." Were they saying what I thought they were saying?

I had to make a decision quickly, because the start of the regular season was coming up, and if I was going to be part of the show going forward, I had to fly out to Toronto right away. In the end, I decided that if my parents thought it was worth the gamble, then I did, too. I got on the plane to finalize the deal.

The CBC building in Toronto is enormous, and so of course when I showed up to discuss my dream job, I immediately got lost. There are so many floors, and on each floor there are all these criss-crossing corridors, hallways, and intersections—it's like a maze. At this point, Joel and I had never met face to face. I wasn't even sure if I would meet him on that first Saturday night of the regular season or not, but I was nervous about it. I had googled him ahead of our meeting, and boy, was his resumé impressive. I couldn't keep track of how many Olympics he had produced for CBC Sports, let alone the many seasons of *Hockey Night in Canada*. As I walked down one hallway, he was coming my way from the opposite corner. At the exact same moment, we both turned our respective corners and literally bumped into one another.

We shook hands and made a bit of small talk. I don't know if he could tell, but I was super nervous. Then Joel said, "Look, you did a great job during the playoffs. Everyone was really happy with the work you guys did. But the truth is we don't have a production budget, let alone a travel budget. And if we were to put out a job posting, there would be a ton of people in Toronto interested in being on *Hockey Night in Punjabi*." He wasn't being mean about it. This was just the reality. I knew he was right.

I thought about what my parents had told me, and then I looked Joel in the eye and said, "Don't worry about it."

He paused for a second. "Are you sure?"

"Yep." I gulped. "I'll be here."

Chapter 6
Hiding from Bob Cole

*W*hat did I just do?

Standing in the hallway of the CBC building in Toronto back in the summer of 2008, I didn't exactly *lie* to my new boss. I told Joel Darling that I would be there for each week's broadcast of the upcoming NHL season, which was true: I planned to. It was a lie of omission. Joel told me that CBC didn't have a budget for the show, and I didn't explain myself. I just said I'd be there. And he had no reason not to believe me.

Once I got back home from that first face-to-face meeting, I sat down with Gurdeep to figure out how on earth I was going to pull this off. There were a lot of details to work out: not just booking flights, but also planning how I was going to get around the city, and even when the best time was to fly in and fly out. Once again, my sister really stepped up, selflessly putting her own stuff on hold to help me. She does that for so many people, not just me. And like before, her experience in the car-rental industry came in handy. When we sat down together, the first thing she said was, "You need to be booking this stuff in advance." Gurdeep knew that holidays and long weekends get crazy expensive if you wait too long. So we made a plan. We waited for airlines to announce their seat sales, and then we booked a whole bunch of flights at once, weeks and sometimes months in advance. We had to stay on top of it, too, because if you were even a little late, the sale prices would disappear. Over time, those savings added up—hundreds or even thousands of dollars per month.

When the season started that fall, my strategy was to spend as little time in Toronto as possible. The less time I was there, the less money I would spend—or at least that was the idea. Luckily, I had pored over and scrutinized every detail of the weekend with Gurdeep, so I was hopeful that I could pull this off.

So, that very first Friday of the *Hockey Night in Punjabi* broadcasting season, I boarded my red-eye flight from Calgary, ensuring that I would arrive in Toronto first thing Saturday morning. It was too risky to try to fly in on the day of the show due to delays and cancellations, not to mention the time difference and all of the prep that I needed to get through. Plus, had I flown out any earlier, I would've needed to arrange a place to stay the night. Overnight flights can be horren-dous, given that you're already tired from being up in the middle of the night. Add in the time spent packing and get-ting through security and not getting a proper sleep on the plane—you could say I was a bit anxious about it all. After landing bright and early at Pearson International, I made my way through the terminal to rent my car and eventually arrived downtown at the CBC building. I spent hours scouring a number of articles for stats and facts, and created sheets and sheets of notes, including the lineups for the games we were going to call. Finally, by 7:00 p.m., it was game time, and

Parminder and I called the double-header that evening. Yup, the same broadcast crew called both games, meaning six hours of live TV! By the time the second game finished, it was around 1:00 a.m. Toronto time. That's a long day, especially when you factor in the flight the night before, and it wasn't over yet. After finishing up at the CBC, I went right back to the airport and started looking around for a quiet place to nap while I waited for my flight back home.

Toronto's Pearson Airport is the busiest airport in the country—during the day, at least. At night, it's a different story. By the time I arrived there at around 2:00 a.m., there were no flights running, and security wasn't even open. It was just me and the custodians in the main terminal area. I had my choice of benches to lie down on, keeping my luggage close to me, to try to grab a couple hours' sleep. Over time, I learned where the best washrooms and benches were, and where the background noises were the least intrusive. But sometimes it was a long wait until four o'clock, when security opened and the airport came back to life. I caught the first flight back home, at 7:00 a.m. Toronto time (5:00 a.m. in Calgary), and landed about four hours later. Back in Alberta, Gurdeep would pick me up—at that point, she and I both lived in a house with our parents, who had recently retired—and, in a pattern that would become familiar, we would head straight from the airport to temple, where we'd meet Mom and Dad and the rest of the community. I'd go on stage to play the tabla, sing hymns, and visit with people until after lunch. And that was my weekend.

I'm an emotional guy, and reflecting after the first weekend that we were going to be doing this all season long, it was surreal. I was extremely tired, but it all felt worth it given that my dream to be a part of *Hockey Night in Canada* had somehow come true. Even though the long-term future and viability of the show was uncertain, I wasn't going to give it up for anything. I decided to take things one season, or even one game, at a time.

But it became clear to me that the Friday-night red-eye was not the right strategy. I was hardly getting any sleep on the plane, and then I landed in Toronto way too early on Saturday, with nowhere to go for hours. It wasn't working. Soon, the weather became a factor as well. Despite Canada's reputation, sometimes winter takes a while to show up; so many times, even in Alberta, we used to end up with a brown Christmas. But by January and February, the snow and ice get really bad. My mom was always, and still is, the first one to say to me, "Don't take a risk. If the weather is bad, you need to go earlier." So in mid-season, I started flying out on Friday nights and sleeping on a friend's couch in Toronto. A couple of times, I spent the night at my colleague's house, then in the morning we would do our prep together before heading over to the CBC building.

Meanwhile, I was still working at CBC Calgary as a reporter during the week, picking up as many casual shifts as possible to help pay for my flights to and from Toronto each weekend. But I was clearly not at my best, especially first thing on Monday mornings, when I needed to bring ideas to our story meetings. I was *exhausted*. Fridays were difficult, too, because I was always trying to get ready for my flight out that evening. As time went on, I started taking only mid-week shifts.

Since I was paying for my own flights, I had to be so careful. The margins were razor-thin. If I wound up booking a flight that cost an extra $200 or even $500, that came straight out of my pocket. Gurdeep and I made this Excel spreadsheet that listed every weekend in the season, and I used it to keep track of which flights I'd already booked, which ones I was still waiting on, and how much each one cost. That way I could look at current prices, compare them to what I had paid in the past, and decide if it was worth waiting around for another seat sale. I also had a policy of checking in to my flights as soon as possible, so I could pick my row (three-quarters of the way back is ideal) and therefore have the best odds of having at least one empty seat in my row. That way I could sleep better, or at least stretch out a bit. In terms of in-flight entertainment, I like watching movies, but I also fly a lot, and I know that time is valuable. Sikh scriptures and hymns teach us to really value our time, and use it wisely. So more often than not, I would listen to Sikh music, and would also bring along reading material or research for work. Luckily, *The Hockey News* still counts as research.

Over the course of that first season, my little arrangement seemed to be working, but I was constantly scared that someone in Toronto would find out that I was paying for my own flights. First, I was worried that I might be breaking some kind of CBC rule, and that I'd get in trouble. Second, I didn't want them to think that because I was coming in from so far away that I was somehow unreliable. I was hopeful that the

Punjabi show was going to grow into something much bigger over time. I decided I had to wait it out, and keep everything to myself.

Given that I was spending so much time at the Pearson Airport late at night, I regularly wandered around and explored. On one of these trips, I noticed that there was a hotel, the Sheraton Gateway, attached to the airport. I went up to the hotel lobby, and I thought to myself: *Hmm, this place is technically open to the public.* The leather couches and chairs they had in the lobby were a lot more comfortable than the ones in the rest of the airport, where I usually attempted to get a couple hours of sleep. I decided I'd try sleeping there instead. The first time, I was a bit self-conscious, because I clearly wasn't a paying guest at the hotel—it was 2:00 a.m., and instead of going up to a room, I was using my laptop bag as a pillow. I was worried someone who worked at the hotel was going to come over and kick me out. To my surprise, while some hotel employees looked over at me a few times, nobody said anything. From that point on, I tried to get some rest in the Sheraton lobby as often as I could.

One night, I was settling in on this fancy hotel couch when all of a sudden I spotted long-time *Hockey Night in Canada* play-by-play commentator Bob Cole across the lobby. I could recognize him from a mile away, and there he was in the distance, chatting with someone. I had never met him before, or even seen him in person, but I found myself frozen in place—he is an absolute legend in the industry. I wanted nothing more than to go up and talk to him. But it wasn't so simple. I felt I couldn't, because I knew right away how the conversation would go: I'd tell Bob that I was also a *Hockey*

Night broadcaster, and since it was the middle of the night, eventually he would ask if I was also staying in the hotel, and then what? How was I going to explain to him that I was camping out in the lobby because I couldn't afford a room? I played over a variety of different scenarios in my head about how I could introduce myself and the broadcast to Bob Cole, but they all seemed to lead back to me possibly jeopardizing my role at *Hockey Night* or being embarrassed in front of someone I admired. So, I just kept staring in his direction from across the lobby, slumped down in my seat, until he left.

I regret that moment now. It would have been such a cool opportunity to develop some kind of rapport with him, especially in those early years of the Punjabi show. Bob is such an approachable person. I learned this years later after reading his autobiography, *Now I'm Catching On*, and after finally meeting him in Edmonton at the last ever Oilers game in the iconic Rexall Place, formerly known as Northlands Coliseum. Meeting him before was difficult simply because we were both always working on Saturdays, oftentimes in different parts of the country. Plus, I realized years later, we have more in common than I first thought. It's well known that Bob lives in Newfoundland but flew out every week to call games in Toronto. He was able to make a career for himself in sports broadcasting without leaving his home behind. In my own way, I was doing that, too. But, hiding out on the couch in the lobby of the Sheraton Gateway, I just didn't realize it at the time.

There were other awkward airport encounters in those early years. Kelly Hrudey and Cassie Campbell-Pascall, both of whom work for the English side of *Hockey Night in Canada*, also live in Calgary. Every once in a while, I would see one of them at the airport, too, getting ready to board the same flight I was getting on. Now, I'm not shy—obviously—but when it comes to certain situations, I get cautious. By this point, I knew Kelly a bit, and Cassie is such a nice person, so I would definitely say hello. But I didn't go out of my way to talk to them too much. Partly because I didn't want to wear out my welcome or come off as some kind of superfan. But, again, I was also scared that it would somehow get out that I was paying for the flight with my own money, whereas all of their travel costs were covered by the show. Travel details are such a common part of small talk. I didn't want to risk it.

At the time, I was so new to flying that I didn't know anything about loyalty perks, either: how you can use your points to upgrade to business class and things like that. So even if I kept my distance at the gate, when we boarded the plane, I ended up having to walk right past Kelly or Cassie anyway, as I walked past the good seats up front to my coach seat way at the back. It was a bit awkward—but to be honest, part of me was just happy to be on the same plane with them. In those moments, I felt that we were all on the same team, doing the same kind of work, travelling together to cover the same games. The difference was that their show paid for them to be on that plane, and mine—for now, anyway—just couldn't.

Our lack of budget on the Punjabi side meant we had to be extremely creative. For instance, in those early days we didn't have anyone creating or handling social media for the show. One day, I decided to sign us up for a Twitter account, and a close friend of mine from Surrey, Sukhpreet Singh Heir, a passionate community activist, gave the show a presence on Facebook. He saw what the show meant for the Sikh community across Canada, and how engaged people were, so he created a Facebook group for us. Before long, we had thousands of members from all across the country.

One of the issues with the show, right away, was that *Hockey Night in Punjabi* wasn't on the same channel across Canada. If you had Shaw, we were on one channel, but if you had Rogers, we were on another one. Same thing with Bell, or Telus, or Cogeco in Ontario and Quebec. It was different for literally every cable company, because we were shown on digital channels that didn't have anything else airing on them except for our show.

Another big issue was that we had no real way of telling people in advance which games we would be calling that weekend. That job fell to me, and, again, I ended up doing it organically. The first games we called were the Stanley Cup Final, so that was simple. But as soon as we started calling the Saturday-night double-headers every week, I started thinking long term. The show needed to grow. We needed people to watch. It was really important to get the word out. I started by contacting everyone I knew personally. I went through the contact list in my Hotmail account and sent mass emails to everyone I could find in the Punjabi community, telling them how to watch that week's show. Once we had the social-media accounts up and running, that helped, too. Every week, I would send messages through Twitter and Facebook, letting people know how they could tune in. When people had questions, or even technical problems (a certain cable provider would often answer callers asking why the game wasn't on by saying they didn't provide the program, even though viewers were watching every week!), they would inevitably ask us through social media—so I would take care of that myself as well.

The Facebook group was clearly fan-created, but everyone knew it was the place to go if you wanted the correct information. The Twitter account, meanwhile, looked like it was coming from the show, but really, it was just me. In a way, I didn't feel like I had a choice. We didn't have a budget for anything. Plus, my colleague at the time was in school to become a doctor—in fact, all of my colleagues had other careers on top of the show. But for me, the show was everything. I didn't really have a Plan B. So I felt I had to go above and beyond, and do everything I could to make it a success.

As clever as I had been up to that point, I knew my plan of secretly paying for flights wasn't going to stay a secret forever. Especially if I kept blabbing in the makeup chair.

I didn't realize when we started that makeup is essential if you're on TV. When you're sitting under bright lights for multiple hours, the shine on your skin really comes through. In Toronto, there is a fabulous woman named Lianne Harrower who's been doing makeup for the entire *Hockey Night in Canada* team for the past 20 years. Because the English side of the show already had their makeup room up and running, it was offered to us on the Punjabi side as well. So every Saturday, I'd go sit in the chair and chat with Lianne while she put my makeup on.

Over time, we got to know each other—she's a great person, always super friendly. She also has a really good memory for details. We would be casually chatting, and Lianne would make small talk: "What time did you get in? Was Cassie on your flight this week?" These conversations added up over time until, one week, I guess I got a bit too relaxed. Now, in my defence, I *was* sitting in a very comfortable chair as Lianne put makeup on my face. It's quite a relaxing experience, sitting in that chair with your eyes closed. But I must've not been thinking about what I was saying, because one minute we were chatting like always, and the next I heard this gasp come from her. My eyes shot open, and I looked over at Lianne to see what was going on. She looked around the room, then whispered to me, *"Are you paying for your own flights?"* She had pieced it together over time, and whatever I had just said must have been the final piece of the puzzle.

All I thought was: *Oh shit.*

Right away, I said to her, "Look, I haven't told anyone about this." I listed all the reasons why it had to be that way. I asked her not to tell anybody else, and thankfully she didn't. But Lianne was the very first person on the *Hockey Night* staff to know the truth.

Soon there were others. One day during the third season of the show, I reached out to Kelly Hrudey, because I needed to discuss a very serious but sensitive issue that I was having at work. At that point, I was scared to reach out to anyone in management. But Kelly was gracious enough to meet me at a Tim Hortons in Calgary. In that conversation I laid down everything that was going on at work, and I also told him all the things I was sacrificing for the show: how I was doing all of our social media myself, and how I was even paying for my own airfare. He couldn't believe it. But that was just a small piece of our conversation that day, and Kelly ended up giving me a lot of good advice. He said I should talk to Joel, because that was the only way I was going to sleep at night.

When I finally got the courage to explain the whole story to Joel, it took him a minute to process it all. The issue at work was news to him, but so was the part about the flights. He thought I was in Toronto often enough to make it work without too much difficulty. When you are an executive producer like Joel, you are dealing with so many different issues while also having to manage so many people. So, of course, I didn't blame him at all. Besides, he had never heard of anyone doing something so absurd—it was so far-fetched that he never even considered it a possibility.

I later learned that Kelly went to bat for me with his bosses on the English side, too. He told them that *Hockey Night in Canada* is the cream of the crop in the hockey world, that it is the best and most prestigious position in our field as broadcasters, and that even though I was on the Punjabi side, if I was good enough to be on the show then they should be paying for my flights, too.

By year three, Joel and the CBC bosses had graciously signed off. It was a tremendous relief for me, to say the least. Joel put me in touch with the late Forrest MacKeigan, a lifelong CBC employee, to manage my travel bookings through the company. Forrest was so impressed by the manner in which Gurdeep and I booked all of my travel the first two years that he gave me special permission to continue to book my own travel, adding that I would be saving the company a lot of money given how efficient we were in looking out for sales. By year four, my accommodation was being paid for as well.

And can you guess which hotel they ended up putting me up in? The very same Sheraton whose couches I used to sleep on, just a few years earlier—and the same hotel Bob Cole stayed in.

———

The other big hurdle we had to figure out on the show was advertising. I knew early on that if we could find a way to get advertisers for *Hockey Night in Punjabi*, that would go a long way to proving that the show was worth keeping around. I used to sit at my desk at CBC Calgary and dream of a time when the show might even attract commercials that would air *in Punjabi*—a rarity back then. As I had done with our social media, I decided to go out and try selling ad space myself.

It didn't go well. I learned that the sales world isn't the kind of place you can easily access from the outside. I had made a list of some massive companies and brands, and after looking up their sales departments, I would cold-call them. But it doesn't work that way. Salespeople really only talk to other salespeople. They don't take calls from some random person trying to pitch them a show to sponsor. I did identify myself as being from *Hockey Night in Punjabi*, but maybe they didn't understand the value, or maybe there was just less work being done at the time in terms of marketing to specific ethnic groups. Or maybe my calls went to a general voicemail that nobody checked. Whatever the reason, I didn't get any responses.

Within the CBC, too, I kept asking who I could talk to about this, until finally I landed a meeting with some of the *Hockey Night in Canada* salespeople in Toronto. I flew out there earlier one week, on a Friday, and I said to them: "Look, the Punjabi market in this country is huge, and we know they watch our show. We could be selling ads directly to them." I told the salespeople that I was already meeting people from local businesses who were interested, but I didn't have any figures to give them, even as a ballpark. The English side had established rates for ads, but no company was going to spend the same amount for our show. We were much, much smaller. In that meeting, the salespeople gave me some actual figures that would work for the Punjabi show. That made a big difference. Once I had those numbers confirmed, I created an entire marketing presentation, which I then took around to companies to try and pitch the show to them.

I'm not a sales guy, and I was new to the whole concept. But I was successful—once. I noticed Telus was doing some commercials in Punjabi, and after some searching, I was able to talk to an individual who had his own company, and it turned out Telus was one of the clients he worked with. Through that connection, Telus ended up buying commercial space on *Hockey Night in Punjabi,* specific to our audience. That was a really cool experience. I wish I had been able to do more of it.

Oh, and I don't run our social media anymore, thank goodness. It was time-consuming to do that stuff all throughout the week—almost like another job. When the show moved to Rogers, our new management team asked if I would hand over the accounts I'd been running to them, so that way they could hold on to the audiences I'd already built over the years, and they wouldn't have to start from scratch. I was happy to do that. Anything for the show.

———

Hockey Night in Punjabi has steadily grown in popularity over the years, but I'll never forget the moment when I realized we were really onto something big.

Early on, for the 2010–11 season, CIBC came on as a sponsor. As part of that sponsorship, they arranged a promotional event for us at one of their branches in Brampton, Ontario. If you didn't know, Brampton is home to one of the largest populations of Sikh Canadians in the country; as of 2011, approximately 100,000 Sikhs lived there—it was an obvious choice for the show's first-ever in-person event. By this point, I had transitioned from doing the colour commentary to play-by-play. My colour commentator at the time, Amarinder Singh, and I went down to be a part of the event, and as we were driving up to the branch, traffic was an absolute nightmare. It took forever to get there, but as we approached, we could see the branch in the distance, along with a bunch of signs advertising the event—some even had our names and faces on them. Even finding parking was extremely difficult. Finally we parked a ways off in a spot that wasn't even an actual parking spot and walked over. As we approached the branch, we saw a lineup of people that stretched out the front door and onto the sidewalk. From a distance, people started calling and waving to us. It was only then that we realized the cause of the traffic jam: us.

After we made it through the line and finally entered the bank, we encountered a gigantic hockey-themed cake for members of the community. They had also set up a bunch of hockey nets and sticks out front for the kids to play with.

And there was a seating area with a fantastic backdrop for us to take pictures, sign autographs, and chat with people. It was surreal, and I was blown away that so many people would take the time to show up in person to say hello. When *Hockey Night in Punjabi* first started, we had received a bunch of media attention, but we had never done anything at the community level before, so we weren't really exposed to the effect the show was having on a person-to-person basis.

The event was a lot of fun. We were sitting there, chatting with people and signing autographs, when I noticed this elderly grandmother approaching the table. She was using a walker and was clearly having some trouble getting around. Out of respect, I folded my hands together, as we do in our culture, got up to meet her, and helped her over to our table. She was wearing her traditional Punjabi outfit, but overtop of that she was wearing a bright blue Toronto Maple Leafs jersey. I noticed that she was teary-eyed, so I asked her if she was okay. She said, in Punjabi, "I can't thank you enough. I finally have a relationship with my grandkids because of your show."

I said, "What do you mean?"

She said she couldn't speak English, and her grandkids didn't speak Punjabi that well. "We didn't have any kind of connection," she said. "They didn't even want to sit with me." But the grandkids were big hockey fans, and because of our show, the grandmother was able to start watching it as well. "Now," she said, smiling, "we sit and watch the show together—and now they think it's cool that Grandma's a Leafs fan. It has changed our family. It's changed my life."

It was a short conversation, but I will never forget that moment. It was the first time I realized that we were bringing together not just families or groups of friends, but entire generations of Punjabi speakers. *Hockey Night in Punjabi* wasn't just a novelty show. What we were doing went so much deeper.

Chilling with Gurdeep on the front step of our home in Brooks.

Rocking my favourite childhood pajamas.

With Harjot and Gurdeep on the morning of Gretzky's last-ever game in Calgary (February 22, 1999).

Living out my hockey dreams with my favourite toy.

Hosting *PowerPlay* in my college years on Mount Royal's radio station.

Hockey Night Punjabi team on the *Hometown Hockey* set with Ron MacLean and Tara Slone.

In the broadcast booth at Rogers Arena in Vancouver with Bhola and Inderpreet.

Thumbs up to the fans screaming "Bonino Bonino Bonino" at Pittsburgh's 2016 Cup parade.

Meeting "The Great One," who was just as advertised—humble and gracious.

With friend, mentor, and former NHLer Kelly Hrudy of *Hockey Night in Canada*.

With the man himself, Nick Bonino, after the Penguins Cup victory in June 2016.

My first love . . . the tabla!

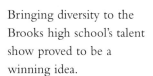

Bringing diversity to the
Brooks high school's talent
show proved to be a
winning idea.

The most influential person in my childhood, Bhai Jiwan Singh Ji. His grace and
humility shaped me into the person I am today.

With legends of the Kirtan world Bhai Niranjan Singh Jawaddi and Bittu Ji.

Such an honour to do Kirtan with Atamjot and Gurpreet at the Golden Temple in Amritsar.

The day I married the love of my life, Sukhy, the newest member of the family.

Marriage is all gains, especially when you have fun-loving in-laws like the Sidhus!

Hockey Night with the Singhs—our unique take on an engagement photo shoot.

Taking a slice out of Lord Stanley. Don't worry, that's our wedding cake!

Being our true, silly selves during a family trip to Seattle.

Ready for Gurdwara with Aparjeet and Mohun.

There's no one I'd rather explore the world with than Sukhy.

With the 2019 Chevrolet Good Deeds Cup Champions in Ottawa.

Turban-tying demonstration to kids in the HEROS hockey charity.

Inspiring the next generation to be proud of who they are is so important and a ton of fun!

Chapter 7
Searching for Harmony

With *Hockey Night in Punjabi*, I feel so fortunate to have found success working in hockey in a way that I could never have dreamed of as a kid. But my biggest blessing has come away from the rink (well, kind of). It's finally time to talk about my wife, Sukhjeet!

Before I even get into our journey together, I have to begin with her family. Our families have known each other since before either Sukhy or I were even born. Some people hear that and, putting it together with our cultural background, automatically assume: arranged marriage. But no. The story of our relationship is a little more complicated—and a lot more interesting.

Our families knew each other through Bhai Jiwan Singh Ji, who, as I've mentioned, used to stay with my family in Calgary when he came to Alberta. But other families would invite him to their house as well, for prayers and musical ceremonies. As the family that organized his trips, we went along to whichever house he visited. That's how my family first met Sukhjeet's.

As a kid, when I travelled to Calgary every weekend to attend services and participate in classes at Gurdwara, one of my closest friends was a guy named Tejinder. He was two years older than I was, but we always got along really well. Each of us was the only boy among our siblings, and we were both sports fanatics. There was a cul-de-sac near Tejinder's house where a bunch of us would get together and play ball hockey after we finished at the temple. Tejinder always wore a Flames jersey and pretended to be Theo Fleury—which was funny, because he was the tallest kid in the group, whereas Fleury was notably short for an NHL star. He also owned road-hockey goalie equipment, too, not to mention a legit hockey net with metal posts as opposed to plastic ones. We spent countless hours on that street, living out our imaginary hockey dreams.

Over the years, Tejinder and I grew closer, and I spent more and more time at his house on the weekends and in the summertime. We would play Super Nintendo, always renting the exact same car-racing game, *Top Gear 3000*, or horse around with mini-hockey sticks in his basement or at the basketball hoop on his driveway. It was at Tejinder's house that I first saw *The Exorcist*, when I was probably way too young.

Tejinder has three sisters, Jagdeep, Manpreet, and Sukhjeet, so whenever I went over to his place, I would always say hello to them. That was about the extent of our relationship, and it went on that way for years, until one day I dropped by to watch the TV show that Tejinder and his sisters were obsessed with at the time: *24*. When I got there, his youngest sister, Sukhjeet, was home, too. We were both in our early 20s, and she was studying to become a teacher at the University of Calgary. The three of us settled around the TV in such a way that Tejinder was on a separate couch a little ways in front of where Sukhy and I were sitting. For some reason, during the show, Tejinder looked away from the screen and started staring really intensely at his thumb. Sukhy and I both saw him do it, and we looked at each other, like, "What the heck?" That one little moment broke the ice between us, and for the rest of the episode, we kept making fun of her brother and chatting with each other. Despite the fact that I'd been in her house many times over the years, we'd never really talked before—and the first thing I realized was what a great sense of humour she had. Sitting there talking with Sukhy was just hilarious. It also didn't hurt that she was a huge hockey fan.

After that, I wanted to spend more time with her, but I wasn't sure how to do it. I guess I saw my chance when Tejinder switched cellphones and gave Sukhy his old one, which still had his old number attached to it. I happened to have tickets to an upcoming Flames game against the Colorado Avalanche, and I had already asked Tejinder if he wanted to go. He said he was busy, so I called his old cell number, and when Sukhy answered, I said, "Oh, whoops! I thought this was Tejinder's number." This, of course, wasn't really an accident. "But while we're talking . . . do you maybe want to come to this hockey game with me?"

That night was the first time we hung out together, just the two of us. Sukhy took public transit to the Saddledome, and she ended up running a little bit late. When I met her at the entrance, I jokingly gave her a bit of a hard time about it: "This is the first time I've ever missed the national anthems at an NHL game!" But that turned out to be the one and only time in our relationship where *she* was the one who made us late for something. We had a lot of fun at the game, which wasn't a surprise, because Sukhy really knew her stuff. From a young age, Tejinder had treated Sukhy like the little brother he never had, mentoring her in all things NHL until she was just as obsessed with it as he was. She was wearing a Flames jersey, while I wore an Avalanche one. Paul Kariya was one of my favourite players growing up, and I had followed his career as an Anaheim Mighty Duck. When he signed with the Avalanche to reunite with Teemu Selanne, the team was absolutely stacked, so I picked up his jersey in excitement— and because this was just before I began my career with *Hockey Night in Canada*, it turned out to be the last ever game I wore a jersey to. Sukhy and I were excited to discover that each of us could carry an in-depth conversation about hockey for hours. Plus, we both loved to laugh. It became clear right away that Sukhy was an incredibly positive person, with a personality that was both vibrant and down to earth.

From there, we started hanging out more often. When she wasn't in school, Sukhy worked at a Real Canadian Superstore location as a cashier in the electronics department and photo lab. Whenever I needed to get photos printed, I made sure to go to Sukhy's location—I'm sure I printed way more pictures than I needed.

One day, Sukhy was invited to join the University of Calgary's interfaith club, but when she showed up on the first day, they said, "Where's the other person?" It turned out they were expecting a male and a female from each faith. She needed to find a Sikh guy willing to go to these meetings with her, and because I was so involved in the community, she asked me. I was glad she asked me, and so on Sundays, we would go to these club meetings together. It was a really positive-minded group, full of other young people from different faiths, and the woman who organized it, Afroza Nanji, had a great heart. In our time there, we worked on a number of different projects, including volunteering for a local homeless shelter, a seniors' home, and Habitat for Humanity. Sukhy and I bonded over our shared desire to make the world a better place—and whenever we had nothing else to talk about, we would go back to talking hockey.

In 2008, by the time I started at *Hockey Night in Punjabi*, Sukhy had begun working for WestJet, a Canadian airline headquartered in Calgary. After finishing her undergrad, she was waiting to see if she'd be accepted into the Faculty of Education at the University of Calgary. One perk of working for WestJet is what's called a "companion fare," which means you can pick one person to get a really cheap deal on all of their flights for the year. Sukhy was one of the few people I had told that I was secretly paying for all of my flights to and from Toronto each week, and she was shocked, asking how this was even possible. That summer, she surprised me by making me her companion so I could save some money that upcoming season. It was a very generous gesture, but not as simple as it looked. Since neither Sukhy nor I had discussed the technicalities of *what* our relationship was by this time, I worried what would happen if someone else in Sukhy's family were to ask if they could be her companion instead—what would she say? Being listed as her companion fare didn't mean we had to travel together, but it did look suspicious, even though it made practical sense. And in the end, her eldest sister *did* ask about it, and we quickly decided to change it around so Jagdeep could be the companion instead of me.

The most unfortunate part was this all happened before the hockey season had even started, so I never even used the discount. But at least the two of them got a cheap trip to Vegas out of it.

———

As Sukhy and I got closer, I was being torn in two different directions. On the one hand, *Hockey Night in Punjabi* was on the air, and I was focused on trying to make it a permanent gig. But on the other I had a completely separate career developing in the world of Sikh music. And in that moment, I seriously considered choosing Kirtan.

Let me back up a bit. My favourite musician ever is Bhai Niranjan Singh Ji. He's from Jawaddi, an area in Punjab, and he, along with his tabla player, the late Bhai Harjit Singh, more popularly known as Bittu Ji, revolutionized Sikh music in the '90s. They brought a totally different style to the music that was far more modern than the simpler way it had been previously performed. Niranjan Singh would sing a Sikh hymn, but he would often switch between different *raags* seamlessly. A raag is essentially a set of specific keys from which one can improvise and create a melody, allowing for endless variation. Niranjan Singh would also combine several different styles, beat scales, and genres of Kirtan into one hymn. Prior to Bittu Ji, tabla in Kirtan was often quite simple and more of an afterthought accompaniment, whereas he brought in a much more entertaining and riveting style, with trends from Western music, along with more intricate and energetic rhythms and beats, which inspired countless Sikh youngsters around the world to play the same percussion instrument. Both of these musicians were legends in my eyes, and they became a dynamic duo that I adored, kind of like Gretzky and the Finnish sniper Jari Kurri. I looked up to them, and whenever I dreamed about becoming a musician, it was them I wanted to emulate.

When I was a teenager, my mom, recognizing my clear obsession, went out of her way to get in touch with the Jawaddi musicians and even helped organize their tour and hosted them when they came to Calgary. I had kept in touch with Niranjan Singh over the phone since then. Finally, in 2006, after a number of years of touring outside of North America, they announced they were coming back to Canada that December. At that time, I was still unsure whether I could make it in broadcasting. I was working at CBC Calgary and running a Calendar Club franchise in a local mall on the side to make some extra money. A friend of mine, Balwinder Marwaha, owned several franchises, and he thought it would give me a taste of the business world, in case I decided to switch paths. But when I found out that the Jawaddi group was going to be touring Vancouver, I dropped all of my work and flew out to the west coast not only to hear them but also to stay with them. I guess I wouldn't make for a great businessman. I asked Niranjan Singh when he was going to arrive from India, and I secretly made sure my flight landed just before, so that I could be there when he arrived at the airport. Sure enough, when he and Bittu Ji walked out, I was the first person they saw.

A group of three musicians together is common in Sikh music, but for that trip, only Niranjan Singh and Bittu Ji came.

They decided that for each performance, they would find a local musician who could accompany them on vocals. After I met up with them, we all stayed together with a friend of mine, Tanvir Uppal, who organized the Vancouver tour. I was there because I was organizing their next stop in Calgary—just like my mom had done in years past. In fact, my mom was one of the first-ever female committee members of a Sikh temple in North America, or maybe even the world. I learned how to fulfill the duties of a Gurdwara secretary from her.

The Jawaddi group was performing every night that week at Sikh temples in and around Vancouver. One day, as we were driving around in the van, I was acting like the super-fan I was: reminding them of old tunes of *shabads* (Sikh hymns) I'd heard and seen them play, and other details I remembered from their performances over the years. They didn't even remember some of them. I mentioned that I had once heard Niranjan Singh singing a hymn live in a particular way, and to jog his memory, I sang a part of it back to him. I noticed Niranjan and Bittu Ji look at each other. And once I started, I couldn't stop: "Remember this hymn? What about this one?"

Later that night, when we were home again after the performance, they called me into a room to talk. I thought I might be in trouble—maybe all my questions since they'd arrived had annoyed them. But instead they asked, "Why don't you accompany us onstage?" They told me that I sang well, and I clearly already knew their music like the back of my hand. "We think you'd be a great fit," they said.

So from 2006 to 2008, right up until *Hockey Night in Punjabi* started—and even a little after that—whenever Niranjan and Bittu Ji came to Canada, I would travel and perform with them. I have to repeat myself: these are Sikh music legends we're talking about, and sitting next to them is some random Canadian kid? It was nuts! They gave me a lot of freedom during the performances, too. There's something in Kirtan called an *alaap*, which is a solo vocal performance within the music, and they allowed me to sing these solos, which was very generous of them. The performances went really well, and the group was so popular that there were always lineups of people to host us for lunch or dinner and show us the sights in each city.

Around that same time, I received an even more unbelievable phone call. It was from Bhai Harjinder Singh, the head of the immensely popular Sri Nagar Kirtan group. If you haven't heard of them, the best comparison I can make is that they are to Sikh music what the Beatles are to rock and roll. I knew Bhai Harjinder Singh because he, too, had stayed with my family in Calgary. He was calling because he was supposed to come back to Canada for another tour, but the musicians who were supposed to accompany him were having a problem getting their visas. He told me he knew that I played the tabla pretty well, and he asked if I would consider joining his tour instead.

What do you even do in that situation? *Okay,* I thought to myself, *the fricking most popular Sikh musician in the world is asking me to accompany him live on stage.* It was so far-fetched, so ridiculous, that I almost felt like laughing. But I held it together long enough to say yes.

All of a sudden, I had become a professional touring musician—something else I'd dreamed of since I was a little kid tapping along with the performers at Gurdwara while sitting in my dad's lap. And even more improbably, it was for two different roles: I had been touring with the Jawaddi group as a vocalist on the harmonium, and now I was going to join the Sri Nagar group as a tabla player.

There was hardly any downtime between gigs, either. Once, after the Jawaddi tour finished in Toronto, I had to fly straight to Vancouver to join the Sri Nagar group. The day I was scheduled to leave, I remember Niranjan Singh from Jawaddi giving me a farewell speech. He told me that it had been a lot of fun having me around on tour, but he cautioned me that things were about to get a lot more serious. "You're about to be an accompanist with the most well-known performer in Sikh music," he said. "The Sikh community worldwide respects Harjinder Singh so much. So make sure you act accordingly." That was the moment when it really hit me, just how extraordinary this was.

And Niranjan Singh was right. The crowds on the next tour were enormous—we performed at Sikh temples across Canada, never for fewer than 1,000 people, and often into the several thousands. And because it was the first time I was accompanying Bhai Harjinder Singh, a lot of people just assumed that I was his son. We did have a physical resemblance: he wore glasses and had a longer beard, just like I did. In fact, he looks like a younger version of my dad. I was humbled to share the stage with a man of his status and to see how much love and respect every congregation gave him. This was before YouTube, so I unfortunately don't have much video of it, but I do have a lot of audio recordings of those performances, which will always be treasured memories for me.

It was nerve-wracking to join such a prestigious group, but the thing was, I knew their music inside and out as well. I knew their tendencies when they performed live, and I also had all of their studio recordings memorized—and do you know where I memorized them? Back on those weekly drives from Brooks to Calgary! I knew the music so well that it only took a couple of days of practising before Harjinder Singh told me, "We don't need to practise anymore during this tour. I'm comfortable singing any hymn that I've ever sung with you."

But we still weren't equals. Not even close. As Sikhs, we are taught that we receive blessings from serving our elders, and I saw the tour as an opportunity to do just that. I helped carry their instruments, brought them tea, ironed their clothes—anything to help. I was so committed to these jobs that sometimes the other band members jokingly called me *Bebe*, or the grandma of the group.

I'll never forget the moment when Bhai Harjinder Singh and I were getting ready for a performance and standing in front of a mirror tying our turbans together. He told me he used to tie his turban in the exact same style I did when he was young. We were chatting and reflecting on our respective journeys, and that was when he posed the question to me. He said, "You know our music inside and out, and it's been a great fit having you a part of the team on tour. If you've always wanted to do this, then why don't you join me as my full-time tabla player?"

I was absolutely stunned that he would even consider that. Once again, for context, the most famous Sikh musician in the world was offering this to *me*. I had to think quickly, though, as he was waiting for a response. Right away, my mind went to hockey and the opportunity I had with *Hockey Night in Canada*. Although the Punjabi version was in its infancy, being a part of it was a dream come true. Thinking on my feet, I responded by asking Bhai Harjinder Singh if I could be his North American tabla player and join him on tours during the summers. Right away though, he said that wouldn't be fair to the tabla player he kept on in India. Whoever was accompanying him had to live in India and travel with him worldwide. I realized then that, while it would've been an absolute blast, it wasn't in the cards for me. While it was immensely difficult to turn down a full-time career as a musician with the top Kirtan group in the world, I knew that a career in hockey was what I had to go for.

Looking back on it, these musical opportunities came along at the perfect moment in my life. I wasn't married and didn't have kids yet, so I was free to travel and dedicate myself entirely to the music. My day job at CBC Calgary was flexible, too, letting me take time off whenever I needed it— even when Bhai Niranjan Singh from Jawaddi invited me to come to India with him, where I stayed at his house with his family in Ludhiana and we performed Kirtan in little villages, big cities, and everywhere in between. My parents eventually joined us, and Niranjan Singh arranged their travel and accommodation in places we wouldn't have been able to see on our own.

Nowadays, I've been able to keep my Kirtan dreams alive through people like a young fellow born and raised in California by the name of Atamjot Singh Dosanjh. After hearing recordings of him performing, I organized events to have him sing in Calgary on an annual basis. Due to the vast reach of our audio and video recordings on SoundCloud and YouTube, the congregation not only locally in Calgary but also globally was wowed, with many in the Kirtan world viewing him as "Jawaddi 2.0"—he's an incredible talent. One of my best friends, Gurpreet Gill, happens to be one of Canada's best tabla players, so the three of us have formed our own group, performing together across Canada. We've been fortunate to have been invited to perform all around the world, highlighted by performing Kirtan at the Golden Temple in Amritsar, which was a surreal experience. It's rare for an all–North American Kirtan group to travel the world to perform.

Another one of my passions in music has been organizing a type of event known as an Atam Ras Kirtan, where I invite popular Sikh musicians to combine their talents in a unique collaboration at Guru Ram Das Darbar, the Gurdwara my family and I attend. Through live recordings of the performances, the week-long event has garnered a global following, helping me put together in Calgary one of the can't-miss Kirtan events in the calendar year. In fact, international Sikh musicians routinely contact me wanting to get in on the collaborations. One particular moment that stands out for me was helping to arrange the entire Canadian tour for Taren Kaur, a young female guitarist and vocalist born in the U.K. It was rare in the past for females to try to make it full-time in Indian music, so to have her perform in collaboration with other famous Sikh musicians made for a very special event. The atmosphere and intimate vibe of these Kirtan programs created memories I'll cherish forever, and I have friends all over the world who say they listen over and over again to the live Kirtan recordings from those events. It's amazing to get that type of feedback, because I devote my time and effort for all of this as seva, without financial compensation; to pass on my passion for Kirtan to future generations is really rewarding.

So many of the close friendships I have in my life are from the world of Kirtan, and the love I've received from the Sikh congregation is very near and dear to my heart. And all of this happened because of that one blessing Bhai Jiwan Singh Ji gave, telling my mom, before I was even born, that her love for music would come to fruition through her children. A saint's words can come true. I really believe that, so I can't even take credit for anything at all. It's really just blessings from some brilliant souls through the grace of the Almighty.

—

Back in Calgary, meanwhile, things with Sukhy were going well. We got along great together, and I had a feeling that our friendship had the potential to go a lot further. But I knew that I wasn't interested in getting so close to someone just to have fun. My thinking was, it only made sense to go through all of the highs and lows of a relationship if there was the potential of getting married.

One day, I asked Sukhy to meet me at a park, to have a friendly but blunt conversation about our future. In her words, I basically interviewed her. "Okay," I said, "it's been great getting to know you more and more . . . and I want this to be forever, but if this is going to go any further, I want to know if you think our relationship has potential, too." In the

Sikh faith, one of the purposes of a couple's journey together is to help each other progress spiritually. This was important to me. Also, in Punjabi culture, you don't just marry the person—you marry the family as well. And not just symbolically, either. Oftentimes you end up living with them. I wanted to make sure we were doing things the right way, and that each of our families would approve of the relationship. Even though she already knew a lot about me at that point, I re-listed some of the most important details: that in my home, we kept Sikh scriptures, the Sri Guru Granth Sahib Ji, and had a dedicated prayer room. My family was very involved with one of the local Sikh temples in Calgary, Guru Ram Das Darbar. On top of that, I travelled a lot for work—for both *Hockey Night in Punjabi* and the Kirtan tours—and I didn't see that changing in the near future. All of these things were important to me. Was that something she wanted to be part of? "If not," I said, "then no problem, and we can just continue as friends."

I wasn't necessarily nervous asking Sukhy any of this. I was fairly confident because I knew the type of person she was. There wasn't a topic under the sun that we hadn't already discussed, be it realistic or hypothetical. We also shared so many likes and dislikes in life—we were just so in sync. But I wanted to be respectful to her. If we were going to take the next step, we needed to be up front about everything, to ensure feelings weren't hurt down the road. I could tell Sukhy was a little caught off guard and nervous, but at the end of the day, I think she appreciated it.

It was a frank and honest conversation. And thankfully, Sukhy's response was exactly what I was hoping to hear. She told me she felt the same way I did, and she reminded me that her family followed the Sikh faith just as strongly as mine did—they also kept scriptures in their house, for instance, and followed many of the same practices.

But we weren't out of the woods yet. For me, the next step was talking to my parents and asking for their approval. Sukhy said that was fine, but she didn't want to rush anything on her end just yet. That was where we left it. But I was unfazed. That day, I went home with the world's biggest smile on my face.

My parents responded really well to the idea. They were extremely happy to hear that Sukhy was becoming a teacher— not only were they both teachers but so were many of my aunts and uncles. They also loved the fact that our families already knew one another.

Her side was a bit trickier, however—even though there seemed to be good signs everywhere. Sukhy still hadn't brought up the subject when she and her dad flew to Ottawa to visit her cousins. While they were waiting to board their flight, I sent her a text wishing her a safe flight. Her dad noticed her checking her phone, and asked, "Who are you messaging?" She told him what I had written, and he said, "Whoever marries him is going to be a very lucky girl." At around the same time, Sukhy's mother brought up another boy for her to consider marrying; in Indian culture, arranged marriages aren't as prevalent as they once were, but so-called introduced marriages are still quite common. This guy lived in England, and he was studying to become an engineer. The funny thing is that her mom pitched the idea to her by saying, "He looks like Harnarayan."

Sukhy realized she was going to have to say something. Finally she asked her mother, "Well, if this guy looks like Harnarayan, then why not Harnarayan?" That was not what her family was expecting to hear. As soon as she suggested marrying me, her father, Jasbir Singh Sidhu, stepped in with some serious concerns about how suitable I was as a match— and I have to admit, they made a certain amount of sense. Looking back, I can see where he was coming from.

One thing he was worried about was my job security. I was on a one-year contract with *Hockey Night in Punjabi*, not making any money, really, due to the fact I was paying for my own flights, and he wasn't sure how much of a future the show had. Heck, at that point, I wasn't, either. None of us were. Plus, during the season, I was flying in and out of Toronto every weekend, not to mention travelling all over the place for the summer Kirtan tours. Sukhy's father was concerned about the toll that so much travel would take on our relationship. When she relayed those concerns to me, I knew I had to do something to prove my commitment. So I went back to school and got two certifications: as a mortgage agent and as a real-estate agent.

That might sound extreme, but I was calling hockey games only on the weekends. At the same time, I was fairly well known in the local Sikh community in Calgary. I figured that the real-estate industry would be an option for me on the side. In reality, however, I was mostly doing it to win over my potential father-in-law. Whenever I made a batch of mortgage agent business cards, or little postcard-sized ads, Sukhy would always bring them home and leave them around the house in hopes her dad would notice them.

It was hard to know if anything was working. After a couple of years passed, Sukhy's dad still seemed to have his concerns, and it wasn't clear whether he was ever going to be persuaded. At one point, my parents went out and found the equivalent of character witnesses—people they knew Sukhy's family respected—and sent them over to her house to advocate on my behalf. But that didn't seem to help, either.

This process stretched out for a long time, and to be honest, I was getting discouraged. Sukhy and I had thought these conversations would be relatively simple, but it was starting to feel like it would never happen. Neither of us had anticipated so much resistance from her family, even if their concerns were totally justified. And if her parents never came around, then marriage was out of the question. In Indian culture, the parents' blessing for a wedding is incredibly important, because the marriage is bigger than just the bride and the groom—you're linking two families together, forever. Without that blessing, the chances of a marriage working out are rare.

This all weighed so heavily on me. Throughout the process, I hadn't allowed myself to think about the possibility of not marrying Sukhy, but one night, I went to my mom's room to spill the ugly truth that maybe this wasn't meant to be. Up until then, my mom had always been my outlet for what was going on in my life, and the topic of marriage was no different. But that night, she wasn't hearing any of it. "Stop this nonsense right now," she told me. "It's a rare thing to find a girl willing to wait this long for you. If Sukhy is willing to fight for your relationship, then you can't back away. You're never going to find someone like her again." Like always, Mom was right, and what she told me that night totally changed my mindset. From that moment on, I knew I had to stick it out, no matter how long it took, and do what I needed to do to be with Sukhy.

Luckily, the tide seemed to be turning at last. My father had called Sukhy's dad to try to further things along. A little while later, I was at the Gurdwara, reading Sikh scriptures as part of a ceremony I was volunteering at. It was a Saturday morning, in the summertime, and as I was reading aloud to the congregation, I felt my phone buzzing like crazy in my pocket. Something was going on, and part of me was worried something bad had happened to someone at home. I signalled to another volunteer to take over for me, and when I checked my phone, I saw I had more than a dozen missed calls from my sister Gurdeep. She had also sent some strongly worded texts: "You need to come home. Now. Sukhy's dad is coming over."

Holy shit, I thought. *It's finally happening.*

I drove home as quickly as I could, and Sukhy's parents, Jasbir and Harbans, along with her brother, Tejinder, and sister-in-law, Bismaadh, were already there. Naturally, as soon as she heard there were guests coming over, Mom started cooking up a storm in the kitchen. She'd brought out the best dishes we owned and had made her signature dessert, a sweet appetizer called *vesan,* made of chickpea flour, sugar, and butter. The way she makes it, the vesan is like fudge that melts in your mouth. Meanwhile, Gurdeep had tidied up, and by the time I got there, the house was sparkling clean and filled with the scent of freshly cooked food. Everyone was already sitting down together, and I took a seat on an island bar stool, directly across from my potential father- and brother-in-law. It was quiet.

Once I was seated, Sukhy's dad looked at me and started asking me question after question. It felt a bit like being on the witness stand. Everyone else in the room was completely silent. But, again, I respect him for being direct. All of his questions had to do with my job, my travel situation, and other logistics that would affect Sukhy. She's always been very close with her dad, and he was doing his due diligence. I answered each question to the best of my ability, but I was still nervous. A lot, maybe even everything, was riding on getting the answers right.

Finally, Sukhy's dad asked me the question that seemed to matter above all else. He said, "Sukhy is going to be a teacher, working Monday to Friday. Meanwhile, you leave every Friday to do the show, and you come back home Sunday. Then, when school lets out in the summer, you're off on all these Kirtan tours. When would the two of you even see each other?"

I knew that, no matter how wonky our schedules got, Sukhy and I would find a way to make things work. I said to her dad, "The moment she tells me that being on *Hockey Night in Punjabi* is a strain on our relationship, I'll quit. My relationship with my wife and my family is more important than my work."

There was a silence in the room. After that, he didn't have anything else to say. No one did. Then my mom stood up and said, "Let's have some vesan!"

Things were clearly looking up, but the real turning point came when my family was once again hosting Bhai Harjinder Singh and his group from Sri Nagar at our house while they were performing in Calgary. Sukhy's family invited them all over to their house for a meal, as they always did, and my parents, Gurdeep, and I went along, too. There were so many of us in the group that we had to drive there in multiple vehicles, and for whatever reason, my car got there first—but there was no way I was going inside by myself. I was worried about how awkward it would be for me to walk in without the rest of my family and the musicians there, and sure enough, I could see members of Sukhy's family looking out at me through the living-room window! I frantically called Gurdeep's cellphone, and it turned out she'd taken a wrong turn. *Oh great.* I looked over to Bhai Harjinder Singh and told him that we couldn't go inside until the rest of my family had arrived. After what felt like an eternity, the other vehicles arrived and we all went inside together.

The mood inside was one of anticipation, but it was unclear how exactly everything would unfold. At one point, Bhai Harjinder Singh addressed the entire room. "We're all here together," he said. "Why don't we meet upstairs in the Sri Guru Granth Sahib Ji room and say a prayer for Harnarayan and Sukhy? That will be a beautiful blessing for this couple." He led us upstairs, and we read a hymn from the Sikh scriptures together. Then Sukhy and I sat next to one another and received blessings from both of our parents and family who were there. This turned out to be our *roke*, which is kind of like a pre-engagement—it's an acknowledgement that the two families have agreed to a marriage between their children sometime in the near future. It's a way of announcing that you're no longer on the market. And from that moment on, all of the difficulties Sukhy and I had faced were out the window. Completely forgotten. Her family welcomed our relationship with open arms.

In the end, I could not have asked for better in-laws. My father-in-law has such a big and kind heart. As I've said, his concerns about my career were completely valid, and I know that all he wants is what's best for all of his kids, including me. If you ever have any sort of good news, he's the guy you want to tell, as he gets so excited and shows so much passion that he makes you feel so good about yourself. And my mother-in-law is very understanding, has a great sense of humour, and is a fantastic cook! Every time I go over, she spoils me with food like *sholay bhature* and is always making some sort of dessert. She always believed in the idea of me and Sukhjeet together, and for that I am forever grateful.

But, before anything else could happen, I knew what I had to do.

Chapter 8
My Big Fat Hockey Wedding

I can't recall where I got the idea, but I had envisioned what I thought would be a fabulous way to propose to Sukhy. So one day, we made plans to meet up, but I didn't tell her where we were going. Also, she loves surprises, and I of course was more than happy to oblige. We drove out to Springbank, an area just outside of Calgary, which has a tiny airport mostly used for personal airplanes and helicopters. I could sense Sukhy's excitement when she realized what we were doing, but she still didn't have a clue what would happen when we were in the air. The pilot did—I had told him ahead of time—and the three of us jumped into the helicopter. I remember exactly what Sukhy wore; she looked fabulous that day. Up in the air we went, taking in breathtaking views of the city of Calgary and eventually the nearby Kananaskis region. I loved how we were wearing the special helicopter headphones, so we could hear one another well despite the noise of the chopper and the wind. The original plan was to land on top of a mountain and get out, and then I would surprise her and propose. But due to windy conditions, we weren't able to stop during the flight. I had to alter my plans on the fly, and as Sukhy looked out her window, that was my chance. I pulled out the bright new engagement ring that I had so carefully kept with me for the past little while. With as much excitement and love as a man can have at any moment in his life, I spoke straight from the heart and asked her to marry me. Sukhy was thrilled and full of emotion and, most importantly, she said yes! She was beaming and couldn't get over how much she loved the ring, which I'd designed with the help of my long-time friend, the late Mandeep Chandna, whose family has owned and operated a jewellery store called Kohi-Noor in Calgary for decades. It hadn't exactly gone as I'd originally planned, so when we landed back at the Springbank Airport helipad, I jumped out and immediately went down on one knee to propose again. The romantic in me felt like the mid-flight proposal didn't do justice, so I decided to redo the moment—minus the ring, though, since she wouldn't agree to take it off. I was able to give my entire heartfelt speech about how much she meant to me, so it was well worth it. I could hardly believe it: Sukhy and I were finally getting married! After so much uncertainty, the reality took a while to sink in.

All of a sudden, there was so much to plan that we didn't really have time to dwell on anything. Plus it was Sukhy's first year teaching, and the wedding was set for July 9, 2011—right after classes let out. She was juggling all of her regular work on top of the wedding prep.

The first thing to sort out was our engagement ceremony. In a stroke of good luck, my Kirtan mentor, Bhai Niranjan Singh from Jawaddi, announced he was coming to Vancouver that October and asked if I could accompany him on the tabla for the duration of the tour. I agreed but also asked a favour: Would he be willing to skip one day of his tour so he and I could fly back to Calgary and perform at my engagement? It was a big request, but we had known each other for so long at that point that I was hoping he would consider. To my relief, he said yes, but the organizers in Vancouver asked that we fly out and back in the same day, so that we would be disrupting the schedule as little as possible.

There were several hundred people at the ceremony, and Niranjan Singh put everything he had into the music that morning. In fact, he literally would not stop playing—when one hymn finished, he jumped right into the next one, and the next one, and the next one after that. During this, I noticed my dad looking down at his watch, because the rest of the ceremony couldn't go on until the music had finished. So, after five or six hymns, a message came to the stage: "Okay, that's enough now." The sender? My mom!

Next up was our engagement photos, and to keep things on brand, we decided to have them taken inside a hockey rink. Couples typically go somewhere picturesque, like Banff or Lake Louise, but we wanted to do something a little different.

We took two different sets of photos. In one, we wore our favourite team jerseys (me representing the Oilers, Sukhy the Flames) and pretended to be rival players: taking a faceoff, or pushing and shoving in front of the net, or mouthing off while sitting in our respective penalty boxes. It all went hand in hand with Sukhy's competitive nature! In the other set of pictures, we both put on Team Canada jerseys and acted more sportsmanlike. Sukhy hired Azad Dhaliwal, known as the best photographer in the city for South Asian weddings. To get some of the shots just right, he even climbed inside and on top of the net. I think I wore every single Gretzky item I own, and Sukhy had a chance to bring out all of the Iginla gear from her closet. I put on my old ice hockey jersey, too, as well as a jersey I had gotten specially made. On the front was a maple leaf, in a bunch of different colours to represent Canada's multiculturalism, and on the back it said "KHALSA," as a tribute to the tenth Sikh Guru. To be a Khalsa is to be the purest form of a Sikh. It refers to someone who has all of the values our Gurus have taught us: selflessness and a commitment to justice and serving humanity. Later in the photo shoot, I even wore my Team Canada jersey signed by Gretzky, which is how you know it was a really special occasion. If you're thinking, *Wow, this guy has a lot of jerseys*, well, you're not the only one. Sukhy always gave me a hard time about this, even before we began living together: I had an entire closet full of them. Hey, she has a lot of shoes and purses. So what if I have way too many jerseys, right?

Before we knew it, the morning of July 9 was upon us. Wedding days are always emotional, but there's an added layer in Punjabi culture, because according to our traditions, that's the day that the bride and groom officially begin to live together. It can be a lot for anyone to process. That morning, I wrote Sukhy a full-page handwritten letter and had one of her nieces deliver it to her before she came to the temple. In it, I reaffirmed my commitment to our relationship and tried to reassure her that I would do everything I could to make her feel welcome and a part of our family. Our photographer captured the moment that Sukhy read it, and that picture sits inside our wedding album. We've kept this up as a tradition since then, leaving surprise notes in each other's pocket or bag, or under our pillows.

Before the ceremony, while Sukhy and her family did a traditional prayer together at their house, I was getting ready at my place. I had my usual protein shake for breakfast and got dressed in an outfit Sukhy and I had custom-made in India. The traditional Indian wedding colours are red and gold, but we decided to go with royal blue and gold instead, as blue is our favourite colour and also one of the official Sikh colours (and, of course, it didn't hurt that blue is a part of the Oilers' threads). My Punjabi shoes, meanwhile, were so slippery that I almost fell down the stairs, only barely catching myself on the bannister. Sure, I was vibrating with nerves and excitement, too. But I still blame the shoes.

A Sikh wedding is full of tradition. For instance, when both families arrive at the temple, they meet outside and have a formal introduction called a *milnee*—this dates back to a time when families wouldn't necessarily have known each other before the wedding. The funny thing is, I use that term on *Hockey Night in Punjabi*. When the first scrum of the game breaks out, and players are getting in each other's faces, I'll say, "Oh, they're just having their milnee."

The ceremony was fairly traditional. To honour the teachings of our faith, Sukhy and I arrived ahead of schedule, ensuring we had enough time to relax and listen to the Kirtan and to focus our minds on the hymns. More than 700 people were there at the temple, and more than 400 attended the reception later on. One particularly special guest was, again, Bhai Niranjan Singh, who flew in from India just for the occasion, which was a real honour. When I asked him to perform at my wedding, he made a joke, saying that if one of his own guys was about to make the ultimate sacrifice and get married, the least he could do was be there to witness it! But he also knew I was close with other Sikh musicians, and in humility said that even if he didn't perform at my wedding, he would still not miss it and would attend as a part of the congregation. There was no way, though, that I was going to get married without Niranjan Singh singing there.

Even though the ceremony was traditional, we found ways to incorporate hockey into the day. There's another Punjabi custom where, after the temple ceremony, the groom arrives at the bride's house to take her home for the first time. It's a fun event, because the bride's sisters and cousins all line up at the entrance, and the groom has to find a way to get in—usually he ends up paying them off, one by one, or else has to win some kind of game before they'll let him past. Sukhy's family had a lot of fun with it. They offered me plates of traditional sweets, but they had changed the flavours around, so the ones that were supposed to be sweet were super salty, and vice versa. Others were spiked with really intense spices. At one point they held up a sign that read, "Out with the Oilers! In with the Flames!" Then they showed me this massive Flames flag that had been on Sukhy's bedroom ceiling when she was a kid, and told me that if I would wear it like a cape, then they'd let me in. However, there was no way I was about to do that. Our photographer captured the moment by grabbing a picture of Sukhy watching everything that was going on from a bedroom window. It was a stalemate, and I backed off the driveway for fun—before sneaking into my in-laws' house through the back door instead.

That night, to contrast the traditional feel of the ceremony, we hosted a looser, more fun Sikh musical performance. I free-styled on the tabla and on vocals alongside Niranjan Singh. Sukhy even performed, too, singing a hymn while I accompanied her on the harmonium. Being able to share that stage with her, alongside all of the other musicians, who by that point were like brothers to me, was a really special moment. It came as a shock to the both of us, though, when we found out that our videographer somehow decided not to record the hymn we sang together, and later blamed it on a low battery. We lost many nights of sleep over this and were so disheartened after watching the draft of our wedding video that it's one of the many reasons we don't have a wedding video at all. Absolutely devastating.

The next day was our reception. Sukhy and I aren't into drinking, dancing, or heavy partying—common occurrences at South Asian weddings. But we still wanted to make sure our reception was fun for everyone. In the months leading up to the wedding, we threw around other ideas but couldn't agree on anything. Then it dawned on both of us: *What if we had it inside a hockey arena?* Suddenly, everything else clicked. *The invitations can be tickets! The guestbook can be a blank hockey jersey! The cake can be the Stanley Cup!* We both loved the idea. Our families might have taken a little bit longer to come around, but we convinced them to trust us and go with it. Our invitations read "Stanley Cup Final, Game 7," and even had a Ticketmaster logo, for authenticity's sake. (Sorry, Ticketmaster!)

We rented a rink in Calgary called the Acadia Recreation Complex—without the ice, of course. We wanted the older folks who weren't as steady on their feet to still be comfortable, and besides, I had already done enough slipping around in my wedding shoes. When people showed up, we served them appetizers and showed them to their tables, which were set up in each of the offensive zones. Once everyone was seated, the two of us came out as the old *Hockey Night in Canada* theme song played over the loudspeakers. We walked out to centre ice, where Kelly Hrudey did the ceremonial puck drop. I didn't know he was going to do this, but right after dropping it, Kelly bodychecked me out of the way so Sukhy could win the faceoff. (To this day, she claims she didn't need his help and would've won it anyway.)

One of the many memorable items at our reception was definitely our life-sized Stanley Cup cake. I can't take credit for it, though—that was all Sukhy's idea. She had approached different cake-makers around Calgary to figure out how it could be done. Sukhy likes chocolate, and I like vanilla, so the cake was half and half. I'm pretty conservative when it comes to choosing what to eat or drink. I usually stick with what I know I like—you're setting yourself up for disappointment by trying something new, right? You can't go wrong with vanilla. Nevertheless, Sukhy has had her way in getting me to try all sorts of new food over the years, especially when we travel together. As for the wedding cake, it was a massive hit. It looked so realistic that people kept wanting to touch it. The only downside is that the cake was so popular, by the time I got there to have a piece, my beloved vanilla side was all gone. I didn't even get to taste my own wedding cake!

After dinner and dessert, we all went to the neutral zone for some hockey-related games, as well as the classic musical chairs, which was good for the elders in attendance. The idea was that once you were eliminated, you had to go sit in the penalty box. As we got near the end of the game, I looked over and saw the box was jam-packed with people from my side of the family.

We had two MCs that night: Sukhpreet, my friend who had started the first *Hockey Night in Punjabi* Facebook page, and Inderpreet, who later became my colleague when the show moved to Calgary. Both of them are from British Columbia, so they found ways of bringing their Canucks jerseys into whatever they did that night, along with their wireless mics. At one point, Inderpreet went up to my uncle, Raghbir Jassal, who had flown up from San Diego for the wedding, for the equivalent of an in-game interview after he'd been ousted from the game.

"How do you feel about your guys' performance so far?" Inderpreet asked him, gesturing to the overflowing penalty box. "It looks like Harnarayan's side is losing pretty badly."

But my uncle had the perfect answer. "Oh, we don't care about winning this game," he said. "We've already won—we got the girl!"

There were other things for our guests to play around with, too. Nowadays it seems like every wedding has a photo booth, but we had one at ours before that trend had really taken off. We also sold our own 50/50 tickets, which are part of every hockey game. The idea was that 50 per cent of the money would go to the winner, and 50 per cent would go towards a student of Sukhy's who had vision problems but whose family couldn't afford the surgery she needed. A cousin of mine from Edmonton, Satwinder Sran, ended up winning the draw, but she announced that she was going to donate her half of the proceeds to the student's family as well. It was a beautiful moment.

On each of the tables were hockey-themed decorations, like mini-hockey sticks engraved with our names and the date—another one of Sukhy's great ideas. We also gave away special hockey cards of Sukhy and me that included jokes like calling Sukhy "Rookie of the Year" because she had just finished her first year as a teacher. To help decorate, I brought in my collection of hockey pucks that I had gathered over the years, displaying them around the Stanley Cup cake on a platform that was painted to look like a hockey rink. But because everything else on the tables was meant to be taken home, all of the kids just assumed the pucks were free, too. You should have seen the look on my face when I came around at the end of the night and realized they were all gone! But I'm sure the kids got more use out of them than I ever would've.

Sukhy's idea for the reception was that if we kept everyone busy and entertained, they wouldn't notice they were missing all the alcohol and dancing. And based on the feedback we received, it totally worked.

———

Back then, Sukhy enjoyed watching the TV show *The Bachelor*. When we were deciding where to go on our honeymoon, she kept coming back to the island of Saint Lucia, where some of that season of the show was filmed. Now, I'm a cost-conscious guy—Sukhy would instead say I'm a *penny-pincher* (hey, I've had to be!)—but she kept bringing it up, and eventually I got the hint. Your honeymoon is a once-in-a-lifetime trip, right? I ended up surprising Sukhy with the news in the parking lot of a Dollarama, of all places, and after the wedding, we flew down to enjoy a week in the Caribbean.

After we got back from our honeymoon, it was still August, and starting in the fall, Sukhy and I would both be back at work full-time. So we started a pattern that continued up until our kids were born: whenever we had some free time together, we'd go travelling. Over the next few years we went all across the United States and Jamaica, and even a couple of month-long trips all around Europe.

We've had our fair share of adventures and misfortunes. We once got to Paris after spending a week in Barcelona and Madrid, where the temperatures were in the sweltering mid-30s Celsius. Paris was the exact opposite, with cold winds and rain. Sukhy was starting to feel under the weather, but we had no idea how bad it was about to get. We ended up deciding to jump on one of those double-decker tour buses and sat at the top, even though the weather wasn't great. After that, we climbed the famous Arc de Triomphe, which has a total of 387 steps. It's steep and tight, with no real places to rest along the way. The view at the top makes it all worthwhile, but maybe not when you're feeling ill. Sukhy's health got much worse that evening, so we called a doctor to our hotel room. The doctor ended up calling an ambulance, and all of a sudden we were in a Paris hospital, with neither of us knowing any French. I remember being so scared because they separated us and later quarantined Sukhy when they couldn't figure out what was wrong with her. Given the language barrier, it was difficult to determine what exactly they were doing or thinking, but they ended up taking fluid from her spine, thinking she might have meningitis. Thankfully, the tests came back negative, and she was released at the end of the day and told to rest. But again, thanks to the details being lost somewhere in translation, we didn't understand that a person is supposed to lie down for several hours after getting a spinal tap. So for a couple of days afterwards, Sukhy continued feeling dizzy and nauseous.

After the scare, she was feeling a lot better as we carried on into the Netherlands and Berlin. In every city we went to, we took a bike tour so we could learn the sites and historical significance before we ventured out on our own. Thinking a bike tour might be too cumbersome in Berlin, with Sukhy just recovering from her ordeal in Paris, we decided to try a Segway tour instead. Before the tour, we had to take some training on how to steer and stay balanced. There were about a dozen of us in the group, and everyone seemed to get the hang of it, except for one person: me. First and foremost, I had trouble getting on even their largest-sized helmet because of my turban, even though I had already prepared for this by wearing a smaller-sized version. Second, due to the rain, we were told to wear ponchos, but for some reason, I couldn't get mine on properly, never being able to locate where my arms were supposed to go—all to Sukhy's absolute amusement. Third, I ended up needing extra training with the Segway transporter, which took place in front of everyone on the tour. At one point I lost my balance so badly that the Segway began swinging violently forwards and backwards, at which point the instructor had to save me from a major accident. Sukhy was embarrassed to even know me. When I looked back, she was covering her face because she was laughing so hard. Eventually, I was able to control the Segway just enough for the tour guide to let me come along, and despite a few hiccups, I even escaped without any injuries.

After Berlin, we made it to Italy and the awe-inspiring Colosseum, not to mention the streets of Rome, where something happened that Sukhy will never let me forget. We were walking back to our hotel late at night through an area where the street lights were dim. You have to remember, I'm from Alberta, which has been rat-free for decades. Well, as we were walking, we noticed something rather large move abruptly about 20 feet ahead of us. It was an enormous rat, and it caught us both off guard. Instead of shielding her from danger, my first instinct immediately was to pull Sukhy in front of me. This has been justifiably thrown in my face countless times since.

However, I did make up for it on our second trip to Europe, when we visited Lisbon, Portugal. We continued our tradition of getting tours in each new city, but this time decided to try something new: an electric bike tour. Neither of us had ever driven an electric bike before, and we didn't realize how fast they can go. We were also unaware how steep many of the streets in Lisbon are. Nonetheless, we began our tour with a group of a dozen other people, and it was a lot of fun—until we turned down a particularly steep street. The brick road seemed to have no grip left at all, and I was barely controlling my bike when I heard Sukhy yell from behind our tour group that her brakes weren't working. Instinct kicked in, and as she whizzed by the rest of us, I leaped off my own still-moving bike in an attempt to save her, hitting the pavement forcefully and landing on my leg. It's the effort that counts, right? I was out cold! The next thing I remember is waking up to a crowd of people looking over me—and, astonishingly, Sukhy was one of them! It turns out the tour guide, who was used to this kind of thing, had grabbed the handlebars of Sukhy's bike and guided her to safety. Meanwhile, in attempting to impersonate Superman saving Lois Lane, I had injured myself badly. After realizing Sukhy was okay, I tried getting up but couldn't put any weight on my right leg. The tour guide recommended I get checked out, and so instead of Sukhy in a French hospital, now it was me waiting to be seen by the doctors in Portugal. Luckily, no bones were broken, but I had suffered a contusion, which meant that putting weight on my leg was going to be problematic until it healed. So much for walking around Europe. I had to take it easy, but we still managed to see and do everything we wanted.

Whether we're travelling through Portugal or hanging around our house in Calgary, there's so much that I appreciate about Sukhy. She is so kind and generous, and she still makes me laugh as hard as anyone ever has. She's also a renowned prankster. In fact, Sukhy is known among her colleagues at her elementary school as the best prankster the school has ever seen, whether it's taping other teachers' chairs together, filling colleagues' cupboards with balls that come pouring out, or covering an entire office in Post-it Notes. She somehow even incorporated some of her pranks into her writing lessons with her students. But her best prank to date was on one of her colleagues at the time, a Buffalo Sabres fan named Josh Miller. Josh had performed his fair share of pranks on Sukhy as well, one of which included turning every inch of her classroom literally upside down. Imagine walking into your classroom in the morning right before class starts and seeing every table, chair, bench, basket, stapler, you name it, flipped over. To top it off, her keys were hanging from the ceiling. Sukhy's good friend and colleague Carrie Root helped her frantically get everything back in order. As they were doing so, Sukhy knew that, to get Josh back, she needed to step up her game. She took out an ad saying a car was being given away for free and listed Josh's phone number. His phone lit up for an entire day, and he couldn't figure out what was going on. In fact, he still doesn't know who did it, but he'll find out after reading this. Sorry, Josh. That was my wife!

When you're in the sports-broadcasting industry, the travel can take a toll on your family. I've been fortunate that Sukhy has been so understanding, given how much I am out of town and how unpredictable my schedule can be—I can be gone for days or even weeks at a time. It's no easy task to be apart from one another so much during the hockey season, but we are blessed to have the summers off together.

Sukhy loves her job, and her passion for education shows. She is a phenomenal teacher to all of the students who have been lucky enough to be in her class. I can't count how many times she's gone above and beyond to help her students and their families, from buying new Canadians winter jackets, mittens, and toques, to donating furniture to families who had nothing in their home. There was even a time she encouraged me to try teaching as a substitute at a Punjabi class at Khalsa School Calgary (Khalsa schools are private schools that teach Sikh music and scriptures on top of the regular curriculum). I've taught Punjabi and Sikh music on a volunteer basis at the local Sikh temple, but never in a formal classroom setting. This was before we had kids, and when I got home after the first day, I told Sukhy I needed some time to decompress before I could even tell her what had happened. Handling twenty-plus children for the day had taken every-thing out of me. Apparently, I told her I couldn't talk at all because I was so exhausted and I needed peace and quiet. I'm not sure I've ever needed to say that before! I still have no idea how elementary-school teachers like Sukhy do it on a daily basis. Not only is she an awesome teacher, but she's also a great chef. What's funny is, the quality is on point but the quantity is usually way off. If four guests are coming, she accidentally makes enough for about sixteen people. I feel so blessed to have her in my life. I wouldn't know what to do without her, especially since she keeps everything neat, tidy, and organized. Those are skills I'm still very much learning.

The only real sticking point between us comes back to—you guessed it—hockey. And it only got more complicated when we started to talk about having kids. Would they be Oilers fans or Flames fans? At one point I tried pitching a neutral team, like Ottawa or Winnipeg, for them to root for, but Sukhy vetoed both options. Then I said, "Well, what about the Canucks? We visit Vancouver all the time, and we both have family and friends there." She looked me square in the eye and said, "I would rather have them be Oilers fans than Canucks fans." Which just goes to show you how intense the recent rivalry between Calgary and Vancouver has gotten—or how brutal the Oilers were for over a decade.

One of Sukhy's fears was having a child born during the hockey season. She knew how committed and busy I was with travelling for work (70 to 80 flights a year), but it also made sense for her as a teacher to try and have a baby in the summer. Thankfully, the due date for our eldest was at the end of July. I was covering the Stanley Cup playoffs, so I was away from home from mid-April to mid-June, coming home for only a day or two between rounds. It was a lot for us to be apart while Sukhy was pregnant with our first child, and Sukhy began having this recurring nightmare. When I came home between the conference finals and the Stanley Cup Final, she sat me down and told me it was really bothering her. Even though the baby's due date was in July, it was possible that she could deliver in June, during the final—and in her nightmare, that's exactly what kept happening. She would be in the hospital, in labour, and I'd be forced to decide whether to come home and be with her, or miss calling a Stanley Cup Final game. Each time, the dream would end before I gave her an answer, which was giving her some anxiety in real life. You also have to understand, up until that point, I'd never missed even a regular-season game, let alone one in the Stanley Cup Final! After hearing Sukhy's concerns, I immediately reassured her that if it came to that, I would be at the hospital with her every step of the way. But in all honesty, a Stanley Cup Final game was something I had never imagined that I would have to give up, and I just hoped that everything would work out in the end.

And it did. I came home after the playoffs, and things were moving along as scheduled. The due date even passed, and finally Sukhy went into labour in mid-August. Going through that entire experience shows you how much of a miracle life is. During the pregnancy, Sukhy kept saying that she couldn't wait to meet the baby. That line stuck with me, and so when it was time for the hardest part of her labour, I pulled out my secret weapon. I had made a sign that read, "I can't wait to meet the baby!" with a baby smiley face at the bottom. I pulled a secret roll of tape out of my backpack of supplies and pasted the sign on the wall right in front of her delivery-room bed. She absolutely loved it, and eventually, with the blessings of the almighty Creator, our daughter, Apaarjeet Kaur, was born in 2015. Two years later, our son, Mohun Singh, was born—thankfully, another summer baby, which again helped me avoid missing any games. On top of her other amazing qualities, Sukhy's love and generous spirit shine through when she's with our two beautiful children. She plays with the kids so enthusiastically that it makes any adult want to participate in whatever activity they're doing. Her creativity is second to none, and the kids can't get enough of her. In fact, I've heard other kids say they wish she was their mom. Sukhy has the ability to make any task, no matter how mundane, the most fun in the world and to somehow incorporate learning into it, whether she's reading to the kids, cooking with them, cleaning up, or playing. She is truly the best.

As for the debate about which team the kids would cheer for, in the end we decided we wouldn't buy them anything with a specific team logo on it. But they've ended up with a lot of hand-me-down Flames stuff anyway—mostly thanks to Manpreet, Sukhy's sister, who lives in Toronto. And then, of course, once I started working for the Flames, I realized it was silly to keep fighting it. The way we look at it now is that our kids will be Alberta hockey fans. What that means in reality, however, is that whenever we receive as a gift, say, a set of Flames dinner plates, it's only a matter of time until a matching set of Oilers plates shows up to help balance things out.

While it is difficult for us as a couple and as a family to be apart so much during the hockey season, I'm so grateful for the love Sukhy and I have for one another. Anytime I'm on a plane, she's the last person I send a message to before take-off, and it's always the same words: "*Love you, Sukhy. Ang Sung Waheguru*," meaning, "May the Creator always be with you, guiding your way on." I began doing this years and years ago, thinking that if something were to ever happen to me on the plane, those are the last words I want her to read from me.

Sometimes it seems like my relationship with Sukhy came together against all odds. But there were some people in our family who knew we were going to be together even before we did. At our engagement ceremony in 2010, a family friend from our parents' generation told us both a story. Back when we were still in elementary school, I was over at Sukhy's house for a prayer ceremony with Bhai Jiwan Singh Ji. The ceremony had just finished, and people were hanging out and eating the langar, the free community meal. This woman, Bhajano Kaur Chauhan, happened to be sitting near Bhai Jiwan Singh Ji and his wife, and she noticed that they were laughing about something. She asked, "What's so funny?" He pointed at me, then at Sukhy. We were sitting in opposite corners of the room, each minding our own business.

He said, "I'm laughing because it's written in their destinies that these two are going to get married, and they have no idea."

"Ever since," the woman said to us, "I would watch the two of you whenever we were all in the same room, and to be honest I wasn't sure it was going to happen. I didn't see any signs of anything. But now it's happened. Bhai Jiwan Singh Ji was right all along."

Chapter 9
Coast to Coast

T he story of Sikhs in Canada is one of struggle, but also
of perseverance and success. Our community has such
a rich history in this country, dating back more than a
hundred years. Pioneers like my great-grandfather didn't
have the right to vote. They struggled with racism, even from
their own federal government. And when things did improve,
it didn't all happen at once. I remember when I was a kid
in the 1990s, Baltej Singh Dhillon made national headlines
for trying to become the first Mountie to wear a full beard
and turban, both of which went against the RCMP dress
code at the time. None of it made sense to me. I remember
thinking: *How is this even an issue? If someone wants to serve their
country, isn't that a good thing?* Of course, for some people, it
had nothing to do with the policy and everything to do with
Dhillon's appearance.

When *Hockey Night in Punjabi* started airing across the
country every weekend, I used to sit and think about how
our show fit into that larger story about Sikh Canadians,
and the progress we have made. A lot of it had to do with
the fact that we aren't just covering any old sport. It's hockey—
our national pastime and easily the most popular sport in the

country. And it's being broadcast in a language like Punjabi? That's huge. Seeing the show in the TV listings each week gave me, and I think the community as a whole, a feeling that in some sense we were validated as Canadians. All of a sudden, Punjabi speakers were able to experience the same Saturday-night ritual that English and French speakers in this country had been experiencing for decades. If my great-grandfather could see how far we have come as a community, I don't think he would believe his eyes.

The funny thing is, hockey was already quite popular in the South Asian community before our show came along. Many large Canadian cities are diverse places, and if you go to an NHL game in Canada, you will see that reflected throughout the stands, and even up in the private boxes. It also helps when the teams are good, which is why so many new Canadians fell in love with hockey in 2004, when the Flames went on their magical run to the Stanley Cup Final, and again two years later, when the Oilers did the same thing. These playoff runs brought together so many different ethnic communities, including Punjabis, all cheering together. When Calgary was in the final, Punjabi families paraded their Flames flags through the streets. The same thing happened in Edmonton in 2006, and on the coast during the Canucks' near-miss in 2011. When I remember that the Gurdwaras in the Alberta capital held prayers for the Oilers, it still puts a big smile on my face. Of course, I myself had hockey in my prayers for years and years!

Another reason the NHL has been popular within the Punjabi community is ball hockey. While it doesn't get the same adoration that ice hockey does, Canada does very well at ball hockey—and whenever we send a team to the Ball Hockey World Championships, it's often comprised of many South Asian players. You will also find us in recreational ball-hockey leagues in every major Canadian city. Why? In large part, it's because my generation grew up in Canada loving hockey, but most of us never skated when we were young. Instead, we grew up playing hours and hours of hockey on the street or the driveway (and, in my case, on the living-room floor). We have plenty of skill, though.

Plus, for a long time, India was a powerhouse in the world of field hockey. The national men's team won five Olympic gold medals in a row, from 1928 to 1956. It even used to be the country's national sport. The majority of those players were Sikhs from the state of Punjab. Sukhy's uncle, Naib Singh Brar, for example, used to play on a field-hockey team in his youth, and he can still tell you the names of all of his old teammates. That's true of a lot of the older generation of Punjabis. When you show them an NHL game, they intuitively understand it, because they all grew up following, and maybe even playing, a very similar sport. While there are some obvious minor differences, the idea of putting a ball or puck into a net with a stick is something that anyone can understand.

———

Hockey Night in Punjabi was not intended to be a groundbreaking TV show, and I don't think anybody realized how much of an impact it would end up having. I have already told the story of the grandmother in Brampton who used our show to connect with her kids and grandkids, but the truth is, we have had so many people over the years tell us the same thing.

Usually it goes like this: the kids were born in Canada, so they are exposed to hockey immediately and, in turn, usually become fans of the sport. Their parents are interested because they're the ones who chose to live in that particular city, so it's only natural that they cheer for the local team. But for the grandparents, hockey is unfamiliar. Our show is really a way to connect with a totally different culture. I think that's why we receive so many positive messages from our viewers every week. Our show has become a Saturday-night tradition for these South Asian families, just as it has been for Caucasian families for so many years.

You can see the effect the show has had on the ice as well. One day when *Hockey Night in Punjabi* was still in its infancy, I was at the Don Hartman Sportsplex in northeast Calgary, where there is a large South Asian population. I was standing around in the foyer, waiting for someone, and I noticed this Punjabi couple looking over at me and whispering to each other. Eventually they came over and told me that neither of them was a hockey fan growing up, but now they never miss an episode of the show. We chatted a bit more, and I asked them what they were doing at the rink. They said they had become such NHL fans, they decided to put their kids in minor hockey. Amazing! This was first-hand proof that we were reaching people in a special way—here was this family investing not just their time but also their hard-earned money in the sport of hockey.

This ties in to a larger conversation you often hear about the state of the sport in this country: how hockey is getting too expensive, how Hockey Canada's enrollment numbers are stagnant, and how the percentage of Canadian players getting drafted into the NHL keeps dropping. When you think of all the Canadians who have never really been exposed to hockey properly, I think there is a real opportunity here. Demographics in this country are changing, and hockey hasn't traditionally been as accessible to non-white Canadians. Or maybe it just hasn't been introduced to them properly. Whatever the reason, realizing that our show wasn't just a source of entertainment—that it could help grow the sport—changed my whole perspective.

I can think of so many similar stories in the years since then. I once received a Facebook message from a fellow in Winnipeg who told us that when he first came to Canada for work, he was having a hard time finding things to talk about with his colleagues. There was no common ground. He was seriously considering going home to India because he was having such trouble connecting to people here. But somehow he found our show, and from then on he started joining in conversations about the Jets. It changed his whole standing in the workplace. The term "water cooler conversation" is a cliché, but it can be of real importance, especially when you're new to a place and don't know a lot of people.

And sometimes it's the little details that really make you smile. For instance, I know a Sikh family here in Calgary, the Chanas, whose kids play and love hockey so much that they sometimes show up to the Gurdwara wearing jerseys. Or take my friend Sukhpreet, who helped promote *Hockey Night in Punjabi* through social media way back in the day. He has kids of his own now, and he told me that when they play hockey around the house, they do their own play-by-play, just like I did—only when they do it, it's in Punjabi.

One of the things that I love about our show is that we aren't just copying the English show in a different language. Instead, we make a point of putting our own spin on things, giving the games a Punjabi flavour so that our broadcasts have a different taste than anything else you might see on TV. That's a big reason why our audience has responded the way it has—there's nobody else out there calling hockey the way we do.

The best example of this is the vocabulary we use on the show. When *Hockey Night in Punjabi* first started, in 2008, I sat down and made a list of every hockey term I could think of. These were all well known in English, of course, but I needed a Punjabi equivalent for each one. Take the goal post. Should I just call it the Punjabi word for *post*? Or is there a better word? In Punjabi, the word for a metal pipe is *sareeaa*, which is what we've occasionally used. Penalties were another difficult area. For instance, the Punjabi words for penalties like *high-sticking* or *hooking* don't really work in the context of sports, so we've used the English terms for those.

And that's just the actual hockey terminology. Broadcasting involves so much more than that. You end up using a lot of complicated and creative turns of phrase—like calling someone "a magician with the puck," if they're good at stickhandling. Some of those translate to Punjabi, but again, because hockey commentary had never really been done in that language before, I had to find a bunch of new metaphors that would make sense for our audience. Not just one time, either.

The same things can happen again and again over the course of a game, so you need multiple ways of describing these events. That's why I needed the lists.

Of course, you can plan as much as you like, but in the end, what worked best was my colleagues and I being creative as we went along, and then noticing which words and phrases worked and which ones didn't. I remember having a discussion with my colleague Parminder early on about how to translate *he shoots, he scores*. It's a classic hockey phrase, and we knew we'd need our own version. Together we came up with *mareya shot, keetha goal*—keeping *shot* and *goal* in English because that's what happens in field hockey in India, so our audience would already be used to it.

One of my favourite phrases we have come up with is our term for the penalty box: *saja dha daba*, which translates back into English as *box of punishment*. Everyone loves this one. It's so fun and dramatic, and also similar in some ways to the other English nickname for it, *the sin bin*. Sometimes, I'll emulate English broadcasters, too. There is a legendary broadcaster in Buffalo named Rick Jeanneret, who always says, "And he goes top shelf, where Mama keeps the cookies!" I started saying my version of that—but again with a Punjabi twist: "Top shelf, where Mom keeps the vesan!" That's a tribute to my mom, who's spent so many years supporting my passion and career—and whose vesan is world famous!

But the phrase that's caught on the most within the Punjabi community, especially with the kids, has to be *chapared shot*. This is our translation of *slapshot*, and it's unusual because *chapared* in Punjabi means a slap to the face. I said it for the first time without really thinking, but as soon as I did, it just took off. For a long time, when I went to live events, that was the most common phrase people would ask me to say.

Sometimes, however, there can be a bit of a language barrier, which can be funny as well as a bit embarrassing. There are several Swedish NHL players with *lund* in their names: Mikael Backlund, Henrik Lundqvist, and others. Well, in Punjabi, *lund* means penis, which puts me in a tough spot as a broadcaster, because it's not like I can avoid saying their last names, right? When this came up in the early years of the show, I sometimes felt like I was in high school again, being on the verge of giggles as I said, "Backlund takes a shot on Lundqvist, but Lundqvist makes the save!" And goalies are the hardest. You have to say their name so many times during a game. I'm just grateful that Lundqvist at least is called *King Henrik*, a G-rated nickname that I convert into Punjabi as *Raja Henrik* as often as I can.

We've even had details get lost in translation among our own staff. I remember a former *Hockey Night in Punjabi* producer, the late Wayne Craig, coming up to us at the first intermission of one game and saying, "Remember, it's 'Bob Cole.' You've got to say it right." I was confused, because I couldn't remember mentioning Bob's name during the broadcast. But I said I'd do my best, and he left. When the second intermission rolled around, Wayne popped his head in again, more frustrated than before. "Look," he said. "He's a legendary broadcaster. You can't be saying his name wrong! It's not *Bill* Cole—it's Bob."

Now I was getting a bit heated. "I know who he is, Wayne! We weren't even talking about him!"

Wayne was a lovely guy most of the time, but after that game was over, I came out of the booth and he was standing there once again, this time with his arms crossed.

"C'mon," I said. "Not again."

"I cannot believe you kept butchering his name like that," Wayne said. "I told you two times!"

Now that the game was over, I had a chance to think. "Bob Cole . . . Bill Cole . . . Bob Cole . . . Bill Cole" and suddenly it hits me: *bil-kul*! It's a Punjabi word that means *okay* or *that's right,* and it's common enough that we'd probably said it dozens of times throughout the broadcast. We had a good laugh over that. I was glad we figured out the miscommunication before we both went home and stewed on it even more. But I'll admit that when I picture Wayne sitting out there for hours, losing his mind because he thinks we don't know how to say *Bob Cole,* it still makes me smile.

I love that the creative phrases we use on *Hockey Night in Punjabi* have become popular with our viewers. To me, hockey commentary *should* be entertaining. It doesn't have to be business all the time. Depending on the moment, you can have a lot of fun with it. Besides, people in the Punjabi community tend to be loud and proud and colourful anyway. Why shouldn't the language of our show reflect that?

———

I do a fair amount of public speaking, often at schools, and whether I'm in a big city like Toronto or a smaller city like Lethbridge, there are always children from diverse backgrounds in the audience. Afterwards, they often come up to me and tell me that hearing my story gives them hope for their own future. That's why I say yes to these opportunities whenever possible. I'm very proud that I can show kids that you don't have to compromise who you are to succeed in life—that your career and your faith aren't competing with each other. In these events, I like to repeat a saying that helped me a ton throughout my childhood: "What is popular is not always right. What is right, is not always popular." The more kids who hear that message and are inspired by it, the better.

It can stick with them for a long time, too. There's a young man here in Calgary, Taranjot Vinning, who went to a Khalsa school that I've spoken at several times. Taranjot's teachers always told me, "He wants to be you when he grows up." So I always tried to act as a mentor to him, and to spare a few minutes to chat whenever I could. Well, now he's in high school, and he's got a large social-media following for his creative and well-designed posts about the Flames. It's amazing how well he's doing, considering how young he is. I think he has a really bright future in the broadcasting industry.

Or take last year, when I got a phone call from a guy in Surrey named Parm. He told me he was getting married, and he asked if I would consider performing Kirtan at his wedding. At first I was confused, until he told me that when he was in junior high, I came to speak at his temple. I was there because of *Hockey Night in Punjabi*, so I spoke about my journey, but I also performed Kirtan. Parm told me that day changed his life. At the time, he was struggling with the fact that his family wasn't as into the Sikh faith as he was. But hearing me speak gave him the encouragement to follow what he believed in.

What's great is, he told me he was now an RCMP officer— following in the proud tradition of Baltej Singh Dhillon!

Parm's wedding was the same weekend as my son's first birthday, and I told him it would be tough to get away. I also knew it wasn't going to be an easy sell to my wife, who I was away from too much as it was. But he wouldn't give up. One day Parm left me a long, emotional voicemail, explaining again how much he wanted me there and how much it would mean to him. I forwarded it to Sukhy, and then waited a few days before sheepishly bringing it up. She said, "I don't know how you can say no to him." I ended up flying in and out that same day, and made it back in time for Mohun's birthday party after all.

———

Of course, as more and more kids from minority backgrounds get signed up to play minor hockey, it's all but inevitable that more of them will make the show. In fact, we're seeing that start to happen already. The first player of South Asian descent to play in the NHL was Robin Bawa, who played 61 games in the late '80s and early '90s—including two with his hometown Vancouver Canucks. Given the amount of adversity Robin faced, it is great to see him finally being recognized for the pioneer that he is, recently being inducted into the B.C. Hockey and Sports Hall of Fame. Carrying on his legacy, it's cool to see Robin's son, Arjun Bawa, being selected by the Red Deer Rebels in the 2020 WHL Bantam Draft. After Robin Bawa's last NHL game, it took four years for another player of Punjabi descent. The second was Manny Malhotra, who grew up in Toronto and is half Punjabi. He had considerably more success: he was drafted seventh overall by the New York Rangers in 1998, and went on to play nearly 1,000 games for seven different NHL teams.

In 2010, Malhotra signed a three-year contract with the Canucks, and a big South Asian magazine in the Vancouver area called *Darpan* asked me to come out and write a cover story about him. It was a big deal that he had decided to come play in the Lower Mainland, where there's such a prominent South Asian population. At the time, Malhotra was well regarded as a faceoff specialist, and the Canucks were trending upwards, big time. They'd had some playoff success— but then they kept getting beat by the Chicago Blackhawks, year after year before finally breaking through, reaching the Stanley Cup Final in 2011. I knew that storyline well because I had called all of those games for *Hockey Night in Punjabi*. When I interviewed Manny, it turned out he knew all about our show. I remember asking him if he could speak any Punjabi. "Yeah," he said, "but the words I know, I can't use in this interview."

Another great moment came years later, when a Western Hockey League junior team in Washington State called the Everett Silvertips had an all-Punjabi line. It included Jujhar Khaira, who went on to play for the Edmonton Oilers in the NHL, as well as two other players named Manraj Hayer and Tyler Sandhu. Three Punjabi guys on the same team, at the same time! Seeing Khaira play his first game and eventually go on to score his first goal were truly significant moments for the community. Meanwhile, the president of the Surrey Minor Hockey Association, Harbs Bains, once told me that over 80 per cent of the kids in his program are now of South Asian descent—and the majority of them say they watch *Hockey Night in Punjabi* every Saturday night. Even if those kids don't all make the NHL, the talent level just keeps rising.

Unfortunately, the same issues that I dealt with as a kid, and that my Sikh ancestors did for generations before me, are still with us—and since the election of Donald Trump, those ugly incidents seem to be on the rise once again. In 2018, the coach of a minor-hockey team in Brampton reached out to me over social media. The players on that team are predominantly South Asian. But when the team travelled to more rural towns in Ontario, they dealt with an incredible amount of racism from players on the other teams, and even from spectators in the stands. The coach could tell it was really starting to affect the kids, some of whom wore turbans.

That was a really hard message to read. But I showed it to my colleagues, and we decided we should do something. As it happened, there was a *Hometown Hockey* broadcast coming up in Brampton, so a few of us went out there to meet the players, and to let them know they have our full support. It's frustrating that things like this are still happening. But it's important for us to use our platform to let people know that racism, in any form, has no place in the world today.

———

If it wasn't for *Hockey Night in Punjabi*, my weekly Punjabi-language videos for Flames TV wouldn't exist. I have to give full credit to my sister Prem, who came up with idea and encouraged me to pitch it to the team's vice president of communications, Peter Hanlon, who is one of the best, if not *the* best, in the business. Our show proved that there was a demand for hockey content in other languages. And the videos I've made for the Flames have given me special insight into how hockey and Punjabi culture connect on a local level. It was significant for the Flames to be the first NHL team to offer this type of content, catering to a specific community. But it also made me feel proud that it was the team in the city where I lived that first realized how important it was to grow the game and their fan base in this way.

I often try to keep things light. For example, when the NHL cracked down on the size of goalie equipment, I went into the Flames dressing room and did my best to squeeze myself into a pair of the new goalie pants. When the NHL first began venturing into the world of Esports, I used the big TV screens in the Jumbotron control room to play some *NHL 19*. Another memorable video involved asking players which teammate they thought looked the most Punjabi (Mark Giordano won in a landslide). Over the years, I have also brought in other sports, like lacrosse, with the help of the Calgary Roughnecks, also owned by the Calgary Sports and Entertainment Corporation. This was an effort to introduce not just myself but Calgary's entire Punjabi community to another sport they might not know much about.

One of our most popular videos was when I tried to teach Flames players various Punjabi hockey terms. Seeing stars like Sean Monahan and Johnny Gaudreau attempt to pronounce words in Punjabi was a hit with our viewers—it also just made me crack up. I was really impressed with Reto Berra, a goalie from Switzerland, who nailed virtually all of the terms, from the pronunciation to the intonation. (He later told me that he knew five languages, so it made a bit more sense.) Having renowned fighter Brian McGrattan try to say *bootha bhuntha,* meaning *smash his face in,* was also a blast.

Because of these videos, I have become quite familiar with the Saddledome and the many great people who work inside that iconic building. Being able to sit in Brian Burke's office when he was with the team, and hear first-hand how he orchestrated one of the most amazing feats in NHL draft history—drafting the Sedin twins back to back when he was with the Vancouver Canucks—was definitely cool. Having general manager Brad Treliving come up to ask how I'm doing or assistant coach Martin Gelinas tell me how proud he is of the work I do are just some of the things that make the Flames organization such a great place to work. Everyone genuinely respects and appreciates me, even after I accidentally texted one of my superiors, Jason Johnson, an overly detailed description of how badly I needed to use the bathroom—thankfully he took it in stride and has told only one other person about it. As far as I know.

The great thing about working in a hockey market like Calgary is how welcoming and supportive the rest of the Flames media have been. People like Rob Kerr and Pat Steinberg, from Sportsnet Radio 960 The Fan, have been incredible sources of encouragement, as has the current voice of Flames radio, Derek Wills. And if there's one current NHL play-by-play commentator whose work I try to emulate the most, it's Rick Ball, who calls Flames games on TV. I'll never forget a text I got from him during the 2018 playoffs, when he watched *Hockey Night Punjabi* and told me that despite not knowing a single word of Punjabi, he thought I sounded great, just based on my tone, energy, and inflection. Hearing that from one of the best in the business meant a lot.

The Flames videos have also had an effect on Sikh families in Calgary. I often get invitations to local hockey tournaments and other events where South Asian kids are participating. The fact that the videos are on the official Flames website, and promoted by their social-media team, is truly important—it shows that this is something that the Flames really stand behind. Sometimes I see the occasional boneheaded comment on Facebook or Twitter, but underneath that is usually another Flames fan writing back on our behalf, giving eloquent answers about how these videos help grow the sport. And of course the social-media team is vigilant about getting rid of the truly hateful comments, which I appreciate.

Thanks to the popularity of our videos, I have been able to bring the Flames brand out into the local Punjabi community. We even brought the team mascot, Harvey the Hound, to the *Vaisakhi* parade, a festival to celebrate the creation of the Khalsa in the Sikh faith, with more than 30,000 Calgarians in attendance. Sometimes the smallest gestures can go a long way. People were so excited the team was participating in an event specific to their faith.

———

Despite the enthusiastic reception, however, our show has gone through its fair share of ups and downs over the years. The first time *Hockey Night in Punjabi* was cancelled, it was in the lead-up to the 2010 NHL season. The entire CBC was dealing with a budget squeeze, and our show, still operating out of Toronto, took its funding directly out of the existing *Hockey Night* budget. When times got tough, we were the first to go. Although it might have made sense from a business perspective, it's hard to take the emotional aspect out of something that you've invested so much time and heart into. Being cancelled hurt, especially when you could see the positive effects the show was having on the community. It wasn't until December of that year, when the season was already well underway, that CIBC came on board as our first title sponsor, and we were able to come back on the air. The timing worked out, because we were able to cover the Vancouver Canucks on their run to the Stanley Cup Final—and picked up tons of new B.C. viewers along the way.

Of course, we all know what happened at the end of that series, and it was surreal to be a part of it. By the time we got to game seven, there was a lot of bad blood between the teams. On the one side you had the Big Bad Bruins, led by guys like Zdeno Chara and Milan Lucic, and on the other you had the Canucks, led by the Sedin twins, who always played the game totally clean. Brad Marchand had continuously picked on the Sedins, many times without penalties being called. People always say that the referees put their whistles away during the playoffs, and had they not done that, Vancouver would have had more of a chance. But that's not what happened, and the Canucks ended up losing game seven. I was on Toronto time, so the games went extra late, and by the time I got back to my hotel room and turned on the TV, there was breaking news on every station of . . . well, at first I wasn't sure what I was watching. It looked like the kind of thing you would see during a violent political protest. Eventually it sank in that I was seeing downtown Vancouver, full of rioters and flames and general mayhem. *This is happening?* I thought to myself. *In Canada?* I couldn't shake how strange it felt to know that the game I'd just called could lead to something as dark and chaotic as this.

As soon as the season finished, though, we were in trouble again. It turned out that CIBC wasn't able to renew their sponsorship, so for the second year in a row, the NHL season started, and *Hockey Night in Punjabi* was nowhere to be found.

That was the year Sukhy and I got married, and she had just moved into my house to live with my family. It was a hectic time for both of us—and now I was out of work. This time, however, the Sikh community voiced their support, letting people know that they were not happy that the show wasn't on. People started writing letters to the CBC, petitioning the local media, and calling their MPs. Peter Julian, an NDP MP at the time, even spoke publicly about his support for the show.

Once again, it was Joel Darling to the rescue. Our producer fought for us within the CBC, and when he called me later that fall, it was to say four magic words: "We've found another sponsor." It turned out that Chevrolet had come on board as a title sponsor. That was fantastic news, but even better was when they said they had a long-term vision for the show, which included covering our entire budget. This vision was due in large part to Paul Bailey, the person in charge of Chevrolet's national marketing strategy in those days. I was over the moon. Then Joel told me something else. He said the show still needed to get its costs down going forward—and one thing that stood out was the weekly air-fare. What did I think about bringing the show to Calgary?

I honestly never thought the show would move to another city. After all, everyone knows Toronto is the centre of the hockey universe, not to mention the home of Canadian media. The English *Hockey Night* show is based there. I figured we always would be there, too. But I have to give credit to my eldest sister, Harjot. In the early days, when I was running around scheduling secret flights to and from Toronto every week, she said, "You watch. One day the show will come here." I brushed it off at the time, thinking there was absolutely no way, but you know what? She was right.

If *Hockey Night in Punjabi* was really moving to Calgary, that meant we were going to need some new analysts to join me on the broadcasts. Joel asked if I could find some potential candidates, so I started asking around. It had to be done quickly, because the season was already underway; our first broadcast was scheduled for December 10. As I mentioned earlier, it's not easy to find people who are both proficient in Punjabi—not just reading and speaking the language, but also performing it live on the air—and who know a lot about hockey. But I tried to be as thorough in my search as I could.

In the end, I interviewed several people, from ball-hockey legends to taxi drivers. One candidate was Inderpreet Cumo, who at the time was a gym teacher and had been a hockey fan his whole life. And there was Bhola Chauhan, a Calgary-based writer and radio broadcaster who already had a lot of Punjabi media experience. After I'd met with them and sent Joel their resumés, he agreed that they were the most ideal candidates. Our team was in place, and we were ready to go back on the air.

After the years of going back and forth to Toronto, the seasons in Calgary were an unexpected but enjoyable change of pace. In an effort to promote the show and entice viewers to come out and see its vehicles, Chevrolet brought us to various dealerships in Surrey, Calgary, and Brampton, where people could meet the broadcasters, drink chai, eat samosas, and win prizes. Plus, now that the show was able to support itself financially, our working conditions improved. The studio we used at CBC Calgary was much bigger than the one we'd had in Toronto. For the first time, we had a legit *Hockey Night in Canada* backdrop, and we had more freedom in terms of technology, which meant we could do more pre- and post-game segments, and conduct our own in-studio panel that could show game footage as we talked.

The new on-air team worked together towards the goal of growing the show, making it more informative and entertaining. Inderpreet is a great analyst and a lot of fun to be around. Not only was he able to quickly and effortlessly pinpoint what happened and why, but he also incorporated a lot of humour into the show. In Punjabi culture, people love poetry and quick little rhymes—we call it a *boli*—and Inderpreet is so witty that he comes up with them instantly. Bhola has an amazing command of the language. Whenever there was a hat trick, or guys getting into a fight, he would break out into these poems, off the top of his head, to describe what was happening. Meanwhile, I was trying to keep that special Punjabi flavour in my play-by-play. We all incorporated our own personality into the games we were calling, and after years of uncertainty, the show finally felt like it was on stable footing.

And then the lockout happened.

As any hockey fan will tell you, 2004 was a boring year. A league-wide lockout cost the NHL its entire season. As a fan, I was bummed, but because I wasn't working in the industry yet, it didn't affect me on a personal level.

2012 was different for me. With the length of the previous lockout so fresh in everyone's memory, there was confusion and uncertainty throughout the league—and the media. Suddenly, I found myself without any games to call. And while both the NHL and the NHLPA said they were optimistic their differences could be settled quickly, nobody was sure exactly when that would happen. When the NHL announced in November that all games until the end of the calendar year were cancelled, Sukhy and I decided to book ourselves a trip to India.

We had always wanted to go there together, but because Sukhy is a teacher and my job is tied to the hockey schedule, the only time we were both free was in the summer—and that's not an option, unless you're used to scorching heat. India in the summer can get to 45 degrees outside; when my family and I went together back in 1994, my sister Gurdeep fainted because of the heat. We had also wanted to visit Bhai Jiwan Singh Ji, who hadn't been able to come to Canada for several years due to his old age and health. But all of a sudden, with me out of work and Sukhy with two weeks off at Christmas, we realized we finally had our chance (even though we had to vastly overpay for the plane tickets).

Sukhy had only been to India once, when she was six, and since she had very few memories of that trip, everything was new to her, and I thoroughly enjoyed showing her around like an informal tour guide. We had so much fun, but our highlight of the trip was definitely going to the Harimandir Sahib, popularly known as the Golden Temple in Amritsar, where I wound up onstage, playing the tabla, in front of Sikh pilgrims from all around the world.

This was not planned. While in India we met up with Bhai Harcharan Singh Ji Khalsa, one of the Sikh musicians I am close with, as I spent significant time with him in my youth. He lived in Amritsar at the time, and was the lead singer of a group that was performing at the Golden Temple at the same time we were there. At one point in our conversation, he said to me, "Look, you're here in India. This is a once-in-a-lifetime opportunity. Why don't you just join us?"

I ended up performing in the Golden Temple twice that day, once in the morning and again later that evening. It's hard to describe how much this meant to me. I was nervous to be performing on such a big stage—it's the equivalent of the Vatican having a house band—and there were thousands of tourists, pilgrims, and other people who'd travelled from all over the world to be there. But at the same time, the Gurdwara itself is so sacred that it calms you. As I performed, I reminded myself that this was the place where all of the sacred learnings I'd ever been taught originated. This was where our forefathers sat, and the place that housed so much historical significance for us Sikhs. And Sukhy was there in the audience, watching it all happen. You aren't allowed to take pictures inside the temple, but she was able to convince the staff to let her quickly snap a couple of photos anyway so that I could cherish the memory forever.

—

Back in Calgary, I was relieved to find the NHL and NHLPA had settled their issues, and the lockout officially ended in January 2013—enough time to save half of the season. But, yet again, things didn't settle down for the show. That summer, downtown Calgary—including the CBC building, where our studio was located—suffered a catastrophic flood. It happened right in the middle of the Stanley Cup Final between the Chicago Blackhawks and the Boston Bruins, and we were told there was nothing that could be done. Nobody was allowed into the building. It looked like we were not going to be able to call any more games in the final.

I called Joel and tried to argue our case. "Our viewers have been following along this entire playoffs, and there are only a couple of games left until the Stanley Cup will be handed out," I told him. "We can't just leave them hanging."

In the end, he agreed to let me and one other analyst fly to Toronto, where we would call the remaining games. Inderpreet is a full-time teacher, so unfortunately he wasn't able to come. But Bhola is self-employed, so it was the two of us who got on the plane. We called those final few games right from Studio 42, the famous CBC studio where Ron MacLean and the English *Hockey Night* panel work. I knew the building from my previous years there, and it was special to be back again.

Our show has always been lucky enough to get media

coverage, but 2013 brought our biggest opportunity yet when the *New York Times* wrote a profile on *Hockey Night in Punjabi*. Their writer, David Sax, came out to Calgary and followed us around for a few days—he even came to one of our ball-hockey games. The story ended up on the front page of the sports section and included a history of the show, along with a glossary of our Punjabi hockey terminology. In one of the photos, Bhola and I are calling a game in our studio, and we're reacting to someone scoring a goal less than a minute in. He's shocked and pointing at the monitor, and I've got one arm in the air with an expression of disbelief on my face. It was a funny, genuine reaction, captured for the world to see. The story got a great reception, and it really helped us gain positive attention in the United States.

Meanwhile, changes kept coming. The hockey community knew something big was going to happen by the end of the 2013–14 season, because that's when the CBC's rights to broadcast *Hockey Night in Canada* were set to expire. It was a critical moment for hockey media in this country. Would the CBC be able to hold on to the rights to one of its most iconic shows? If not, who was going to take over? I asked everyone I could think of, but nobody knew for sure. Most of us figured the rights were going to go somewhere else, or perhaps be distributed among several different bidders. The people at our show were particularly nervous. The English version of *Hockey Night* wasn't going anywhere, but the Punjabi version? We had no way of knowing whether the new rights-holder would be interested in keeping us around.

By this point, I had called close to 400 games for *Hockey Night in Punjabi.* If you include our brief debut for the Stanley Cup Finals in 2008, we had covered the league for seven seasons. A lot of blood, sweat, and tears went into all of those broadcasts. And with the recent cancellations, not to mention the lockouts, I had gotten used to that feeling of uncertainty. Still, every time the Stanley Cup was awarded, it was a bittersweet event for me. Calling the final is the absolute peak of covering the NHL, but once the confetti had been thrown and the broadcast was over, I always left wondering if that was the last game I would ever call. At the end of every season, I would walk back to my car, emotional and worried. But I told myself to be thankful that my improbable dream had come true.

After the 2013–14 season, the first sign I received about the show's future came, funnily enough, while I was sitting on the subway in Athens, Greece. It was the middle of the summer in 2014, and Sukhy and I were there on vacation. My phone shouldn't have had any reception. But somehow it started ringing, and I looked down and saw Joel Darling's name on my call display. I knew it meant news about the show, so we jumped off at the next station and I called him back. Joel told me the show was moving again—this time to Vancouver. The play-by-play job was still mine if I wanted it, but it would mean commuting every week. Again. It took a while to sink in. The show had gone from being based in Toronto for four seasons, to Calgary for three, and now it was moving out west for the foreseeable future. My initial reaction was excitement and relief that the show so near and dear to my heart was indeed going to continue. I also knew that it was a lot to ask of Sukhy, as our schedules would hardly ever align during a hockey season. Nevertheless, we had extensively discussed the possible scenarios throughout the summer, so it didn't take us long to give Joel an answer. Sukhy and I were just grateful it would be a shorter commute this time around, and I told Joel that I was in.

As for the broadcasting rights, it was announced that Rogers and the NHL had agreed on a 12-year, $5.232 billion deal starting in the 2014–15 season. It was the largest in NHL history and one of the biggest media-rights deals in Canadian history, and it sent shockwaves through the rest of the industry. And as the rights-holder changed, so did our station. Rogers owns Sportsnet, which is where the majority of their NHL broadcasts air, but they also own Omni, a series of multicultural TV stations across the country. That's where *Hockey Night in Punjabi* ended up. But it was no coincidence. Nathen Sekhon and Bhupinder Hundal were managers and executive producers with Omni and were very excited about broadcasting hockey in Punjabi. They had done so during the 2010 Vancouver Olympics, but one of their main goals at that time was to produce and air NHL games in Punjabi, so they put together a presentation to Scott Moore, Joel Darling, and the rest of the *Hockey Night in Canada* brass. For me, it was exciting because Omni already had a very successful national Punjabi news program, not to mention existing staff and infrastructure, and the managers of that show. Plus, I had actually met Nathen and Bhupinder in the summer of 2012, when they hired me for Omni's coverage of the London Olympics. I called track and field and wrestling competitions and anchored some of their highlights shows. It was a great experience, and once the Rogers deal went through, they told me that they'd had their eye on *Hockey Night in Punjabi* from the moment they heard the CBC's rights were expiring—the London 2012 gig was a way of seeing if I was someone they could work with. I was thrilled that the show was going to a place that would allow it to grow.

That first year in Vancouver was full of exciting change and new experiences. Nathen and Bhupinder were true professionals who had garnered a reputation in the broadcasting industry for being efficient but never sacrificing the final product. Not only does Nathen do a quality job producing our show and dealing with everything and anything behind the scenes, but he's also one of the biggest WWE wrestling fans out there, and so we love incorporating any references to Bret "The Hitman" Hart or the Ultimate Warrior on the show. Plus, Nathen's probably one of the biggest fans of my mom's vesan. Whenever Mom sends some down for the crew, she instructs me to give the very first piece to Nathen, and I never forget to follow that rule. Bhupinder is someone who is just so valuable in this industry—it's extremely difficult to find a person who excels on the production side and can also perform on the air. He's a natural at both sides, which was a major asset for our team. His on-air personality, especially in the host role, made for intermissions that couldn't be missed!

Also on the team the first season in Vancouver was Randip Janda, who originally worked with Omni News as an assignment editor. Randip started as an analyst for us and is a through-and-through sports junkie who can carry an in-depth conversation about almost any sport on the planet. He always comes prepared, so you're never worried when you're on the air with him. Randip's one of the best at giving anyone a ribbing. Boy, can he dish it out good. We've shared some hilarious moments on the air, some of which I simply cannot write here, but one had to do with San Jose Sharks forward Joe Thornton not wearing any clothes during an interview. Randip is a trendsetter too, carving out full-time roles on the English side, becoming a co-host of the afternoon radio show in Vancouver on Sportsnet 650. He is also on the Vancouver Canucks regional TV broadcasts, helping with the intermission walk-off interviews.

Both Bhupinder and Randip successfully helped launch the first-ever South Asian night and *Divali*-themed games for the Canucks. Divali is a day of historical significance celebrated by both Hindus and Sikhs worldwide. The theme nights have become an annual success, but the best part has been how the games have provided our show a way to honour some of the South Asian community's hockey heroes. For example, having Robin Bawa honoured by the Canucks and dropping the puck for the ceremonial faceoff, with Jujhar Khaira playing for the Edmonton Oilers, was a moment we'll never forget.

Harpreet Pandher has been my main colour commentator on the show since it ventured out to Vancouver, and there's no one I'd rather have by my side in the broadcast booth. Not only is he a hockey historian, he is honestly one of the funniest people you could ever meet, which helps make for an entertaining broadcast. His personality seamlessly matches the show's charm and he is invaluable to our call.

A few seasons in, once we began producing our own intermissions, the broadcast team grew to include Gurpreet Sian, a former radio show host who created his own university courses, successfully teaching bhangra at several post-secondary institutions in the Lower Mainland. Gurpreet works as a studio analyst, and not only is he one of the nicest, most genuine people I know, but he does a splendid job in all of our segments. Next to join the squad was Mantar Bhandal, a fellow whose dream, like mine, was to be a hockey play-by-play commentator. He achieved that by calling games for the Merritt Centennials of the British Columbia Hockey League after finishing his broadcasting studies at the British Columbia Institute of Technology. Mantar's hockey knowledge is such a huge asset to our show. He's not only a fantastic play-by-play commentator but also an excellent panellist, bringing a ton of energy and knowledge to every broadcast. Taqdeer Thindal is a long-time friend of mine and another analyst who joined the show a few seasons after it moved to Vancouver. This guy is the epitome of positivity, always smiling and showing his teeth. He can quickly pick up what happened on a certain play and explain to you why a goal just occurred. But Taq, as he's known by most of us at *Hockey Night Punjabi*, is just one of the most generous individuals you can meet.

After moving the show to Vancouver, my colleagues and I worked to fine-tune *Hockey Night in Punjabi* into the show you see now. We all have different routines and varying obligations outside of the show, but for me, between my weekends working on *Hockey Night in Punjabi*, the work I do for the Calgary Flames mid-week, and all of my other family and community commitments, my schedule can get wild. But here's what a typical week looks like.

To begin with, everything I do is oriented around Saturday

nights, when I'll be working the double-header, so I spend all week building up to those two games. That starts the previous Sunday or Monday, when I first look ahead to the four teams who will be appearing on *Hockey Night in Canada* that week. Because of my schedule, I have an actual agenda book that I use to organize my entire life—if it's not written in the agenda, it's not getting done. There, alongside my schedule for other work and family stuff, I make a detailed list of the schedule for each team I'll be covering on Saturday night: who they're playing against that week, where, and what time. Right away, that shows me certain things about each team. Who's coming off a road trip? Who's starting one? For American teams coming through Canada, chances are they are either doing the Toronto–Ottawa–Montreal road trip, or the Western Canadian road trip. That information can help me on the air. I also keep a running list of every Canadian team's matchups, because a *Hockey Night in Canada* broadcast will always include at least one Canadian team. (It is in the name, after all.) Knowing where each team is coming from helps me visualize some of the story I'll tell to our viewers later on.

Then, as the week goes on, I check that handwritten schedule and follow each of those games in depth, so I know everything that happened. Watching highlights is key. That's where I find out about certain milestones, trends in special teams, and other stats about the teams and their individual players. Then there's the reading. I read a lot of hockey articles, from a lot of different sources, for all kinds of background information. That way, when it comes to Saturday night, if I notice something happening with a certain player, I can put it in context: "You know, on Tuesday, this guy took two penalties, and here we go again . . ." Sometimes you need to look at the bigger picture and track a certain piece of information over the course of the season. If a certain player is on pace for a hat trick in the game you're calling, and you know all the times they've come close over the course of the year, you can reference that on air and it helps build the anticipation.

Another key part of my work week is conference calls. This is where my colleagues and I discuss storylines going into the weekend. On the Punjabi side, it depends on what role I have that week—sometimes I'm doing play-by-play, and sometimes I'm hosting the studio panel. There used to be a time, in the early years, where the guys who called the games were also the ones doing the panel, but the show has grown since then, and now those are two separate teams of people. I'm a note-taker, and back in the day, I would jot down everything we discussed on the calls. Nowadays, we have a member of our production team, Raja Shergill, who keeps track of what visuals we will need and, with the help of Google Docs, each commentator can write in their own points and access the file whenever they need to. For instance, if we want to talk on the air about Brad Marchand licking another player's face, then Raja knows he has to have a video clip of that ready to go.

These calls usually take place twice per week. The main thing we have to decide is which storylines we are going to focus on. Is there a player coming back to play against his former team for the first time? Is there a major rivalry? Some kind of crisis on one team's power play? We talk about all of this as a group, and once we have narrowed down our topics, we then have to decide which visuals we are going to show to pair with them.

You can prepare for certain segments in advance of the games. For example, puck drop usually isn't until 10 or 15 minutes into the hour, so we know we have that much time to fill on our own before the game starts. We might do an overview of each team and focus on a couple of important players or storylines for viewers to pay attention to. It's a formula created by Nathen and Bhupinder.

On top of the conference calls, my colleagues and I also have a group chat on our phones. If something major happens during a weeknight game that we think everyone should know about, we will talk about it there, too. I should also say that even though the English and Punjabi shows are both called *Hockey Night in Canada*, they operate independently of one another. On the Punjabi show, of course, we use a lot of English media as material for ideas—like the well-respected Elliotte Friedman's *31 Thoughts*, a weekly blog on Sportsnet that has a ton of insight into what's going on behind the scenes around the NHL. One of our segments on *Hockey Night Punjabi* is called Snichervaar Charcha (Saturday Round-table), in which we discuss the hot topics of the hockey world, but we have our own opinions about them. And when we need visuals, usually it's our own producers who go out and dig them up—they aren't handed to us by the English broadcast or anything like that. Our team edits the clips themselves, too, depending on what we want to show, or how we want to talk about something. That changes every week.

We have a number of other intermission segments on the show, one being called Muqabla, or Battle, where we put one play up against another. Each panellist argues why their play should be considered the best of the month, and viewers vote on it. So, throughout the week, we'll be messaging back and forth about particularly great goals or saves that could make it onto that segment.

Another segment created by Bhupinder, which became his signature, is Meri Gal Sunn, or Listen Up! Here, a panellist looks straight into the camera and addresses an issue with a player, a team, an agent, management, or even the NHL itself. It's a great way to get a point across and drive home your opinion on something. The only trouble is, people remember what you've said. Bhupinder, for instance, was known to absolutely lambaste the Oilers organization for the way they mismanaged their assets, causing the team to continually miss the playoffs; because of that, after one game I had a group of Oilers fans surround my rental car in a busy parking lot outside Rogers Place in Edmonton. Sure, they said they loved our show, but boy, were they not happy with what Bhupinder had said about their team. I got out of there quick, saying, "Hey, it wasn't me!"

But the most popular intermission segment we have on *Hockey Night Punjabi* is called Tu Rehende, meaning Get Outta Here! It's a debate between two panellists about some of the week's hot-button hockey topics—and let me tell you, it can get heated. It's meant to simulate an impassioned argument between two knowledgeable hockey fans, but done using Punjabi flair and style. Nathen—who, remember, is also a die-hard wrestling fan—even helps get things off to a great start by sounding a bell similar to the start of a match in the WWE. For example, we recently debated whether it would be better to have Toronto Maple Leafs forward Auston

Matthews or Edmonton Oilers forward Leon Draisaitl on your team. It was an interesting debate at the time. You could argue that Matthews has the better shot and is a pure goal scorer, but Draisaitl could be considered a better 200-foot player who can not only put the puck in the net but can dish it, too. The debates can get loud and boisterous; we hosts have to moderate the analysts, preventing them from talking over one another to making sure they get equal amounts of time to make their points. As a host, you often get the last word in, and I remember ending off that specific debate about Matthews and Draisaitl by saying, "Well, at least Leon keeps his pants on in public!" My colleague Randip Janda considers himself the undisputed champion of the segment, and I'd have to agree.

For the weekly Flames TV Punjabi video, I follow the Flames schedule throughout the week, too, and I try to attend at least one or two practices if the team is in town. Some of my videos are about individual players, if they are having a career year, like captain Mark Giordano did in 2018–19. Others are about community events, so every week, I write a script and then work with the Flames production team to figure out what day I should come to the Saddledome to shoot it. Once the shoot is done, I sit down with an editor and we put everything together. The videos are then promoted through the team's social-media accounts, and they go up on the team website as well.

So many people who know about my work on *Hockey Night in Punjabi* have said to me over the years: "You only work one day per week!" But there's so much work being done behind the scenes on the other days that viewers don't see. If you're going to try to pull off six hours of live television—two full hockey games, plus all of the surrounding segments—then you need to spend a lot of time making sure you're ready for anything. Every Saturday, by the time I get to the studio or the arena, I've done at least three hours of prep that same morning for the games I'm going to call that night. That starts with the rosters. I have my own system, and I tweak it every year, in terms of writing out the players and their numbers, and making sure the most important information is big enough that I can see it at a glance. Personally, I like to keep the forward lines and the defence pairings together. Other commentators list all of the players in order according to their jersey number, but I prefer visualizing clusters of players. That way I know (at least for the first period) that if Player X is on the ice, then Player Y and Player Z are probably going to be out there with him. I keep a record of all the previous times I've called each team's games, and it's neat to see how the rosters have changed for some of the teams we don't cover as often, like the Arizona Coyotes or the Florida Panthers. The amount of turnover that can happen in just a couple of seasons is crazy.

After finalizing the roster notes, I read every game preview I can find. I make sure I'm up to date on all the stories that have developed during the week. And I take pages of notes about which players are on point streaks, which players are struggling, which players are doing terribly on faceoffs—all kinds of fun facts I might need during the show. If I'm doing the studio panel, I like to handwrite my notes. As I said, I'm a note-taker, and I find I still retain more if I write things out by hand. Saturday is a long, busy day before the puck has even been dropped.

Another unusual thing about this kind of work is the pace. Since the games start in the evening, calling the double-header means you are on the air until late into the night. I need to be at my peak energy levels after dark. It's the opposite of a nine-to-five job. Unlike the players, I don't nap during the day, because Friday is my sleep-without-kids night (yes, my wife is jealous of this). I can sleep in until 10 a.m. on Saturday and then *go go go* until the end of the night. Still, there's a lot of caffeine being consumed. Personally, I prefer tea, and I carry probably 40 different tea bags on me at any given time, depending on what I'm in the mood for. (I carry around so much stuff, from tea to vitamins to allergy medication to Fisherman's Friend lozenges, that some of my Punjabi colleagues jokingly call my laptop bag "the dispensary.") Coffee, for me, is reserved only for those days when I absolutely need it. Then it's time to put on my suit, tie my turban, hit the makeup chair, and before you know it, it's game time.

Play-by-play commentary is a unique job. You have thousands and thousands of viewers who use the game as a way of escaping their reality for a couple of hours. They depend on you to perform for them. And the game of hockey is so special, you want to capture the experience happening in front of you and deliver it to your audience as best as you can. That means being on your toes and staying in the moment the entire time. For me to do my job properly, I have to push everything else going on in my life into the background. Play-by-play isn't something you can do if you're distracted or stressed. People can tell—especially moms. Mine has watched so many of my games over the years that we jokingly say she needs her own Twitter account: @PunjabiHockeyMom. Not only does she have great opinions about what is going on with the Flames and Oilers, but she can also tell if something is not right with me, just by the sound of my voice. But I've learned from that experience as well. When she points out something like that, I think to myself: *If she knew I was thinking about something else, then maybe other people did, too.* That just motivates me to be better for the next game.

Once the final buzzer has gone, and the games are over, I don't feel like talking to anybody. My voice is usually gone, and I'm mentally drained. It takes so long to wind down afterwards, too. Falling asleep on a Saturday after calling two games back to back is such a challenge. I try using sleep herbs and various calming teas, but they only help to an extent. It doesn't help that even when I am asleep, I'm still hearing hockey commentary in my head as I toss and turn. Then, at around 5:00 a.m., I have to be back up again to catch the first flight home to Calgary. This last part of my week turns me into a zombie every time, because I don't get into a deep enough sleep Saturday night after the games. Still, I manage to shower, quickly pack my bag, and head out to the airport. Once I arrive in Calgary, the first thing I do is go straight to the Sikh temple, Guru Ram Das Darbar, because that's where my family is. We are heavily involved in our service—most members of my family get there before it starts and stay behind after it ends. At this point, our entire congregation of a few hundred people knows that halfway through the service, I'm going to show up, half-asleep and dragging my suitcase behind me. Still, I love being there, participating in the music and sharing the community meal and catching up with everyone. Plus, people know where I've been, so the first comment they always make to me is, "Can you believe what happened in the game last night?"

———

There's nothing more gratifying than hearing stories about the influence *Hockey Night in Punjabi* has had on people and on the community—but there's one story that hit extra close to home. As I have already mentioned, we get a ton of feedback from our viewers, and when the show was based in Toronto and Calgary, we used to get messages all the time from a girl named Amrit, who wrote to tell us whenever she and her grandma were tuned in. She seemed sweet, and I was glad the show was a source of entertainment for her.

Back in 2015, Nathen and Bhupinder brought in a young woman named Amrit Gill, who was studying broadcasting at BCIT. She was going to intern by helping us manage and provide content for the show's social-media accounts. I didn't put it together at first, but at some point, she asked me, "Do you remember the Amrit who used to watch the show with her grandma?"

"Yes . . ."

"Well," she said, "that was me!" It turned out that over the lifespan of the show, Amrit had grown up, gone to broadcasting school in B.C., and ended up working at the same show she grew up watching.

That story made me feel so proud—and, I won't lie, a little bit old.

It doesn't end there, though: she did a great job, proving how much we needed her and forcing Nathen and Bhupinder to create a new position on the show. Amrit became the first-ever female to work on-air for *Hockey Night Punjabi*. She also does a ton of work behind the scenes, for which she never gets enough credit. She was doing so much that Nathen decided to bring in another talented up-and-comer, Shubham Arora, to take on some of the responsibilities Amrit had. Not only is Amrit handling social media, but she's become a fantastic on-air personality, providing hockey stories from the community to our viewers. The stories she researches and produces have become one of the most important elements of our show. It's all a credit to her passion for being a broadcaster and for wanting to provide narratives exhibiting South Asians' journey with the sport of hockey. Whether she's telling the story of the only South Asian child on a hockey team, or highlighting players who faced racism growing up, or depicting youth who still deal with discrimination today, or visiting a South Asian family who are devout viewers of our show, she covers it all and does one hell of a job.

Chapter 10
"THEY'RE HERE"

I t's no surprise that hockey media outlets in Canada benefit from having Canadian teams qualify for the NHL playoffs and then making a long run once they get there. Usually, this hasn't been a problem. In fact, ever since we launched *Hockey Night in Punjabi*, there had always been at least one team from Canada in the playoffs, and often more than that.

But in 2016, the unthinkable happened: none of the seven Canadian teams in the league made it. In the entire history of the NHL, that had only happened one other time—in 1970, nearly 50 years earlier. So as soon as that season's standings were finalized, all of us broadcasters got a bit antsy about what this would mean for our ratings—and, in turn, our jobs. We had no idea what to expect. But for our show, at least, it ended up being a total blessing in disguise.

Because *Hockey Night in Punjabi* can only cover one game at a time, we have to make some tough decisions, especially in the early rounds, when there are so many teams battling, about which series we are going to cover and which teams we are going to focus on. Top priority, of course, goes to the Canadian teams, but if there aren't any of them left, we try to pick a superstar to follow—and usually that's Sidney Crosby and the Pittsburgh Penguins. The reasons why should be obvious, but in short: Crosby has been the best player in the league for years, he's Canadian, and people all across the country know who he is and love watching him play. It's really a no-brainer.

By the time we got to the second round that year, where Crosby's Penguins went up against Alex Ovechkin and the Washington Capitals for another of their epic postseason battles, things were getting intense. Of course, Sid and Ovi have been in competition with each other ever since they both entered the league in 2005. They are incredible, generational talents, but they play the game completely differently: Crosby is an elite playmaker with a tireless work ethic, Ovechkin an unbelievable pure goal scorer who will also physically punish you. The two stars have already amassed point totals that will go down as some of the best of all time. For years, however, Crosby seemed to have the advantage, because his team won a Stanley Cup early on, whereas Ovechkin was on a Capitals team that wasn't able to put it all together. Whenever their teams met in the playoffs, both players had a lot to prove.

Before game one, I was sitting around with my colleagues, going over my notes. As I've mentioned, I like to write out the last names of the players on each forward line, followed by the defence pairs, to help me visualize who's playing with who. But in my prep that day, I had made a blatant error. The Penguins' third-line centre at that time was Nick Bonino, and for whatever reason, I had accidentally written his name for all three forward spots on his line: Bonino-Bonino-Bonino. It was such an obvious mistake, but I didn't even notice what I'd done until Nathen pointed it out to me. We all had a good laugh, but it was getting close to game time, so I didn't have a chance to go back into my game file and fix the mistake. Instead, I kept the same sheets with me and figured I would just work around it once we were on the air.

The game itself was thrilling, with the teams trading goals back and forth heading into the third period. Things were tied 2–2 when T.J. Oshie scored his second of the game to put the Capitals ahead. But then, just a few minutes later, deep in the offensive zone, Carl Hagelin of the Penguins threw the puck out front to Bonino, and he shot a knuckler that beat Braden Holtby. With the adrenaline pumping, and my pre-game mistake still in my head, out it came, over and over again: "Bonino-Bonino-Bonino-Bonino-Bonino-Bonino-Bonino-*Boninoooooo*!" I must have said it 10 or 11 times without stopping to breathe.

Sometimes, when you do something like that, there's a small moment of panic in the back of your mind: *Oh shit, what am I doing?* In broadcasting, you have to act on instinct, but there's an element of risk that comes along with it. All you can do is try to capture the moment as best as you can. In this case, it helped that Nick Bonino's last name is fun to say, especially when you repeat it a bunch of times in a row. Amrit posted a clip of the goal and my goal call on the show's Twitter page, and, thankfully, Penguins fans absolutely loved it. That was good enough for me.

Based on that call, we could tell that people in Pittsburgh were starting to pay attention to our show up in Canada. The series had just begun, though, and I knew that if Bonino scored another game- or potentially series-changing goal, then Penguins fans would be expecting something from us.

It turned out that game six of this series was also a nail-biter. The Penguins roared ahead to a 3–0 lead but took multiple accidental delay-of-game penalties in the third period, and the Capitals were able to come back and tie it. The game went to overtime, and none other than Nick Bonino scored the series-winning goal. When he slid the puck past Holtby, and on home ice, to boot, it was a big moment—and it needed a big goal call to go with it. I came up with a variation of my previous goal call, but instead of just saying his name repeatedly, I said "Bonino dha goal! Bonino dha goal!" over and over again. Which translates to: "It's Bonino's goal! It's Bonino's goal!"

That attention from Penguins fans only continued in round three, when Crosby and Co. took on the Tampa Bay Lightning. That entire series was incredibly fun to call, because the Lightning were a high-octane offensive team, led by Nikita Kucherov. As it happens, Kucherov's last name fits in really well with the Punjabi language. At one point in that series, he scored a goal, and in the heat of the moment I rejigged the lyrics to a well-known Punjabi song by a man named Malkit Singh. He's a famous, old-school Punjabi singer, and it's a song that people always dance to at parties. So, to celebrate the goal, I sang a line from the song but swapped in Kucherov's name to imitate the tune.

Again, I was worried afterwards that I might have gone too far. But when my colleagues started to come in to suggest other songs we could adapt in the future, I realized it was another hit. That goal call got a lot of attention, this time specifically from the Punjabi community. It added an extra entertainment factor to games that were already pretty darn entertaining. Everyone I spoke to or met that week was talking about the Kucherov goal call, and, my phone was buzzing non-stop.

But back to the Penguins. Game two of that series ended up going to overtime, and this time it was Crosby who scored less than a minute in. For his entire career, people had called Crosby "Sid the Kid," but by this point, he was nearly 30 years old. Clearly not a kid anymore. Besides, a lot of time had passed since he first won the Cup, in 2009, and he really did look like a more mature player on the ice. So when he scored that overtime goal, I yelled, "Sid, the *former* kid, *Crosbyyyyyy*!"—stretching out his last name as long as I could. It turned out to be Crosby's first-ever overtime goal in the Stanley Cup playoffs.

Now this call *really* took off. It got a ton of love on social media that night, and before we knew it, a bunch of sports websites, including *The Hockey News* and even NHL.com, had written about it. That was already wild, but not long afterwards, a T-shirt company called Sin Bin Apparel contacted me and asked if it was okay if they made a shirt with my call on it. I was extremely flattered and told them of course, go for it. There may have been no Canadian teams in the playoffs that year, but there we were, this specialty show from Canada, making headlines across the hockey world. It was amazing to see—but that was nothing compared to what was about to happen.

In the NHL, nothing matters as much as the Stanley Cup Final. After battling through the physical and emotional turmoil that presents itself through 82 regular-season games and four gruelling rounds of the playoffs, the Stanley Cup might very well be the hardest trophy to win in all of pro sports. You need a combination of skill, grit, determination, good health, and a bit of luck to win it all. Everything that teams fight for all season long comes down to that one last series. For our show, the 2016 final—which featured the Pittsburgh Penguins versus the San Jose Sharks—felt different than it had in previous years. It had a lot to do with the large following we had built up with Penguins fans over the course of the postseason. They were now following our goal calls on a nightly basis, and they were also constantly reaching out on social media with requests—including a unanimous demand that if Bonino scored yet another big goal, that I do his special goal call again. That's another funny thing about broadcasting. Usually you don't plan exactly what you're going to say, because it feels less spontaneous, and sometimes, I think, viewers can tell. But this time it felt like there was a real expectation building.

The momentum we had going with viewers was unimaginable, but no one could have predicted or scripted what was to come. We went into game one in Pittsburgh, and it was tied in the third period, with just two and a half minutes to go. Then the puck came loose behind the Sharks net, and Kris Letang passed it out front to—well, who else? Nick Bonino, who put it top shelf for what turned out to be the game-winning goal. You know the saying *served up on a silver platter*? That's what it felt like, watching that puck go in. It was as if I had no choice. I took a deep breath and went for it again: "*Bonino-Bonino-Bonino-Bonino-Bonino-Bonino-Bonino-Bonino-Bonino! Nick Boninooooooooooooo!*"

It turned out to be the goal call that the entire hockey world would remember. But most people have no idea it was actually the second time I'd done it.

This Bonino call went viral instantly, to a degree I hadn't even believed was possible. I went back to my hotel room that night, watching a mind-boggling number of retweets and shares pile up on social media. When I woke up the next morning, I was bombarded with media requests. Basically every media outlet in Pittsburgh wanted to talk to me. But there were also requests from TV, radio stations, and newspapers all over the U.S. and Canada. I also got a message from Celina Pompeani, host of Penguins TV, the team's official arena and online programming. We ended up doing an interview about the goal call, which aired across all of the team's social-media channels, as well as on their Jumbotron during one of their Cup final home games. Later in the series, Scott Oake did an interview with Bonino for *Hockey Night in Canada*, and he brought me in to be part of it. But one of the wildest moments for me came during a press conference with Penguins head coach Mike Sullivan. I was listening to every media availability I could find for research, and you would not believe how stunned I was when the very first question reporters asked him was: "So what'd you think of the Bonino call?" It's the Stanley Cup Final and the head coach is being asked about something I had done? It was a good thing I was alone, because I was completely shocked. As if he didn't have more important things to think about!

That second Bonino call got all of the attention, but I have to say, we came up with some other great calls in that series, too. For instance, in one game when Brent Burns scored for San Jose, I came out with a classic *Simpsons* reference: "Mr. Burns! *Excellent.*" And a lot of my colleagues on the show are big wrestling fans, so when the Penguins' number-one defenceman scored a big goal, Bhupinder yelled, "Bang, bang, Kris Letang!"—a reference to the popular WWE wrestler Mick Foley.

Throughout the series, Celina from Penguins TV and I stayed in touch. As it got closer to an elimination game, and it looked like Pittsburgh had a real shot to win the Cup again, she asked me: "If the Penguins do win, would you be able to come down for the parade?" She told me the organization really wanted us to be there. I was surprised, but she was insistent. She said, "You have no idea how big you are down here."

Then, on June 12, 2016, the Penguins took game six by a score of 3–1 and won the Stanley Cup. Sidney Crosby won what ended up being the first of two back-to-back Conn Smythe trophies as playoff MVP. I chatted with Joel Darling and our producer, Nathen, and my colleagues and I made our decision. We realized we were never going to get an opportunity like this in our lives again. So we quickly figured out the logistics, and then we all got on planes to Pittsburgh.

We still didn't know what, exactly, we had signed up for, but we were starting to get a hint. On our way to the parade, we had to catch a connecting flight in Chicago—and already we were being recognized. People on our plane to Pittsburgh came up to us and said, "Hey, are you the Bonino guys? Are you *Hockey Night in Punjabi*?" Then, as soon as we landed and were walking through the Pittsburgh airport, we were tagged in a tweet that had a photo taken from someone behind us, along with the caption, "THEY'RE HERE." More people recognized us on the street outside, and more again at our hotel. My colleagues and I were walking around downtown Pittsburgh and cars were screeching to a stop so the drivers could get a picture with us. You could tell the entire city was buzzing about the Penguins' Cup win.

The next morning, we showed up at the Consol Energy Center (now PPG Paints Arena) and met up with members of the Penguins communications team, including VP Tom McMillan and director of event presentation Bill Wareham, by the big Mario Lemieux statue out front. They told us how excited they were that we could join them, and that they had a lot of fun stuff planned for us, starting with a tour of the building. It really is a beautiful rink. They have put together some great tributes to the team's Lemieux-and-Jagr era, and here we were, celebrating its next great era. As we were walking around, one of the communications people paused and repeated what Celina had said to me earlier: "You have no idea how big this is, do you?" We looked at each other and kind of shook our heads. "Every single radio and TV station here has been playing your goal call multiple times a day since it happened," he said. "There isn't a person in Pittsburgh who doesn't know about it."

Next, they took us down to a hallway just outside of the dressing room. All of the Penguins were inside, and we were told to wait there for a couple of minutes. While we were waiting, I looked over to my left and saw, way down at the other end of the hallway, this really tall man, surrounded by his own security detail, headed our way.

We all looked at each other. "Is that Mario Lemieux?"

The man walked a bit closer. "Holy shit, that *is* Mario Lemieux."

You know when royalty approaches, and you're supposed to stand at attention, out of respect? That's what we all did for Super Mario. Physically, he has that kind of commanding presence. As he came nearer, all four of us nodded at him and then moved back against the wall to let him pass by.

Instead, he stopped right in front of us and, with his classic smile, said, "Which one of you did the Bonino call?"

I slowly put up my hand. Then he pulled me away from the wall to give me a handshake, which quickly turned into a hug. "That was brilliant," he said. "You're a part of Pittsburgh Penguins history now." I think I'll remember that sentence for the rest of my life.

Of course, it's extra funny to me, because, as a kid, I was such a diehard supporter of Gretzky, and that meant that the Penguins were the rival team that I despised because they were so good. I thought back to my old binder of hockey cards at home in Brooks, where I would put Lemieux and the rest of the Penguins all the way at the back. And here Lemieux was, all these years later, giving me a hug. How things can change, huh?

Before we went inside, a couple of players came wandering in and out of the dressing room. One of them was Kris Letang, and when he saw us, he came right over to say hello— he knew who we were. He laughed and said Bhupinder's goal call right back to him: "Bang, bang, Kris Letang!" Then he asked for a picture with *us*, which seemed totally backwards, considering that he was the guy who had just won the Stanley Cup.

We also met Celina Pompeani in person for the first time, and I thanked her for all she had done for us: if not for her, I really don't think we would've gotten the invitation to join their celebration. Then Bill and Tom, from the Penguins staff, told us it was time. "Now, most of the players don't know you're here," they said. "Right now they're getting dressed to go take their team picture on the ice with the Stanley Cup. But our idea is you just walk into the dressing room right now and do your thing."

The feeling of nervous excitement kicked in. "We're going to surprise them?"

"Yep," he said.

"Okay," I said. "And by 'do your thing,' you mean, like . . . do the goal call again?"

"Yes! Exactly!"

So they opened the doors and we marched inside. I felt a bit awkward, because I was wearing a shoulder bag with a bunch of my stuff in it, and holding a Starbucks chai latte, and I didn't have time to put any of it down. I was just carrying it all with me. Plus, it seemed so quiet in the room. But then, as we turned the corner, I started to do the call: "*Boninoboninoboninobonino!*" And the players immediately started clapping and cheering. I could feel all of my excitement and adrenaline and energy overflowing when I heard the noise swell in the room. You can be assured that nothing could wipe the smile off my face. What an extraordinary moment that was—one I will never forget. Celebrating with the players in the dressing room before the team had even shared their championship with their own fans really solidified how much the team embraced our broadcast.

We were able to meet all of the team in turn. Nick Bonino himself was the very first person to come up to us, and we all took pictures together. Goaltender Marc-Andre Fleury, who is always such a jovial person, came up right away to shake our hands, too. Other members of the team came over to tell us how much they loved our goal calls. The stall that's front and centre in the Penguins dressing room belongs to Crosby (of course), because he's their captain and hands down their best player. Sitting in front of his stall, on one side, was the Prince of Wales Trophy, which you get for winning your conference in the playoffs. On the other side was the Conn Smythe trophy, for being the MVP of the playoffs. And right there in the middle was the Stanley Cup itself. The whole scene was majestic—like waking up in hockey heaven. I still get goosebumps thinking about it.

Then Mike Sullivan, the coach, came up to me and shook my hand aggressively. "I gotta tell you," he said in his booming voice, "you guys were a part of our Cup run."

"Really?" I said.

"Oh yeah," he said. It turned out that Sullivan used to play our goal calls during the team's video sessions to help pump the players up throughout the playoffs. "The guys just loved it," he said. "It really got them going." How about that?!

Then it was time for the players to have their team picture taken, and believe it or not, they invited us to go out on the ice with them. We first watched from the stands as the team took their group photo, and right after, the Penguins PR folks told us to come onto the ice. Bonino and Crosby skated over, one after another, and we took some pictures together. The other noteworthy thing about Bonino that year is that he was on a line with Carl Hagelin and Phil Kessel that the media had nicknamed the HBK Line, after the 1990s wrestler Shawn Michaels, a.k.a. the Heartbreak Kid. Somehow the Penguins had arranged for Michaels's actual WWE championship belt to be there with the team, so in our picture with Bonino we're all holding onto the actual belt.

As I chatted with Crosby on the ice, I mentioned to him that before the Stanley Cup Final Bonino goal call, there was one I had done about him. I tried to explain it. "It was 'Sid'—"

Then Crosby cut me off. "Yeah, 'The Former Kid'!" he said. "I loved that."

If you ever see the picture of the two of us, I'm grinning from ear to ear. He knew about it! I still can't believe it.

Following the photos, we went along with the team to the Stanley Cup parade. Hearing hundreds of thousands of people yell my goal call back to me on that stage was the pinnacle, but the entire morning was just surreal. To get there, the Penguins put us on a bus that had big windows on each side, but even with the windows all the way open, it was sweltering. As we slowly made our way down the packed streets, I pulled out my phone to record as much of it as I could. There were so many people there. So many Bonino signs. Even some "We Love Hockey Night Punjabi" signs. Once people realized it was us inside, I was being pulled from one side of the bus to the other and back again. My colleague Bhupinder had to direct me: "Quick, come on this side! They want you to wave here! Someone wants a selfie with you there!" It seemed like the drive was never-ending, because it took so long to get down even a single block. Pittsburgh isn't that big of a city—only 300,000 people live there, technically—but the crowd for the parade was estimated at 400,000 as fans from the surrounding area all piled into the city's downtown. No wonder it felt like the parade route stretched on forever.

At the parade, we met a bunch of other Penguins employees, who were all so friendly and excited. We also met the Penguins national anthem singer, Jeff Jimerson, who viewers see on TV before every game—in fact, he's been their singer for more than 20 years. As we walked towards our buses, Bhupinder, Randip, Harpreet, and I all sang a rousing rendition of "O Canada" along with Jimerson. Everyone was having an absolute ball. And when it was our turn to go onstage, I went up to the microphone and did the Bonino call again, as loudly as I could, as my small way of showing how grateful we were to the entire city of Pittsburgh for all the love they'd shown us.

The madness didn't stop after the parade was finished, either. No matter where we went, we saw the news footage of us from that morning, doing the Bonino call again for the crowd. It didn't matter if we were in a restaurant, or walking through a store. It seemed like every TV and radio was playing it, and I kept seeing our faces and hearing my own voice all around Pittsburgh. It was crazy.

By the time we got back to the arena, we figured that everything the team had planned for us was over. And that was fine with us. We saw the Keepers of the Cup come by, and met Phil Pritchard, who looks after it full-time for the Hockey Hall of Fame, and took some pictures. But my colleagues and I were kind of loitering, to be honest, because we'd heard that there was going to be a team lunch for the players and their families. We figured, what the heck? We were already there. We might as well see if we could get in.

Around the arena, we started casually asking whichever staff members we could find: "So what floor is this lunch on, anyway?" Eventually we found our way to this big, beautiful room that had tables and chairs set out everywhere and, of course, the Stanley Cup front and centre, with a beautiful backdrop. The players and their families were already there, lining up for the buffet. We tried to walk in as casually as we could, and sure enough, nobody said anything. So we joined the back of the line and grabbed plates of food, too. But then we had to find a table to sit at, and the closest empty spaces were about six feet away from Mario Lemieux, Jim Rutherford, and their families. They were so close to us that we could almost touch them. That's when Harpreet leaned over to the rest of us and said, "I don't care what you guys say. This is a once-in-a-lifetime moment. I'm going to ask for a picture."

Again, I was nervous, because we weren't even really supposed to be there. I didn't want to overdo it. But Harp couldn't be stopped. We all watched with our hands over our eyes as he went up to Mario—and it worked! Of course, if it worked for him, then we were all going to try it, too. One by one, we went up to him and got pictures together. While we were doing that, Jim Rutherford, the general manager, said to us, "Y'know, it's great that you guys could be here. We love your work."

After lunch, things finally started to wind down. The players were getting pictures taken with the Cup along with their families. We were mingling, too, and chatting with different people. There were only a couple of us left at our table. Then I saw Nick Bonino walking over. There were no cameras rolling and no Penguins PR people around, and he said, "I just wanted to say: thanks for making me famous."

It was just such a genuine, heartfelt moment between the two of us.

"Man, don't thank me," I said. "Thank you for scoring such big goals!"

On our way out, Bill and Tom, from the Penguins staff, came up to us again and said, "Before you leave, head down to the team store and whatever you want to grab, grab it." We heard later that the official Bonino goal-call T-shirt, made by Reebok and the NHL, was the single most popular item in the Penguins store that year. I grabbed a couple of whatever sizes were left and headed back home to Canada, still shaking my head at everything that had happened over the past few weeks.

Not long after that, I got a call from the Canadian Museum of History, which is right by the Gatineau/Ottawa provincial border. They told me they wanted to include something to do with the Bonino call as part of a travelling exhibit they were putting together, and I mentioned I had one of the official team T-shirts. They loved the idea, so I sent it to them, and it was on display for an entire year. When I got it back, I kept it in their fancy museum plastic, so it will stay in mint condition for a long, long time.

—

I've run into Bonino a couple of times since the parade. Most notably, at the Penguins' Stadium Series outdoor game at Heinz Field the next season, thanks to the efforts of Joel Darling, Nathen, and Bhupinder. At that point, I had people yelling the goal call at me non-stop all year long. Being in Pittsburgh, it was once again next-level. I asked him, "Is it the same for you?"

He said yes, and that it wasn't just fans, either. All that season, Bonino had heard other NHL players yell it at him, everywhere he went, on and off the ice! More than one of his family members even had the goal call as their ringtone, so they would hear it blaring at them every time he called.

I asked him, "Man, did you ever think this one weird thing was going to connect us together for the rest of our careers?"

He shook his head. "I had no idea."

Chapter 11

If You Can Make Connor McDavid Laugh, You Can Do Anything

A lot of things changed for me after the Bonino call. Now that I had my moment of going viral, people all around the hockey world suddenly knew who I was, and about *Hockey Night in Punjabi*. The show's platform was raised, and it offered me a number of new and exciting opportunities that I was more than ready for.

In the fall of 2016, the World Cup of Hockey took place—an international tournament held in September, before the NHL season officially kicked off. It was the first time the tournament had been held in more than a decade, and it was a big deal: the hockey world descended on Toronto for those two weeks of games and other promotional events. What added to the hype was the uncertainty around the 2018 Winter Olympics in South Korea, and whether or not the NHL would allow its players to participate. Many people questioned whether we would ever see a best-on-best format again if the

Olympics was not in the NHL's plans, and so the World Cup offered everyone an enticing glimpse into what could be missed.

During the week of the World Cup, I was hired to host an event put on by an Italian men's clothing company called Eleventy. I flew out to Toronto ahead of time and went down to the store to be fitted for a beautiful new suit. (As always, I brought a selection of different turbans with me, to make sure everything would match.) I knew my event was going to feature two NHL players, and sure enough, while I was in the fitting room, in wandered Aaron Ekblad and generational talent Connor McDavid, two of the star members of Team North America—because they needed suits, too. It was neat to be able to get to know them a little bit ahead of time.

The event took place in the Eleventy section of Saks Fifth Avenue in downtown Toronto. My official job was to interview McDavid and Ekblad in front of a live audience, and to ask them questions about hockey, the ongoing World Cup, and their likes and dislikes when it comes to fashion. Really, though, I only had one task: to make Connor McDavid laugh. The Eleventy reps had told me ahead of time, "If you can do that, then we're good."

This was harder than it sounds. McDavid is known to be a reserved guy—and for good reason. He has had such intense media attention on him ever since he was a little kid; I don't blame him for wanting to keep to himself a little bit. But during the interview, I threw in a line about how hockey players are lucky when it comes to clothes, because every time I got dressed I had to make sure my turban matched my outfit, too. McDavid laughed at that, and I snuck a look out to the

Eleventy reps in the crowd. They gave me a nod of approval. Mission accomplished!

I was also scheduled for an event at the prestigious Hockey Hall of Fame. All throughout the tournament, the hall was hosting summits on different topics related to hockey, like environmental sustainability, diversity, and youth-hockey development. Each summit had a keynote speaker, and I was asked to speak about diversity and inclusion in hockey.

Walking onto the stage at the Hockey Hall of Fame was yet another surreal moment for me. I had been there back in the '90s with my mom, and later as a teenager with my sister Gurdeep. Being around so many pieces of hockey history was a cherished memory. I've already written about the Golden Temple in Amritsar, and how it's the most holy place in the Sikh faith—well, in my mind I always thought of the Hall of Fame as hockey's own version of Amritsar.

Evanka Osmak, a popular TV host from Sportsnet, gave me a lovely introduction, and then I was up at the podium, shuffling my notes and getting ready to speak. But as I looked around the room, I started recognizing faces. Lots of faces. Back in the corner, for instance, was Scott Moore, who was then president of Sportsnet. Not far away from him was Bill Daly, deputy commissioner of the NHL. And then I saw the commissioner himself: Gary Bettman, the man in charge of the entire league. Nobody told me so many bigwigs from the hockey world would be in attendance. But hey, no pressure, right?

Luckily, I was telling the story that I knew better than any other. I told the audience all about my personal journey in the industry, from growing up in Brooks all the way to living my dream as an announcer on *Hockey Night in Punjabi*. I told them how being a hockey fan positively affected my childhood, and what my personal success has meant not just for my immediate friends and family, but also for the larger Punjabi community across Canada. I put it all together—and I even found time to work in a couple of funny stories along the way. I don't know if it was what the crowd expected to hear that day, but they quickly got into it. I could hear laughter, and by the end I could tell that my personal story had resonated for them, too. In that moment, I felt as if I really did belong in the hockey world, and that they were happy to have me there.

After my keynote speech, I stuck around Toronto for the rest of the World Cup. During the early parts of the tournament, much of the talk around the hockey world surrounded Team North America, a team comprised of some of the best under-23 players from Canada and the United States—and the team that my Eleventy buddies Ekblad and McDavid were on. The group was intriguing in a lot of ways. Although the players represented the future of the NHL, their lack of experience and the fact that they weren't playing for some sort of national pride led some people to believe that they wouldn't be much of a factor in the tournament. Then the games began, and they were flying! Team North America quickly became must-watch TV, and it didn't hurt that Auston Matthews, playing his first meaningful games in the hockey-crazed city that had just drafted him, was riding shotgun to Connor McDavid. The hockey was so fast and skilled. It became clear that Team North America was not just a sign of things to come—they were the *new* NHL.

Near the end of the tournament, I was sitting up in the media section of the Air Canada Centre (now Scotiabank Arena), watching a game, when I got a text message from Ed Hall. Like my longtime boss Joel Darling, Ed is an executive producer with Sportsnet, and at the time he worked directly under Scott Moore at the English version of *Hockey Night in Canada*. I had met Ed a couple of times before, but I hadn't had the chance to really get to know him yet. So when I saw that his message said, "Do you have some time to talk?" my mind, like it usually does, went straight into worst-case-scenario mode. *Oh no. What did I do?*

It turned out Ed was nearby, so he came up to meet me in the media room. He sat down next to me, and we chatted for a bit. Then he said, "Listen, I have an opportunity for you, and I'm wondering if you're interested."

"Of course," I said. "What is it?"

He said, "First of all, I want you to know this is coming directly from the top of the company." He paused for a second. "We'd like you to be on an English broadcast of *Hockey Night in Canada* in the upcoming season."

I felt my eyes widen with surprise.

"Personally," Ed added, "I'm very passionate about your story." And he wasn't just saying that. In that first conversation, Ed even brought up how my great-grandfather had first come to Canada a century ago—something I had mentioned onstage during my speech at the Hockey Hall of Fame. "This is something we really want to do."

It turned out they already had specific details in mind. It was going to be a hosting gig, on November 30, during a nationally televised game between the Toronto Maple Leafs and the Calgary Flames. That way, I would be working out of the Saddledome, a building I was already familiar with. Plus it would give me enough time to get up to speed and be ready for the broadcast.

I did my best to tell Ed how much the opportunity meant to me, but it was tough to hold back all of the emotions I was feeling. The second he left, I ran to the back of the media room, called Sukhy, and all of those emotions started spilling out of me. When she first picked up the phone, I couldn't even talk properly. Tears were coming down my cheeks.

"You won't believe it," I kept saying to her. "You won't believe it."

———

What does it mean for a dream to come true?

When I was a kid, I spent a lot of time imagining myself as a professional hockey broadcaster. But I wasn't picturing a show like *Hockey Night in Punjabi*—mostly because back then I never would have believed it could exist. The hockey world has changed so much since the '80s, in terms of both representation and technology's role in helping people watch the sport and interact with their favourite personalities. So while I love being part of *Hockey Night in Punjabi*, and I'm so proud of all that we've accomplished on the show and for the community, it's not exactly what I had dreamt about specifically when I was young.

But the English version of *Hockey Night*? Now that was different. Even when I was going to broadcasting school at Mount Royal in Calgary, I kept a postcard pinned to my fridge that showed the entire CBC Sports broadcast team. Every time I grabbed yogurt for my *paraunta* or milk for my cereal, I would look at that postcard and remind myself what my ultimate goal was. I used to think about the English broadcast as I fell asleep at night. It literally was a dream, and now it was coming true.

I'm not sure anything can really prepare you for a job like that, but in my case I had some extra learning to do. Remember, for the past eight years, my job on *Hockey Night in Punjabi* was doing play-by-play. I did hosting, too, but always for an in-studio panel—it's very different than being down at ice level, which is more talking to players who've just stepped off the ice, and managing in-game stories. It's in my nature to over-prepare for things, but what Ed Hall asked me to do as host was going to require a lot of homework.

I decided to go straight to the source. The first people I reached out to were Cassie Campbell-Pascall and Scott Oake, the regular hosts on *Hockey Night in Canada* at the time, whose shoes I would be stepping into for the night. I also talked to Gene Principe, the host for the Edmonton Oilers broadcasts on Sportsnet, who is not only a really approachable guy but also a total pro on the air. Gene is the type of person no one in the entire industry has anything bad to say about. He really, truly is one of the nicest people you could ever meet—one of my mom's favourite memories is the time our family drove up to Edmonton for her 80th birthday to watch an Oilers game at the brand-new Rogers Arena, and Gene took total care of her. He invited us up to his intermission studio and gave us a tour. Sportsnet writer Mark Spector and analysts Louie DeBrusk and Nick Kypreos showed her so much respect. In fact, Louie got up from his chair and had my mom sit down instead, and even gave her his Sportsnet mic. The pictures from that day are just priceless.

When I reached out to Gene about what the hosting role entailed, he graciously answered all of my questions, and even offered to let me shadow him for a day, which was an opportunity I wasn't going to pass up. I drove up to Edmonton first thing in the morning, and Gene and I did everything together, from watching the morning skate to setting up in the hallways during the game to get ready for interviews. Getting to watch such a seasoned pro, completely in his element, was impressive. Even a two-minute segment that looks smooth on TV requires more hard work and planning than most viewers will ever know.

As the in-arena host, your job is to complement the main broadcast by telling little stories that make the main story—the game on the ice—that much more interesting. You are searching players' social-media accounts for any colourful details that you can bring up during the broadcast. If there's a picture or a video clip, that's even better. You're also checking for all kinds of little details: players' and coaches' birthdays, hometowns, where they played their junior hockey, and any connections between the home team and the visitors. Every game can have a narrative, and it's my job as host to find out what I can add to paint a fuller picture. The stats are less vital in this role. It's more about the people.

In preparing for the host role, you also attend the game-day skates. That is when you can talk to the players and coaches to confirm some of the stories you want to tell on the air. Say I want to talk about something that Johnny Gaudreau did while studying at Boston College. A practice or game-day skate is my chance to quickly check with him to make sure I've got all my facts straight and to get more context from him.

You are constantly thinking on your feet, too. There are plenty of stories that develop during the course of the game. For instance, if a player suddenly leaves the bench, chances are it's the host who'll be trying to get to the bottom of it. Is it an injury? An equipment malfunction? Or, in the infamous case of Canucks goaltender Roberto Luongo, an emergency bathroom break? People are going to want to know—fast.

When I went out for coffee with Cassie, she filled me in on all of this, but she also told me her own story of getting into broadcasting. Coming in as a former player, she had to learn things more or less on the fly (though being a two-time Olympic gold medalist surely helped!). I was grateful for how specific and practical her advice was. Cassie took me through an entire broadcast and went over, in detail, everything that I would be responsible for over the course of the night. For example, she told me that when you are doing an interview with a player on the bench, it's a good idea to bring your notebook out with you and rest it on the lip of the bench while you talk. She also broke things down in terms of time, and suggested how often I should be checking in with my producer, when I needed to be moving from one place to another, and things like that. They were minute details, but they can make a big difference when you're performing live.

Scott Oake was helpful, too. We met up for a quick coffee one day after a Saturday night broadcast, and he mostly just told me not to worry, and reassured me that I could do it.

He also reminded me to have fun out there—obvious advice that a lot of people forget to follow.

When the day finally came, I was so busy doing my game-day preparation that when I started getting interview requests, at first I didn't realize what they meant. Why would someone want to talk to me? I hadn't even thought about receiving any media attention. Looking back on it, I suppose it did make sense: I was the first person wearing a turban to appear as a broadcaster on one of the most important TV shows in Canadian history. That *is* worth celebrating! The downside, however, was that suddenly all of the time that I'd usually use to get ready for the broadcast was now filled with fielding interview requests from TV and radio stations all over the country. It was a special feeling, but also a bit overwhelming. All day long, I felt like I was trying to juggle two different jobs at the same time.

I tried to remember all of the advice I had received. There were some funny moments leading up to the game, too. I remember talking with a producer after the morning skate, and he looked at me and said, "So . . . have you decided what you're going to wear tonight?" I knew right away what he meant. The game was between Toronto and Calgary, and I happened to be wearing a blue turban. My blazer and pants also had shades of blue in them.

"I know, I know," I said with a laugh. "Too much Maple Leafs. I'll be sure to throw some Flames red in there for balance."

There was no easing me into the job, either. My very first on-camera job that evening was a one-on-one interview with Maple Leafs coach Mike Babcock. This was before the game, and when I showed up at the prearranged time and place, there was . . . nothing. No Mike Babcock, but also no camera or audio person. I assumed I had made a mistake, and as I was trying to figure out what had happened, Babcock walked briskly around the corner, alongside someone from the Leafs PR team, ready to go. But without a camera, none of that mattered. I told them I needed a minute to figure things out, and I called everyone I could think of for answers. Babcock was a good sport about it, but the PR guy, who was a bit irritated at the situation, told me I had two minutes before they had to leave—it was a game day, after all. Everyone's schedules are incredibly tight. I could understand that. Leafs PR didn't want Babcock standing around aimlessly in the hallway, so they took him back to the dressing room and warned me that they would come out once more in exactly two minutes, and if I wasn't ready to go, there wasn't going to be any interview. The game hadn't even begun, and I was already sweating buckets. Sure enough, when Babcock came back out the second time, I still had no camera with me for the interview, but finally, at the very last second, the camera operator came running around the corner at full speed. We managed to pull off the interview by the skin of our teeth. That's the thrill of TV!

Still, I came away from that first interview feeling a bit shaken. I walked back to my little host studio, and inside was a tech guy from *Hockey Night*, putting some wires together behind the scene. He had heard what had happened, and he asked, "Is this your first game?"

"No. But in this role, yeah," I said.

"Well, it might be your last if you don't figure your shit out."

Gee, thanks for the words of encouragement.

As we approached puck drop, I made my way into the stands of the Saddledome and waited for my cue. I kept thinking to myself that this was a national game, so if someone tuned in, from anywhere across Canada, they were going to see me on their TV screen. It's a responsibility I didn't take lightly, and I recognized just how incredibly amazing this opportunity was. I was surrounded by 18,000 screaming fans, but I had to pay careful attention to the voice in my earpiece as my producer gave me a countdown. That night, Daren Millard was anchoring the panel for Sportsnet from the studio in Toronto, and I was waiting for him to throw to me. But again, I was surprised when Daren started giving this really heartfelt introduction—not of the game, but of *me*. I was so flattered and emotional—part of me was thinking, *How is this happening?* while the other part was like, *Keep it together! You're about to start talking!* I had to hold back the waterworks and get on with things. Then, finally, I heard the words start coming out of my mouth: "Thanks, Daren, and welcome, everyone, to the Scotiabank Saddledome . . ."

It reminded me of the first time I was on CBC Radio in Calgary, where the rest of the newsroom crowded around the radio to hear me make my on-air debut. Now the same thing was happening again, but this time I knew it was my friends and family all tuned in at the same time, cheering me on.

But I couldn't rest on my laurels for long. As soon as that first TV hit was over, boom: it was on to the next thing. I was on my feet all evening. The Flames ended up beating the Leafs 3–0, and all three goals came in the first period—two in the first minute! People working at the Saddledome that night kept saying I was good luck for their team. I decided to interview Matt Stajan, who scored the third goal, at the intermission, and after that, I told various stories throughout the broadcast. Then, at the end of the night, I asked for my own gift. I wanted one of the iconic towels that players wear over their shoulders during the intermission interviews. I brought it home carefully, along with my media pass, so I could add everything to my memorabilia collection at home. That was one evening I didn't want to forget.

The next morning, I got a phone call from Scott Moore. He said, "Harnarayan, that was such a proud moment for me to see you on the show. Just a couple of years ago, our broadcast talent wasn't even allowed to have facial hair. To see you on the national broadcast with a turban and a beard, it made me really proud of how far we've come." Not only was I happy he called with positive feedback, I was also surprised to learn that Scott felt that my first English broadcast was a significant moment.

I thanked him again and told him that I'd dreamed of that opportunity for years but never expected it would actually happen.

———

The full contingent of *Hockey Night in Punjabi* might not have been there to broadcast an event like the World Cup of Hockey, but one of the goals Bhupinder had was getting our show more of a presence at marquee NHL events. We cover the league just like anyone else, and I think we do an informative and entertaining job of it, but the fact that we broadcast in another language, on a different channel or platform, can sometimes put us on the back burner for events. But Bhupinder is a creative, big-picture guy, and he's had some great ideas over the years—none of which worked better than the NHL 100 celebration.

In 2017, the NHL turned 100 years old. To celebrate, that January they announced a list of the 100 greatest players to ever play in the league, and held a bunch of events in Los Angeles, where that year's NHL All-Star Game was being played. To help the show make strides in the sports world, Bhupinder secured funding from a prominent businessman in the South Asian community to pay for our travel, and Bhupinder, Randip, and I flew out to Los Angeles. It was great, because not only did we get to cover the All-Star Game and NHL 100 for *Hockey Night in Punjabi*, we were also able to meet many people from around the league and network, which never hurts. And if I thought the World Cup of Hockey was a big deal, that was nothing compared to the mayhem we saw in California. All that week, every time we turned a corner, we found ourselves doing double-takes at how many NHL superstars were just hanging around. *Oh man, that's Ray Bourque! And there's Pat LaFontaine!* It was almost too much to process. Legendary NHLers were walking around the streets of L.A. like ants. We loved every second of it.

One of the first meetings we had lined up was right after we landed—an interview with Tom Hoffarth, a reporter with the *Los Angeles Daily News*, to talk about *Hockey Night in Punjabi*. We met him for lunch at the restaurant attached to our hotel, and sure enough, as soon as we sat down at our table, we saw Grant Fuhr, the great Oilers goalie during Edmonton's dynasty years, sitting just a couple of tables over. That was very cool, but all of a sudden, from my vantage point, I saw that sitting across from him was the one and only Wayne Gretzky.

Are you kidding me?

I was so excited that I was almost shaking in my seat. It's horrible to admit this as a broadcaster, because you're supposed to be calm and objective in every situation, but I couldn't help it. This was my favourite hockey player of all time—the guy I'd built a shrine for in my childhood bedroom.

We tried to remain calm and get on with the interview. The reporter asked me about how I first got into hockey, and I told him how obsessed I was with Gretzky. In fact, in our pre-interview, which I'd done before we left for L.A., I had told him about the Kings sweater from my kindergarten class photo, and how I had kept it all these years later, in case my own kids wanted to wear it someday. The journalist thought it was a great story, and I'd brought it with me so he could see it, too. So here I was, sitting a few tables over from the Great One, with my childhood jersey of his in my bag.

My colleagues and I tried to be professional as long as we could, but soon our entire table was talking about how we could approach Gretzky at his table and say a quick hello. It was such a big deal and a big opportunity. At the same time, though, he was clearly having a private lunch. Would he think we were being rude? It's different for fans, but for members of the media, you really want to be respectful of any player's private time outside the arena.

We didn't get a chance to find out. While we were still making our plan, and before any of us could work up the courage to get up and walk over, Gretzky stood up and came over to *us* instead. "Hey, you're the *Hockey Night in Punjabi* guys!" he said. "My sons love you guys. They're fans of your work, and they show me clips from your show all the time."

We were flabbergasted. First Mario Lemieux, the year before, and now Wayne freaking Gretzky? But we quickly got over our nerves and had a nice little chat with him. For my part, I tried to talk as fast as possible, because I wasn't sure I would ever have this opportunity again. Of course, I ended up telling him again about how my mom would make parshaadh on his birthday and how we'd do a prayer for him back in Brooks. Next, I had to mention the old Kings sweater from kindergarten, which I then pulled out and showed to him. He said, "That's great! Let's take a picture!" That picture of us together is now a centrepiece of the memory wall my wife created for me in our basement, and I'm not sure how I'll ever top it. After that, Wayne's son Trevor came over and chatted with us about watching our goal calls on the *Hockey Night in Punjabi* social-media feeds. Trevor turned out to be just as down to earth as his dad, and later we exchanged messages online. But Wayne Gretzky coming up to our table is a memory I will cherish for the rest of my life. What a class act.

We were fortunate that so many people in the hockey world recognized us, but buying into your own celebrity can make things humorous, too, as we soon found out. A little later in the trip, my colleagues and I were standing near the media room in the Staples Center, and from a distance, Bhupinder spotted Bobby Orr walking right towards us! Was it possible? Could *another* NHL legend be coming over to say hi? We braced ourselves for another surreal conversation, right up until the moment Orr said to Bhupinder, "Excuse me, do you happen to know where the bathrooms are?" It was hilarious. You can't win them all.

Of course, we got plenty of business done on the L.A. trip as well. As part of the press corps, we were right up front as the NHL 100 ceremony took place, and afterwards went onstage to interview some of the players who'd made the list, like Dominik Hasek, Brendan Shanahan, and Pat LaFontaine. We also recorded a segment for *Hockey Night in Punjabi* from the exact same studio and desk that the English broadcast team was using, with the arena and ice in the background. That was exciting, and really made us feel like we were able to give our viewership the coverage they deserved.

Away from the show, another event had been arranged for me to do, and once again I was paired with Connor McDavid, this time for an event sponsored by Canadian Tire. They had set up an elaborate ball-hockey obstacle course on the rooftop of a high-rise in downtown L.A. The event was going to be streamed live, with the idea that McDavid would run the course while I did lighthearted play-by-play for viewers following along on Facebook Live.

That afternoon, a black SUV with tinted windows pulled up in front of my hotel, and when I got inside, McDavid was already there, alongside a couple of guys from the Oilers PR staff. We had already met at the fashion event a few months earlier, not to mention in a couple of dressing rooms following Oilers games. As I mentioned, he has the perception of being a fairly quiet guy, but on the car ride over, we had a very friendly chat, where I even managed to make McDavid laugh for a second time. We started talking about Gretzky, and I told him the story about making parshaadh for Gretzky's birthday when I was a kid. I added, "I wonder if my kids will do the same thing for your birthday one day."

"That would be awesome," he said with a grin.

When we reached the rooftop, the Canadian Tire crew was already there. The obstacle course was all set up, and I started thinking about how I was going to handle the event. I was used to broadcasting to an audience watching along at home, of course, but this time there was no live audience to feed off. We would have to create the atmosphere ourselves. It probably won't be a surprise to hear that as soon as the cameras went live, McDavid was an absolute magician with his stick-handling. I did my best to keep up, chatting with him as he went and describing what was going on for the viewers. I even got a flash of his competitiveness when he wasn't able to quite put the ball where he wanted, and he became frustrated. I couldn't get a word out of him until he'd figured it out. It just goes to show that phenomenal talents like his never really take a day off.

The other thing I learned that day was how complicated the day-to-day life of an NHL superstar is. As soon as we got back in the SUV, the conversation immediately shifted to how to get McDavid from one place to the next without causing a scene. For our event, he was wearing casual clothes, but he needed to be wearing a suit for his next commitment, which was coming up right away. He listened carefully and then asked, "Okay, so how do I get changed?"

That's the thing about guys like McDavid. He can't even go into a Starbucks to get himself a coffee because of the crowd he would attract. It was fascinating to be a fly on the wall in that SUV, watching how carefully the PR team had to work just to get him up to his hotel room and back out again. It was particularly bad that week, because all of the NHL talent was staying at the same hotel, and word had gotten out to the fans in L.A and those who had come in from all over the world to take in the festivities. The lobby was continuously crawling with fans looking for autographs and photos with their favourite players. It was nuts.

The entire drive back, the Oilers PR people were on the phone with the hotel, asking about back-door entrances and other ways they might be able to get McDavid into the building without anyone seeing him. Eventually they came up with a plan, and asked me if I minded waiting in the car while McDavid was dropped off first, and then they could drive me back around to the front door. No problem! I was fascinated by the whole process and wanted to see as much of it as I could.

The car pulled around back behind the hotel, and McDavid and I shook hands and said our goodbyes. Then he opened the door and got out, and no joke, within seconds there was a crowd of 50 to 100 people yelling his name and rushing over to him. The Oilers PR guys shouted, "Go! Go! Go!" and McDavid sprinted over to an open door, which slammed shut behind him as soon as he was through. And all just so he could put on some new clothes! It's funny, because back in the day, I would have been one of the people in the crowd, waiting to catch a glimpse of Gretzky.

After the dust had settled, they drove back around and dropped me off at the regular front entrance of the hotel. Of course, no throngs of fans were running after me for an autograph, which, after the scene I had just witnessed, was just fine by me.

———

Just as I have found success in my career, I always make a point of finding ways to give back, using whatever name recognition I might have to help others. It's something I was raised to believe from a young age, as part of my Sikh faith, and also based on the example my parents set for me. So when Chevrolet first told me about this new project they were calling the Good Deeds Cup, I knew I had to be part of it, because it followed so closely to the Sikh concept of seva— serving humanity without expecting anything in return.

Officially announced during the 2016–17 NHL season, the idea was the brainchild of people like Paul Bailey, who was in charge of Chevrolet Canada's national marketing campaigns at the time and had been such an advocate for *Hockey Night in Punjabi* ever since they came on as our title sponsor. He'd organized community events for us in the past, including meet-and-greets at dealerships, as well as a fun outdoor ball-hockey event in Edmonton where *Hockey Night in Canada* broadcasters like Kelly Hrudey, Cassie Campbell-Pascall, Mark Lee, and I signed the hood of a Chevrolet Silverado that was to be given away in a contest. I remember pausing with the Sharpie in my hand, thinking: *Does the person who wins this really want my autograph?* But it was all in good fun. For a long time, Paul kept hinting that a big new project was in the works, but he ended up leaving the company before it came to fruition. Luckily, his replacement, James Hodge, a Chevrolet executive (and a big Ottawa Senators fan, might I add), shared Paul's vision and also wanted me to be a big part of it.

That project turned out to be the Good Deeds Cup. The point of the Good Deeds Cup is to inspire and reward peewee hockey teams across Canada for generous off-ice gestures of support for their communities. It's such a brilliant idea. If kids see the value of serving their community at a young age, I really believe that will stick with them as they get older. And it has obvious ties into hockey, too, because what makes you a good teammate is the same thing that makes you a good community member. Everyone looks out for each other. To qualify, teams send in video submissions showing a good deed they did that season. Chevrolet picks a winner, and the team gets $100,000 to put towards a charity of their choice, a bunch of new hockey gear, and their team name engraved on an actual trophy that cost Chevrolet $50,000 to produce. It's legit.

The winner that first year was the Glace Bay Miners, from Glace Bay, Nova Scotia. I was supposed to fly out to surprise the winning team at their home rink, but at the time *Hockey Night in Punjabi* was covering the playoffs every second night from our studio in Vancouver. In the end, we were able to find a two-day gap in my schedule, and I flew all the way across the country: a red-eye from Vancouver to Toronto, then another flight to Halifax, then a third flight to Sydney, Nova Scotia, and from there I drove up to Glace Bay. The schedule was so tight that when I got into town, after 11 hours of travelling, I had to go straight to the event! I had never been to the Maritimes before, and it makes you realize just how massive this country of ours is. I also saw first-hand how friendly the people out in the Maritimes are. It was neat to realize that I didn't need to introduce myself or explain to anyone what I did, or what *Hockey Night in Punjabi* was. Hockey is just that popular in Canada. They all just knew.

Inside, the community hall was completely decked out, and everyone from the town was there, including the mayor. When the team showed up, confetti poured down from the ceiling, and four-time Olympic gold medallist Caroline Ouellette and I presented them with the trophy for their good deed: celebrating Valentine's Day with the veterans at a local retirement home. The team was shocked. They had no idea. Then we paraded around the streets of Glace Bay, showing off the Good Deeds Cup, and ended with a celebration at the seniors' home. Everyone had a great time, and I think it showed Chevrolet how much potential the idea had.

The next year, the cup was won by a team in northern Manitoba called the Pas Huskies, who helped rally to keep a local shelter open throughout the winter holidays. The West Carleton Warriors won it the following year by raising money and helping to organize cleanup efforts for their community outside of Ottawa, which had been hit by a tornado in 2018. I flew in again for this one, and witnessed another event pulled off brilliantly. The kids were brought out to the historic Rideau Canal in Ottawa and told they were going for a team skate. Meanwhile, the Chevrolet team had set up the cup on a podium further up the ice. As the kids got closer to it, they slowly started to realize what was going on. By the time they got to the podium, they were all cheering and yelling like they'd won the Stanley Cup. It was a fantastic moment, and I found it especially inspiring to see how excited and thrilled the kids were to win a championship for something they did off the ice.

As part of the prize, the young players also received a bunch of personalized hockey gear, and it looked so good that when I came home from Ottawa, I texted James at Chevrolet: "Man, I need one of those jerseys for myself." Sure enough, a few weeks later a package came in the mail: a crisp new Good Deeds Cup jersey with "SINGH" written across the back. It may not be a Gretzky jersey, but I hang it in my collection with just as much pride.

Another initiative I am involved with is the NHL's Hockey Is for Everyone program. For the past few seasons, every February, the league partners with teams and other organizations to find ways not just to grow the sport but to also show that hockey is for people of every ethnicity, race, gender identity, and background. A friend of mine, former local Sportsnet radio host Rob Kerr, came up with an idea to invite people who'd never seen live hockey to a Flames practice at the Saddledome, and he asked me to help organize it. We knew there were so many new people arriving in this country, and we knew that one of the best ways to introduce people into Canadian culture is via hockey. The Flames came on board right away, and it was a remarkable success. Throughout the day, we had guests like Cassie Campbell-Pascall come out to talk about the role of women in hockey, and Rob gave everyone an introduction to how the actual rules work. I helped emcee the event and spoke about my role as a broadcaster. We also had Willie O'Ree, the first Black NHL player, come out and tell stories about his incredible journey in our sport. He is such an inspiring individual who has seen a lot in his lifetime within the game. It was really special being able to meet him, and we've continued to keep in touch. (He sent me an autographed jersey when he was inducted into the Hockey Hall of Fame—and, fun fact, his wife is Punjabi!) When we were planning the event, I mentioned that if you wanted South Asian people to attend, you really had to have complimentary food and chai. That's just how it is in our community. So we added a free breakfast, and it worked out great.

Through this event, I met Kevin Hodgson, who was working with a charity that's all about mentorship. HEROS Hockey is designed for kids who otherwise wouldn't be able to play hockey, be it because of financial restrictions or family issues such as domestic violence or drugs—really, anything that would make a child's life tough. The truly amazing thing is that the kids in the program are chosen by teachers in grade four, and they're kept with the program all the way to the end of high school. It's not simply a one-off. These kids are given a sense of purpose and community through the most formative years of their lives. What was even more impressive was that even though the charity had been around for 20 years, and had teams in every major Canadian city—more than 700 kids in total—everything was being run by just two employees.

That, to me, was really impressive. With some charities, you don't know how much of your donation is really going to help and how much is being eaten up in administration costs. Well, there was your answer. Kevin and his friend Norm Flynn, the founder, were doing all of this themselves. That's only possible because many graduates from the program stayed on as volunteers after graduating, having found it such an integral part of their life growing up. After I got to know some of them, they had me come out and volunteer at their programs in Calgary and Vancouver. I felt fortunate to see first-hand how much of an impact the program was having on the kids and their families. Parents told me their children had no friends before this, or that their kids suffered from low self-esteem and weren't getting good grades. But since joining HEROS, everything had changed. The families were emotional talking about just how much the charity had done for them.

After I started volunteering, Kevin and Norm asked me if I'd be interested in joining their board of directors, partly because they were looking for help getting corporate support, and partly so that, with my experience in media, I could help promote the charity. Kevin and Norm are the type of people who go far beyond the call of duty. They have been known to buy kids mattresses to sleep on, out of their own pockets. They have spent entire nights in hospitals with kids whose parents were busy trying to put food on the table or were in some sort of trouble. I had no hesitation being a part of something so inspiring, alongside people who genuinely wanted to help. Since joining as a director, I have been able to visit some of the HEROS teams across western Canada and emcee their first two fundraising events, which were recently held in Vancouver. Can you believe a charity that has been around for two decades had never had a fundraising event before?

Unfortunately, many large corporate charities are focused only on volume. It sounds great to say, "We've served one million kids," but those are usually one-offs: you give a kid a hockey stick and send them away. It doesn't necessarily improve their life in any meaningful way. HEROS Hockey doesn't have huge numbers, but the kids we do help, we help a lot. That's what makes the work we do so special. I'm really proud to be part of it.

The other big outreach project I've been involved with is a bit different but just as near to my heart. It all started when Bindy Dulay, a woman in Vancouver, discovered a video of a group of young women in India playing hockey. Even to her, a South Asian woman, this was surprising. Sadly, it's still not that common in India for women to be playing sports, let alone ice hockey. But these women lived up in the Himalayas, in a northern part of the country called Ladakh, and it turned out they had all come together, borrowed some equipment, and made a team. Their dream was to become India's national women's ice-hockey team.

Bindy reached out to me and told me she wanted to figure out a way to bring the team to Canada to help them train, and also to raise awareness about what they were doing. She thought it was an inspiring example of female empowerment, and I agreed. Bindy had also reached out to four-time Olympic gold medalist Hayley Wickenheiser, who is probably the best female hockey player of all time, and they, along with the help of many others, got the ball rolling. During the initial planning stages, Bindy, Hayley, and I went out to lunch together to chat and brainstorm. Hayley was very passionate about the idea and wanted to bring the Indian team out to the girls' hockey festival she runs each year in Calgary. That way the players would get some experience playing against other teams, which would help them get ready to compete on an international stage.

It was a major project to undertake. The first step was getting people from Canada to fly out to Ladakh, introduce themselves to the team, and give them some basic hockey training. That, of course, meant we needed funding, so we started talking up the project wherever we could. I spoke at a women's hockey gala in Calgary to raise awareness, and Bindy used her connections to get sponsorship from a few McDonald's franchises. In the end, it was Hayley, along with several other hockey people, who flew out to Ladakh to meet the team. She invited me to come along, but it cut too far into my work at *Hockey Night in Punjabi*—we don't have vacation time during the regular season and playoffs. But the videos and photos I saw afterwards were just incredible. The women play outdoors, in the actual mountains. They also do all their own maintenance, waking up extra early to flood the ice themselves. Those visuals were so honest and humbling— a perfect embodiment of what the game can provide.

Not long after that, Prime Minister Justin Trudeau went on a trip to India, and because word had gotten out about our project, he ended up meeting up with the women's team as well, and they all played a game of ball hockey together. Hayley was there, and the Prime Minister's Office invited me to go, too, but it was a lot of travel for just one day of activities, and it would have again meant missing work. So I had to turn it down.

When it finally came time for the women to fly out to Canada, in November 2018, Bindy and Hayley had organized a really fun schedule where they would spend time in Surrey and Calgary, which both have large South Asian populations. The Indian team played games against local women's teams, and we also received some great media coverage—not just from *Hockey Night in Punjabi* but from the English media as well. I shot a couple of Flames TV Punjabi videos with them, and my colleagues Randip Janda and Amrit Gill gave them a tour of our studio in Vancouver. It turns out the women knew about our show, and some of them even followed us on social media, so seeing how we put the show together was a kick for them. This entire experience showed, again, that hockey transcends national and cultural boundaries.

While I was helping out with the women's team, I got a call from the Ontario Sports Hall of Fame—specifically Mark Gravett, the president, who told me I was the recipient of that year's Brian Williams Media Award. I'd been nominated by Scott Morrison, a well-known long-time hockey writer who's been inducted into the Hockey Hall of Fame. There was a gala coming up that fall. Could I attend?

Obviously! What an honour. It worked out that the event didn't fall on a weekend, and Sukhy and I weren't sure if this was the kind of thing worth her flying out for. She was back to teaching full-time, and our kids were one and three years old. Even with my parents helping out, I didn't want to make things more complicated, so we agreed she would stay home in Calgary.

But when I arrived in Toronto for the event at the Westin Harbour Castle, I started to realize that this was bigger than I had thought it would be—clearly I'm bad at judging this kind of thing. Then there were the other inductees, who were also pretty damn impressive. They included former New

Jersey Devils captain Scott Stevens, longtime Ottawa 67's coach Brian Kilrea, Toronto Blue Jays pitcher Tom Henke, and several others. The night started with a cocktail party, but the actual award ceremony was happening in a different room that I hadn't seen yet. As each inductee was announced and then brought in, one by one, I thought it sounded like an awful lot of applause coming from the other room. Then they called my name, and I walked into what turned out to be this massive hall, with spotlights, camera crews, and probably a thousand people in the audience, applauding. It sounded like the cheers you would get at a hockey game. It was unbelievable. (When my wife eventually saw the photos, we both agreed she should have been there after all. Sorry, honey.)

The highlight of the night, however, was getting to meet Brian Williams himself. He is an absolute legend in our industry: among other things, he was Canada's voice of the Olympic Games for so many years. He told me that because of his busy schedule, he hadn't been able to present his award for several years. "But when I found out Scott Morrison had nominated you," he said, "I changed my schedule and arranged to fly in just for the day, to make sure I could be here." He was flying back to Montreal later that same evening. It was an honour to hear him say that. After an incredibly well-made video introduction about my career, Brian gave a wonderful and heartfelt speech about how significant it was for someone like me to be winning the award. I guess I shouldn't have been surprised at how well he captured what the award meant not just for me personally, but for Canada and all Canadians. I felt the exact same way.

Chapter 12
Poppies

When I reflect back on everything that has happened in my life so far, it's hard to believe it all happened to one person. As a kid in small-town Alberta, I sometimes felt like I was living two separate lives: the private one dedicated to my Sikh faith and music, and the public one where I would talk about the previous night's hockey game for hours to anyone who would listen. I feel so fortunate, as an adult, to have built a life for myself where those two passions can now live side by side.

But even more than my personal success, I'm proud to look around and see signs of how far Canadian society has come, to the benefit of all of us. Of course, it's great that we have a show like *Hockey Night in Punjabi*, now entering its second decade on the air, when that idea would have sounded impossible, even ridiculous, when I was growing up in the '80s. But I reflect back even further. To my great-grandfather, who encountered a Canada that was, all the way up to the prime minister, blatantly racist. And to my dad, who wasn't able to vote in Brooks because the polling station was in the Legion, and turbans weren't allowed there—so he just never voted during those years, even though he was a Canadian citizen.

It's obvious how far we've come, and that's worth celebrating.

At the same time, it's just as obvious that there's still so much work to do. More and more kids from diverse backgrounds are signing up to play hockey, but they still face resistance and sometimes horrendous racism from small-minded people who ought to know better. Not that long ago, I got a message from a coach in Ontario. He told me that the Sikh kids on his minor-hockey team are being taunted and bullied when they go on the road to play games. Meanwhile, our Punjabi videos for Flames TV still get comments saying that we should learn to speak English or else shut up. If you need more examples, I can think of things that happened last month, last week, or even yesterday.

One of the most high-profile instances came on what turned out to be the last-ever instalment of Coach's Corner, on *Hockey Night in Canada*, where Don Cherry made his infamous comments about "you people" not wearing poppies around Remembrance Day. Don has staunchly supported the Canadian military, and good on him for doing so—but the issue was how he singled out visible minorities. The night that it happened, in November 2019, my colleagues and I were busy with our own broadcast, but we soon learned from social media what had just occurred. My first thought was: *Oh boy, here we go*. Randip Janda and I agreed right away that we should post a picture of the entire *Hockey Night in Punjabi* team that night, as we were all wearing poppies. Randip said that we didn't need to say much in the post—the picture itself would do the talking. The caption read: "Another Saturday night in the books. See you next week Canada," with a Canadian flag emoji at the end. Not only were we all wearing poppies, but in the spirit of Remembrance Day, Randip also had on a red tie, and Mantar Bhandal's entire outfit had red in it, including a red turban.

Our group picture at *Hockey Night in Punjabi* received a great response and was seen by thousands of people across the country. There were, however, a few people who incorrectly wondered whether the whole photo was a stunt, and that we'd only put on our poppies after hearing Don's comments. Ridiculous! For me, the first problem was that Don singled out the city of Mississauga, which is well known as one of the most diverse places in Canada. And it got worse from there. He criticized "you people" who come here and "love our milk and honey" but won't spend a couple of bucks on a poppy to support veterans. This kind of argument creates an us-versus-them mentality, something that most visible minorities, like myself, have had to deal with for our entire lives. Some people responded to the public outcry over Don's comments by saying those speaking out were overreacting, but when you look at it through the lens of people who have had to justify them-selves as Canadians for most of their lives, just based on how they look, you can see why the words he used cut so deep. It's extremely dangerous to paint everyone with the same brush.

Don's words also conveyed an assumption that diverse Canadians don't contribute to the Canadian military, and that is simply untrue. Not only do many members of ethnic minorities serve the nation, but thousands of Sikhs also fought for this country during both world wars, during a time when they didn't even have the right to vote or buy land. Today, the minister of national defence himself, Harjit Sajjan, is a Sikh gentleman who has served as a lieutenant-colonel in the Canadian Armed Forces and is decorated for his service in Afghanistan. It's an absurd argument.

Of course, this wasn't the first time Don had said something controversial. Over the years, he had taken shots at Indigenous peoples, argued that women should not work in media covering men's sports, picked on French-Canadian and European players, and voiced his displeasure at Canada's refusal to join the Iraq War. Compilations of these comments circulated on Twitter, and I saw first-hand the astonishment of people of younger generations who were not aware of some of the hurtful comments he had made over the years. In hindsight, I wonder how many *Hockey Night in Canada* producers wish they had put their foot down much earlier.

Back in my hotel room that night, however, I rewatched that Coach's Corner and realized just how uncomfortable the whole thing made me feel. Whenever I meet viewers of our show from the South Asian community, one of the most common things they ask me is, "Have you met Don Cherry? What's he like to you?" There was an underlying concern in the community, dating back years and years, that this man might not be the friendliest to people of diverse backgrounds. I always told them the truth: that Don commanded a lot of respect whenever he walked into a room, and that we had chatted a few times over the years. He even threw me a zinger once, when I was calling some Toronto Raptors games in Punjabi, saying, "No one watches the Raptors in English, so who in the hell is going to watch them in Punjabi?" (This was a long time before the era of the Raptors as contenders and eventually NBA champions.) This story seemed to reassure people, but after reflecting on it, it made me realize that South Asians had always been unsure exactly how Don Cherry felt about them. I couldn't say I blamed them.

I woke up the next morning to emails and texts from all over the place, including media requests not just from Canada but also from the United States and the BBC in the U.K. Later that day, I got on a flight back home to Calgary, and as soon as I sat down in my seat, I got a text from Ron MacLean.

I should say that my rapport with Ron goes way back. As a kid, I wanted to be just like him on TV. And he's been a champion of *Hockey Night in Punjabi* since the beginning. Whenever I ran into him at the Toronto CBC studios, he was just as advertised: genuine, courteous, and proud of what we were doing. We also had the Alberta connection— he is from Red Deer—and anytime his Sunday night show, *Hometown Hockey*, comes anywhere near Calgary, my family and I all go say hi to him and his co-host, Tara Slone. My mom always brings along some homemade food, and the first time, Ron came over to our house in Calgary for lunch, I gave him a tour of my hockey memory wall. What's most impressive about him, though, is how good his memory is, given how many people he meets every week. There have been times where Ron has mentioned Sukhy by name on the broadcast. He even once gave my parents a shout-out, calling them the "legends" of Brooks and telling the story of us making parshaadh on Gretzky's birthday, something I had told him a decade ago. He's an amazing human being.

Sunday is a busy day for Ron, too. After hosting *Hockey Night in Canada* on Saturday night, he travels, usually on a red eye and often across the entire country, to the town he's visiting for *Hometown Hockey,* where he meets with representatives and fans first thing on Sunday morning. Then he has to be on the air for the majority of the day. But this specific Sunday would have been especially stressful. Ron was taking a lot of heat for not calling out Don for what he said on Coach's Corner.

Now, in my opinion, it wasn't Ron's fault—and, in fact, Ron has been saving him for decades by cutting in and saying, "Hold on, Don, you can't say that" whenever Don wandered into dangerous territory. I know better than most people that as a TV host, especially near the end of a segment, your producer is talking to you through your earpiece constantly, giving you information and updates on timing, and so sometimes you miss what's being said on the air. The text he wrote me just said, "Thank you." I wrote back, encouraging him to stay positive and saying that no matter what anyone said, I would always respect him and stand up for him.

While thousands of people loved our subtle message in the photo we posted on the broadcast's social pages, it soon became clear that many others expected us to say something more direct about the whole situation. When I landed in Calgary, I had several missed calls and messages from people in the South Asian community, saying that we were among the few people with a platform big enough to make a difference. My friend Balwinder Marwaha said that he had heard from a number of people demanding answers and who were waiting for me to speak out. Some were insisting he give them my number so that they could urge me to say something themselves. Another good family friend of mine, Calgary lawyer Remneek Kaur Sahota, who had talked with me at length about countless Canadian political matters, was impassioned about this incident and hoped I would speak out. She, like many South Asians, was skeptical that Don's bosses would do anything. But soon enough, Sportsnet put out a statement that his comments were offensive and didn't represent what the network stood for. I was still trying to process the entire situation when I received a call from Rob Corte, vice president of Sportsnet, who knew that I was getting a lot of media requests. He was extremely supportive and told me that neither he nor anyone else at Sportsnet management agreed with what was said on Coach's Corner.

Sitting at home that afternoon with my family, I felt like I was in a daze. Don's comments were all anyone was talking about. It seemed to have enveloped the entire country. That evening, Ron addressed the issue at the beginning of *Hometown Hockey*. It had the feel of an official address by the prime minister to the nation. He said right away that Don's comments were wrong and hurtful, and was very candid and honest in admitting that he was upset with himself at not catching what Don had said in the moment. Mississauga's mayor, Bonnie Crombie, called Don's comments "despicable." Toronto mayor John Tory said they were "unfair and just plain wrong." For me, personally, even as the public outcry continued, seeing Sportsnet's statement, the NHL's statement, and Ron's address gave me a sigh of relief.

After thinking about it more and more, I finally decided that I had to say something. I asked Sukhy, Gurdeep, and Remneek to read it first and give me their opinions. Here's what I said:

What makes Canada the greatest and most unique country in the world, is the strength of its citizens, who happen to be the most diverse group of people on this planet. More and more though, I feel I have to justify myself as a Canadian, despite my own family's history in this nation dating back more than one hundred years.

May we continually reflect upon the sacrifices made by ALL our veterans and soldiers. I am proud to call myself Canadian and pray that this country stays strong and united, despite any actions or words that divide us. I hope we can continue onwards and upwards with our classic humble nature and the values of acceptance and respect. I am proud that we have a national platform that allows us to celebrate Canada's diversity and its love of hockey as a unifying force.

One of the reasons Coach's Corner had been a staple of *Hockey Night in Canada* is that it was financially lucrative to advertisers. In the past, Don himself had justified his questionable behaviour by pointing out that he was a star and drove ratings. That's why it was so shocking to hear, soon after, that Sportsnet had finally cut ties with Don Cherry, and that Coach's Corner was no more. But when Labatt, the sponsor of Coach's Corner, released a statement saying that Don's comments were "clearly inappropriate and divisive," that was that. I learned later that Don had initially been given a chance to apologize and reframe his comments, but that wasn't his style.

The same afternoon Don was let go, I got a call from the public relations team at Sportsnet. They asked me what I wanted to do with the mountain of media requests I had received. I told them that I wanted to speak out but didn't want to do anything that would make the channel look bad, because I was proud of how they'd handled it all. To the channel's credit, they encouraged me to speak to the media if I felt I needed to. Personally, I wanted to provide a counterbalance to some of the shocking vitriol that was appearing from Don Cherry defenders. Our group picture at *Hockey Night in Punjabi* had received some ridiculous replies, but that was nothing compared to what happened to a CBC reporter from Manitoba named Ahmar Khan, whose tweet calling out Don was quoted in a column by *Toronto Sun* columnist Joe Warmington. Ahmar got piles of hate mail and was called every racist name in the book. Some people told him he was destroying the fabric of Canada. Others said the country would be better off if every Indian and Black person left. It was all obscene and appalling.

And it didn't end there. Don's firing was an enormous story in the world of hockey media. But just a few days later, more stories broke that revealed similar problems of bigotry, prejudice, and broken power dynamics inside the NHL itself. It started with the dismissal of Maple Leafs coach Mike Babcock and an ugly rumour surfacing about how he had mistreated some of his players: forcing Mitch Marner, back when the star winger was a rookie, to write a list ranking his teammates by work ethic, then turning around and showing that list to the players at the bottom. Once that story was confirmed, Akim Aliu, a Nigeria-born former NHL prospect, was inspired to go public with allegations that he had suffered racism at the hands of Bill Peters, who worked with Babcock and was once Aliu's coach in the AHL. Aliu alleged that Peters—head coach of the Flames when this story broke—hurled a disturbing racial slur several times while insulting Aliu's taste in music in front of the entire locker room, and that he later made sure Aliu was demoted even further, to the ECHL. It was awful, demeaning treatment; I was appalled and devastated to hear this had happened. To their credit, the Flames conducted a thorough investigation based on Aliu's tweets and further allegations of physical abuse towards other players, and Peters resigned a few days later. But these stories, all coming out so close together, sent shockwaves through the entire hockey community. It really felt like hockey was going through a reckoning that was frankly long overdue. These conversations are tough, but they need to happen, out loud and in public, because that's the only way things will ever get better.

———

While all of this was going on, my friend Jeff Marek, an NHL host on Sportsnet, invited me on his afternoon talk show, *Hockey Central*, to talk about the aftermath of Cherry's comments. Knowing I was being bombarded with media requests, he had reached out to tell me that I was an important part of the hockey community and was respected, loved, and cherished by many. Jeff told me that he would stand with me and support me with whatever I chose to say if and when I spoke out—he even said he'd had a big talk with his own family at home about how immigration and diversity makes us stronger as a nation. That interview with him was particularly special because Jeff was so sympathetic and understanding of the situation. At one point he asked me, "How is my friend Harnarayan doing? Are you doing okay through all of this?" It was at that moment I realized that this whole situation was affecting me on a personal level, and I had to compose myself before I could answer. Deep down, I was immensely disturbed at the racism that I realized still existed in Canada. I knew that my country had racism in its past, and that my family and I had experienced it first-hand—but I thought we had come so far since then. I didn't want to believe that some of my fellow Canadians felt strongly that myself and people like me didn't belong here.

Take five Canadians from completely different ethnic backgrounds and put them all in a lineup. Which of them are "real" Canadians? All of them, of course. That is the beauty of this country. It's what makes us unique. Of course, most Canadians know that our differences are meant to be celebrated, not feared or ridiculed. It's up to us to show those close-minded people that this country is at its best when people of all different backgrounds and interests live and work alongside one another harmoniously.

And one of the best ways to show them that is with hockey. Think back to 2010. During the gold-medal game at the Winter Olympics in Vancouver, when Sidney Crosby scored that golden goal in overtime to beat the United States, an estimated 80 per cent of the country had tuned in to the game. I don't care whether you were in a restaurant or at a friend's house or in a bar: when Crosby scored that goal, everyone cheered. Did it matter that the person next to you might have been wearing a turban, or might have been white, or Black, or Asian? No. In that moment, nobody cared. We were all united together. That's the power of sports.

Hockey has done that for me my entire life. When I felt like I didn't have anything in common with my classmates, I learned that we could all bond over the amazing plays made by Gretzky and Lemieux. In the years since then, I have met so many great people, both inside the industry and beyond, all thanks to hockey. We otherwise would have never gotten to know each other. But we did.

And because it worked for me, I know it can do the same for other people. Not only is hockey one of the most exciting sports in the world, but it's also the glue that binds this country together. I think of other kids out there right now, maybe living in a small town, who maybe don't have a lot of friends, and I hope they, too, discover the joys of this sport for themselves—especially if they are people of colour. Because hockey *is* changing. Whenever I speak to groups of kids, I always tell them: Don't let anyone tell you that you can't do anything because of how you look. I tell them to work hard, live an honest life, and go for their dreams. Because we're so lucky to live in a place where the impossible is possible. My story proves that.

Epilogue
Hockey Night with the Singhs

After I've been away on the road for hockey, nothing feels better than coming home, opening the front door, and seeing my four-year-old daughter, Apaarjeet Kaur, and my two-year-old son, Mohun Singh, instantly drop everything they're doing and bolt towards me to give me the biggest bear hug. Having to travel so frequently and be away from my kids and my wife, Sukhy, for any period of time is tough, but seeing Apaarjeet and Mohun run around our home always brings me so much joy and reminds me of the kid I used to be. Remarkably, when I watch them play together in the living room, it's like a flashback to my own childhood. Without any direction, my own kids are choosing to emulate everything they see on a hockey broadcast.

First, they set up their mini-hockey nets and choose which two teams will be battling it out. Next, they use their toy microphone, which is way more advanced than the one I used back in the '80s—it has a Bluetooth speaker, complete with various echo options and disco lights. And because they've learned a bit about my job, they've added some new details to the game. Usually, it's my daughter who grabs a hold of the mic, saying "I'm Apaarjeet, and welcome to the Saddle-dome!"—copying what I say when I am a rinkside host for a game. Afterwards, it's time for their favourite part, the national anthem: they sing "O Canada" at the top of their lungs. Meanwhile, Mohun stands on his imaginary blue line, leaning his chin on the knob of his mini-hockey stick, swaying back and forth, just like the players do on TV. It's absolutely adorable!

Later, it's finally time for the game to begin. This is where it can get heated between the two, because they each like to play the part of many roles. Apaarjeet tries to be the coach and the referee at the same time, and has Mohun get ready for a faceoff. From there, Mohun takes over, stick-handling past the tabla, eventually shooting the puck into the gaping net, screaming *"mareya shot, keetha gooooaaaal!"* On to the intermission, where Apaarjeet once again takes the mic, and asks her brother, "How do you feel after scoring?" and he enthusiastically responds by saying, "Good!"

I look at the two of them playing together and I think: *It's so different, and yet so similar.* Similar because, whether they know it or not, Apaarjeet and Mohun are developing a passion for hockey the exact same way that I did, back in the day. But it's different in the sense that their commentary happens in two languages: English *and* Punjabi. And different as well because they don't have to imagine what it would be like for someone who looks like them to be on TV. When my kids watch hockey on Saturday nights now, they see turbans, they see women, they see people of colour—people who look and sound just like they do, all coming together to be part of the best game you can name.

Afterword

Here I am now, wrapping up after the final episode of the hockey show that I hosted for CBC Sports during the 2022 Beijing Winter Olympic Games. When this book came out back in 2020, I had no idea that my journey would take me here. Then again, I don't think anyone could have predicted what happened in the last two years. Maybe I should rewind a bit.

Back in March of 2020, I travelled to India to perform again at Sri Harmandir Sahib, the Golden Temple, in Amritsar. It was a tour I was very much looking forward to, but it unfortunately had to be cut short, just four days in. Little did I know how much my life, or rather, all of our lives, would be thrown for a loop. As news of the coronavirus began dominating our timelines, my fellow musicians and I found ourselves stranded, away from our homes in North America. Borders all around the world were starting to close as a means to stop the spread, but after some tense days scrambling to figure everything out, I was lucky enough to find my way back to Sukhy, the kids, and my family. It was scary stuff, as at that point so little was known about the virus, and I worried about potentially bringing something back with me into a household with grandparents and young kids.

I was fortunate to make it back home safely, but like countless others, the pandemic did present me with a challenge professionally. On March 12, 2020, amidst the growing uncertainty around the world, the NHL officially paused its season. Like so many others in North America, I found myself in a difficult spot. For my entire career, I had been paid per game—literally making a living one game at a time! With no indication of when the season would start up again, it was definitely a precarious situation to be in.

The hockey world was at a complete standstill. Players, coaches, trainers, and, of course, broadcasters, all went home and stayed home. Then, some hope, as news started coming out about a "Return to Play" scenario. But this would not be any *normal* return. Twenty-four of the NHL's then 31 teams would gather in one of the two hub cities, Toronto and Edmonton, to play in a qualifying series that would determine whether they made the playoffs or not. This gave teams like Montreal and Chicago a second chance—both teams were thought of as longshots to make the playoffs before the COVID-19 shutdown. Another wrinkle: games would be played with no fans. Bubble hockey took on a whole new meaning!

After months of anticipation, not to mention the time spent confined at home with little to no interaction with others outside of immediate households, it felt like everyone was ready to welcome back the NHL, no matter how different it was going to look. Everything about this situation was new and intriguing, but it was the action taken off the ice that stood out as a true game-changing moment. To paint the full picture, I have to go back to the summer, when

46-year-old George Floyd, a Black man, was murdered by a white police officer in Minneapolis. This wasn't the only racially charged incident during 2020, but it was definitely the most shared, as social media blew up with the tragic footage. All across the world, the reaction was instant, and the effects were massive and lasting—for people, for companies, for entire industries. It forced all of us to rethink and talk about systemic racism and police brutality in a way that hadn't been done before.

Fast forward to August, and Jacob Blake, another Black man, was shot seven times by police in Kenosha, Wisconsin, leaving him seriously injured and paralyzed. In an emotional and passionate response, the sporting world, and most importantly, its professional athletes, took a stand. The NBA players first forced their league to postpone playoff games. Similarly, in the NHL, it was the players themselves that initiated a shutdown during the Stanley Cup playoffs. Even now, I have the powerful image seared in my mind of players in the Edmonton bubble, led by Ryan Reaves, Nazem Kadri, and Pierre-Edouard Bellemare—all players of colour—addressing the media together, with the support of many of their teammates behind them.

It's no secret that hockey is a predominantly white sport, so this was an especially moving moment for everyone to witness. It was during this sudden postponement, with no games to broadcast, that Sportsnet made the important decision to still air live programming, but to use it to address racial inequality. I was asked to join the discussion, which, for me, turned out to be a one-on-one with Ron MacLean. Without having anything prepared in advance, I just spoke from the heart. My message was one of urgency and a response to sports fans out there who had communicated that they didn't turn on a sports channel to hear the media talking about racism. I emphasized that racism was an important topic, not only to many athletes, but to so many of us who work in sports media. I felt deeply that this discussion was necessary because it was bigger than any sport itself.

All of this was such a whirlwind for me, but the Return to Play scenario for the NHL playoffs also provided me with an opportunity—one of the biggest breaks of my professional career up to that point. There were a ton of restrictions that the league had to enforce due to COVID-19, which severely limited the amount of people that were allowed into either the Edmonton or Toronto bubble. The players couldn't even have their families there with them! But, amazingly, I was asked to be a rinkside host for *Hockey Night in Canada* from the Edmonton bubble. It was a huge thrill and honour to be part of the English broadcast again, but at the same time, the experience was rather eerie. Rogers Place in Edmonton's Ice District was devoid of its normal rousing crowd. The building was completely empty, and everything just felt uncomfortably quiet during the playoffs. Even my role as the host was entirely different, because I had to talk to players through video calls, even though we were in the same building together. A great takeaway of this time though was that I got to work alongside, and watch, Chris Cuthbert and former NHLer-turned-analyst Louie DeBrusk every single day. Chris is a legend in the industry, and the commentator who called Sidney Crosby's iconic "golden goal" for Team Canada at the Vancouver Olympic Winter games. I was able to soak in everything he was doing—watching, learning, and even getting to pick his brain. During this time, Chris even bestowed upon me some incredibly heartwarming blessings, words that I'll never forget, saying that he was just keeping the play-by-play seat warm for me and that I would some-day be in that chair. I couldn't believe it! To be encouraged and mentored by him meant the world to me, and little did I know how quickly his wisdom would pay off.

I stayed in Edmonton for just over a month, hosting into the second round of those playoffs. It was such a great expe-rience, and I loved being back on the English broadcast, but I still had my ultimate goal that I was constantly hoping and praying for. Fast forward a few months and it was December of 2020, still the offseason before the NHL was set to kick off a new schedule in January. This was when I was given the chance of a lifetime to audition for play-by-play commentary alongside Louie. But there was nothing normal about this audition. We were both inside our own homes, hundreds of kilometres apart, calling a previously played game between Toronto and Edmonton, virtually. I remember thinking how bizarre everything felt, while also realizing how much was riding on this audition. On one hand, it was a serious mock setup, yet still humorous as I could hear Louie's dog, Tampa, barking in the background. But on the other hand, I was so nervous because this audition felt like it was the closest oppor-tunity I was ever going to get at making my dreams a reality.

I wasn't sure what would come of that audition, but I was given some long-awaited stability. For the first time in my life, I was offered a multi-year contract by Sportsnet. I didn't know exactly what role I'd be given, or if everything would remain status quo, but at that exact moment, it didn't really even matter. Up until that point in my career, I had always been paid per game, and therefore, getting more games was pivotal for me and my family—with this news, I would no longer have to worry about that. All of the risks of jumping at opportunities, from the early days of paying for my own flights to piecemealing broadcasting gigs wherever possible, had finally paid off. I was at a loss for words and beyond emotional when I received the news of my contract, but as it turned out, it wasn't the only surprise ahead.

The NHL was planning a drastic change to its regular season format due to the ongoing COVID-19 restrictions across North America. Unlike the most recent playoffs, teams would be able to travel and play in different cities, but with one small caveat—every game would be played within your own division, meaning any given team would only face six or seven opponents throughout the entire regular season, albeit a shortened one. Oh, and because of border restrictions, for the first time ever, there would be a division made up entirely of Canadian teams. The fans, media, and even the players were all excited to get the season going, and I definitely wanted to be part of the excitement. But the season was set to begin in January, and it was already late in December.

And then, all of a sudden, it finally happened.

On January 13, 2021, the Vancouver Canucks were set to face off against the Edmonton Oilers, at Rogers Place in Edmonton, in the season opener for each team. When I heard the news from Sportsnet management that my audition had been received positively and that *I* would be the one calling the game, in English, I was in complete disbelief. Once again, I found myself without words (and I should remind you, that's rare!). My first English play-by-play broadcast, calling two Canadian teams, on the opening day of the NHL season! Holy shit! It really was finally happening.

Everything about that first game was completely different from any normal situation hockey media had ever encountered before. First, the workflow in English was quite different compared to calling it in Punjabi. Second, I was physically not allowed to meet with my producer with whom I was working for the first time in this role. Third, even the location in the arena where I was calling the game from was new because there were no fans allowed inside and we had to be a certain distance away from the players, not to mention having to call the game while looking through plexiglass! COVID-19 protocols were constantly throwing curveballs at us, one after another, which made for a very overwhelming debut. On top of all that, it didn't help that there was a freaking snowstorm!

When I arrived at the arena, I quickly panicked, because there was no one else in sight. I was thinking to myself: *It's game day, and less than two hours until puck drop. Where is everyone?!* It was getting closer and closer to game time, and I was a nervous wreck. I finally got in touch with some Sportsnet staff, but they weren't telling me all that much. It turns out that management was working frantically behind the scenes to make sure I wasn't going to end up calling the game on my own. This was the first ever NHL game where media had to be tested for COVID-19 prior to entering, and my colour commentator for the night, Louie, and all the rest of the media that day, were having trouble getting into the building, waiting for the results of their COVID-19 tests. I was already in the arena, so as a backup plan, Sportsnet had asked Kelly Hrudey to drive up to Edmonton from Calgary in case Louie couldn't make it in time, but the blizzard was so intense and there were so many cars in the ditches along the highway that he was forced to turn back halfway through. After that failed attempt, Cassie Campbell-Pascall's home in Calgary was being prepped to remotely be my colour commentator as a precaution. It's hard to fathom how much was going on behind the scenes before my first ever play-by-play game in English and the season opener between the Canucks and the Oilers!

Eventually, Louie managed to get in just in the nick of time, but all of this added stress had thrown me off that first game. I know I didn't perform at my best, but if there was one thing I was happy with it was my goal calls, which I had fun with. A moment of celebration occurred when rookie Nils Höglander scored for the Vancouver Canucks. In many South Asian cultures, it's tradition to hand out homemade treats for significant occasions such as weddings or the birth of a child. I didn't plan on making this call going into the game, but when Höglander scored, it came out as, "It's time to hand out the sweets!" It was a unique celebration of a rookie's first ever NHL goal in his first ever NHL game, and it was a neat way to share a part of my culture with hockey fans across the country. And in my first English call, without me realizing it at the time, that moment also proved the importance of having representation in hockey broadcasting to help make viewers from diverse backgrounds feel included in the game.

Calling that first game was such a tremendous milestone in my life. I stayed in Edmonton for the duration of that week as that's where my next game in English was scheduled, but given the restrictions, I was completely alone. I compiled all the feedback I was getting from Sportsnet management, new producers, colleagues, and from the Punjabi side, too. It was a lot to take in. I was putting a lot of pressure on myself to perform at a level that was satisfactory to everyone, and it felt like I was carrying the weight of not only my own journey, but also of so many people from my community and beyond. It's obviously not easy to succeed like that. I was fortunate to have the support of Bob Babinski, a performance coach hired by Sportsnet, who went above and beyond to really help me out. Not only does he focus on the technical side, coaching me on pace, cadence, and when to—and when not to—include statistical information, but he also puts a great emphasis on training your mindset. He has taught me so many things that I have been able to incorporate professionally and personally. Struggling with confidence and dealing with doubt are challenges I've had, especially when it comes to opportunities on the English side, and Bob was able to pick up on that. After getting to know me so well through our sessions, he asked me to reflect on experiences in my life where I exude confidence. I realized that playing the tabla is always a moment where I feel confident, and so he advised me to bring a tabla with me to Edmonton to have in my hotel room. He wanted me to channel that same mindset in my play-by-play. It was such a great tip, and just one example of countless different ways he's been able to create strategies for me to progress and improve.

As the condensed season went on, I was assigned games on both the English and the Punjabi side. During games, I often found myself battling my own mind. I've called over 700 games in Punjabi, and during the English games it was hard not to think of Punjabi terms midway through a play. This is definitely one of the challenges of being a multi-lingual play-by-play announcer. There were times I didn't feel like I was performing as well as I wanted to, but thank-fully everyone at Sportsnet was extremely supportive. Slowly but surely, I began feeling more and more comfortable as the season went on and was stunned when I learned I had been assigned the first round of the all-Canadian Stanley Cup playoff matchup between the Edmonton Oilers and the Winnipeg Jets. However, while my profile and visibility were ramping up during the season, so too were comments on social media about my diverse appearance. Obviously, this wasn't new, but as I was preparing to call the playoffs, I could feel the notifications starting to plant more seeds of doubt in my mind. I wanted to be doing this so badly, but I also really wanted hockey fans to enjoy my calls. Twitter, especially, can be a vortex of negativity, and Chris Cuthbert and Bob Babinksi both wisely suggested that I completely shut my Twitter off for the duration of the playoffs. Chris basically said that it wasn't healthy for any play-by-play commentator to read those comments during a series and have it affect the way they call the game. I was able to check in with Chris every few months during that first season to ask him questions, and he'd give me some pointers as well. I'm lucky that I have someone as gracious as he is to lean on and look up to.

Looking back, I've been blessed so many times in my life. I have a family that loves and supports me unconditionally, and they've allowed me to chase my dream for so many years. And now that I've achieved that dream, I'm not going to take anything for granted. I know that there will be some tough times ahead—that's always the case—but I also know that I can be a positive influence. It's amazing to think of how far we've come since my great-grandfather made the journey here all those years ago. A few years ago, I never would've imagined that I would have a one-on-one conversation streamed live with Canada's prime minister about Guru Nanak's Gurpurab, an important day for Sikhs worldwide. I also understand that I have a social responsibility to be a voice for change and to try and foster a space that is safe for anyone and everyone. I take great pride in this role, and it's why I'm so grateful to be part of groups like the NHL's Fan Inclusion Committee, where we are planting the seeds for real change to make the game more welcoming for diverse fans. It's so encouraging to see that my efforts to speak up were recognized in May of 2021 when I was named the recipient of the Mosaic Institute's Peace Patron Award for dismantling prejudice in sport. And to top it off, winning a Canadian Screen Award in the same year for Best Sports Play-by-Play Announcer was something I never could have imagined.

Heading into the 2021-22 season, I was really excited to build on the momentum from the previous season. The hockey world was also buzzing with the 2022 Beijing Winter Olympics just around the corner. All indications were that the NHL players were going to participate this time around after sitting out the 2018 PyeongChang Winter Games, but everything had to line up perfectly for it to work out. In the end, with the Omicron variant spreading rapidly around the NHL and the world at large, it wasn't meant to be. Even without NHL players participating, the Olympics are a special time in sports and something I have always loved watching. CBC Sports had expressed some interest early on about me joining the Olympics broadcast in some capacity, and with the NHL pulling out, I thought perhaps it would be a role where I would call play-by-play for a winter sport, but since details hadn't been discussed, I wasn't sure what they had in mind. What CBC Sports proposed was something beyond my expectations. My previous hosting experience was different, as on *Hockey Night Punjabi* we always had a game to throw to after our pregame chat. However, for this opportunity, I was asked to host a daily hour-long show with panelists to discuss anything and everything to do with men's and women's hockey. Unsure if I'd even be able to pull it off, I reached out to a few different people close to me for advice. But it was only when I called Canada's most respected hockey host, Ron MacLean, that things started to come together for me. He told me that the ability to call play-by-play but to also host a panel show like this would put me in a unique category as a broadcaster, and that being part of the Olympics would open so many doors for me down the road. When Ron offers advice, you listen, and it sealed the deal.

I accepted the role and flew down to Toronto for what would be a three-week stint as an Olympic host. As I was guided through the halls of the CBC building, the production staff told me that I would be getting my very own dressing room; a first for me. They led me to my room, and after I had a moment to myself, I took it all in. I noticed that there was a hand-written note on the mirror, and I quickly sent a photo of it to Ron. He immediately texted back saying that he couldn't believe that the note was still there. I was stunned. This was Ron MacLean's old dressing room! That meant that every Saturday night, when I was sitting in front of my TV in Brooks, Ron was here, getting ready to speak to millions of Canadians tuning in to *Hockey Night in Canada*. An overwhelming feeling of fate and gratitude swept over me in that moment. Everything that had happened in my life had led me here. On the mirror, the note read, "Every shift is a gift." And amazingly enough, it was attributed to Louie DeBrusk, my broadcast partner for the majority of my games in English, and someone who has always had my back. How perfect was that quote to my typical mantra, of taking everything one game at a time.

So why am I here? I'm here because this is where I belong.

Guide to Watching
Hockey Night in Punjabi

T hough this is by no means a comprehensive or all-encompassing guide to all the things we say on *Hockey Night in Punjabi*, I thought it would be fun to list some of our more common and popular phrases here. Tune in to a *Hockey Night in Punjabi* broadcast and see how many words you recognize!

ਟੀਮ ਨੂੰ ਤਾਂ ਚਾਹ ਚਾਹੀਦੀ ਐ
Bad Period – *team noo tha chaa chaheedhee ai*
"the team needs some chai tea to wake up"

ਕੁਰਬਾਨੀ ਦੇ ਦਿੱਤੀ
Big Defensive Play – *kurbaanee dhay dhithee*

ਖੁਲ੍ਹੀ ਛੁੱਟੀ
Breakaway – *khulee shutee* – "home free"

ਫਸਮੀ ਟੱਕਰ
Close Match – *fasmee tukkar*

305

ਲੱਕੜ ਦੀ ਸਬਜ਼ੀ ਖੁਆ 'ਤੀ

Cross Check to the Face – *lakarr dhee sabjee khuaa thee*
"fed them some wood curry"

ਮਿਲਨੀ ਹੋ ਗਈ

First Scrum of the Game – *milnee ho giee*
"Referring to a Punjabi wedding tradition where
representatives from each side are formally introduced"

ਜਿੱਤਵਾਂ ਗੋਲ

Game-winning Goal – *jithvaa goal*

ਮਾਰਿਆ ਸ਼ੌਟ, ਕੀਤਾ ਗੋਲ

He/She Shoots, He/She Scores – *mareya shot, keetha goal*

ਸ਼ਾਨਦਾਰ ਗੋਲ

Highlight-reel Goal – *shaan-dhaar goal*

ਗੋਲਚੀ ਦਾ ਹਰਮਨ ਪਿਆਰਾ ਦੋਸਤ ਹੈ, ਪੋਸਟ

Hit the Post – *goalchie dha harman piaara dhost hai post*
"the post is a goalie's best friend"

ਖੜਕਾ ਦਿੱਤਾ

Huge Body Check – *kharrka dhitha*

ਜਾਦੂਗਰ

Magician with the Puck – *jaadhoo-gaar*

ਸੱਜਾ ਦਾ ਡੱਬਾ

Penalty Box – *saja dha daba* – "box of punishment"

ਪਨਲੱਟੀ ਨੂੰ ਮੌਤ ਪਾ ਦਿਤੀ

Penalty Kill – *penalty noo mauth paa dhithee*
"murdered the penalty"

ਸ਼ਕਤੀ ਪਰਦਰਸ਼ਨ

Power Play – *shakthee par-dharshan*

ਚਪੇੜ ਸ਼ੌਟ

Slap Shot – *chapared shot* – "slap to the face"

ਬੂਥਾ ਭੰਨਤਾ

Smashed His Face In – *bootha bhuntha*

ਕਮਾਲ ਦਾ ਬਚਾ

What a Save – *kamaal dha buchaa*

ਲੜਪੇ, ਲੜਪੇ, ਲੜਪੇ

When a Fight Breaks Out – *larrpay larrpay larrpay*
"They're fighting! They're fighting! They're fighting!"

ਵਾਹ ਜੀ ਵਾਹ

Wow – *vaa jee vaa*

ਜੁਤੀਆਂ ਖਾਣੀਆਂ?

You Want a Piece of Me? – *jutheeaa khaneeaa?*
"you wanna eat my shoes?"

Acknowledgements

hat an individual becomes in life is often not all due to his or her own efforts. This is definitely the case in my life, where I simply cannot take credit for everything I have achieved thus far.

First and foremost, I must thank Waheguru, the Almighty Creator, for all of the blessings I have received in my life. Thank you Waheguru for making all of my dreams come true and for taking care of me throughout this entire journey. Any greatness in me is from you. Any faults in me are my own.

Mom and Dad, you have both worked so hard throughout your respective lives to ensure every opportunity I have ever wanted was available to me. I'm incredibly proud to have been able to tell some of your story in this book. The obstacles you overcame while maintaining your faith when the world was a completely different place over half a decade ago, is something I will admire forever. You've gone above and beyond to teach me so much and have been extraordinary role models in how to live life. One of the biggest lessons I've learned from you has been in your commitment to seva. Anything you've ever taken on, you've given it your all, no matter what the challenges or conditions were, and these are all traits I strive to achieve.

Sukhjeet, thank you for being my rock of positivity and for making me smile each and every day. Your creativity and zest for life continues to wow me in all of our years of marriage. There is no one in the world who understands me better, and I appreciate how much you've sacrificed in allowing me to fulfill my dreams in the worlds of hockey and Kirtan. You are a phenomenal teacher to your students and an even better mother to our kids. I especially admire how much you are instilling a passion for *simran* (meditation) in their lives. Our journey together has been so special and I'm so grateful that Waheguru brought you into my life.

Apaarjeet and Mohun, your shining smiles and jubilant personalities have made me absolutely love being a father. You both have brought so much joy and energy into our family and there is no limit to how much I love you and how proud I am of both of you. Given your shared love of reading books, I'm excited for you both to grow up and read this memoir. I have such a blast playing mini hockey with you and jamming together on the tabla and harmonium. I thank Waheguru for being given the seva and privilege to be your dad.

Gurdeep, it warms my heart when I hear from readers of this book who say, "wow, she sounds amazing," because it's so true! I don't think I could've asked for or even imagined a better sister. The unconditional love you've given me my entire life is something I will forever be indebted to you for. To my elder sisters, Harjot and Prem, it's great to see strong, confident, and independent women be so successful. You both are living examples of how hard work and determination can prove to serve the greater good of humanity.

To my in-laws, Jasbir, Harbans, and the entire Sidhu, Brar, and Gill families, thank you for supporting me in no matter what I do and for always encouraging me in such a positive and uplifting way. I am grateful for your devotion to seva and simran, so much so that it inspires me to try and become a better version of myself. Plus, you raised Sukhy, the best wife a guy could ask for! To my nieces and nephews, Prabhkee, Harjun, Araadhna, and Maha Singh, thank you for being such great role models to your younger cousins. It's always such a joy to play sports together, especially hockey! To all of my own cousins who have been with me since day one, thank you so much for always cheering me on!

I would also like to acknowledge someone with whom I will share a special bond with for the rest of our careers. Nick Bonino, thank you for scoring such big goals during the 2016 Stanley Cup playoffs. Your generosity and willingness to make time for me and my family has meant a lot to me over the years and I hope that maybe someday we'll be back in Pittsburgh together. Hey, why don't we open a cafe there? I have the perfect name, too: *IceSingh's: Bonino, Bonino, Bonino* of course!

Mike Hingston, thank you for a fantastic job in compiling and beautifully laying out my endless stories, which were full of way too many details and tangents. The chapter titles you came up with are epic! Our visits to Red Deer and Brooks are ones I won't forget! To my editor, Joe Lee, I cannot thank you enough for coming up with the idea for me to write this book and the hours spent working on it with me where I'd go off topic telling countless stories. Thank you to my publisher, Jared Bland, for believing in me and the message of this book and for going the extra mile to support me. Thank you to Andrew Roberts for the amazing design and to Candice Ward for the awesome cover photos. To Erin Kelly, Dan French, Sarah Howland, and the entire team at McClelland & Stewart and Penguin Random House Canada, it has been my pleasure to work with all of you.

Along this journey, the following people have done so much to help open the doors, paving the way for me and assisting in any way possible: John Petrie, Marc Chikinda, Al Lamb, Helen Henderson, Bernard Graham, Scott Dippel, Joel Darling, Kelly Hrudey, Ron MacLean, Marc Crawford, Gene Principe, Cassie Campbell-Pascall, Scott Oake, Christine Simpson, Scott Moore, Ed Hall, Jeff Marek, Elliotte Friedman, Tara Slone, Rick Ball, John Bartlett, Kevin Quinn, Dave Randorf, Jim Hughson, Derek Wills, Ken Volden, Rob Corte, Bart Yabsley, Peter Hanlon, Paul Bailey, James Hodge, Jim Scott, Laura Pacey, Danielle Ellis, Celina Pompeani, Tom McMillan, Bill Wareham, Scott Morrisson, Brian Williams, Mark Gravett, Bob Babinski, Jason Johnson, Ty Pilson, Calya Spiess, Rebecca Orr, Kyle Mack, Brett Munro, Manuel Fonseca, Johnny Michel, Caroline Oullette, Gary Bettman, Willie O'Ree, Rob Kerr, Pat Steinberg, Kristen Anderson, Matthew Malady, Courtney Szto, and Naheed Nenshi.

Thank you to my friend, confidant, and manager, Jeff Jacobson, for your unprecedented support, and a huge thanks as well to your Talent Bureau co-founder, Jeff Lohnes. You have both gone above and beyond to support me and help me fulfill so many of my career aspirations. I must also thank Deidra Dionne and Nathalie Cook, who first agreed to take me on and did an admirable job, along with Graeme McIntosh,

Paul Drake, and Russ Gray. I am grateful for your hard work and belief in me.

To Kevin Hodgson, Norm Flynn, Casey McCawley, and the entire team at HEROS Hockey, thank you for welcoming me into your world of giving and charity. I'm so proud to be part of an organization that impacts thes lives of youth in such a powerful and special way.

During the process of this book, a select few friends, without hesitation, offered their valuable time to give me their thoughts. Remneek Kaur Sahota, you were the first person to read this memoir outside of my immediate family. Thank you for your feedback and for always helping me with anything and everything on a whim. Dr. Michael Hawley Ph.D. from Mount Royal University, thank you for your expertise when combing through the book. I knew you would be the perfect person to vet it. Amrit Gill, thank you for being such a down-to-earth and genuine colleague and friend. What you have done in the background for *Hockey Night Punjabi* cannot be understated. Your feedback was immensely important to me. Sukhpreet Singh Heir, the help and support you gave during not only the initial years of *Hockey Night Punjabi* but also the rest of the years we've known each other is something I will never forget.

To the many people I've worked alongside over the years, nothing from my journey would have been possible had it not been for your efforts, creativity, and guidance. I've benefited from great producers including Trevor Pardy, Wayne Craig, Joe Scarcelli, Nathen Sekhon, Paul Gris, Larry Isaac, and Scott Carruthers. And I couldn't have done it without my colleagues, Parminder Singh, Amarinder Singh, Inderpreet Cumo, Bhola Chauhan, Bhupinder Hundal, Randip Janda, Harpreet Pandher, Amrit Gill, Gurpreet Sian, Taqdeer Thindal, Raja Shergill, Mantar Bhandal, and Shubham Arora, thank you so much for the camaraderie and for all of the fun times.

So many families have opened their doors, hearts, and kitchens to me over the years and I would like to acknowledge a select few who have done so much in helping me. To the Harry Mann and Harman Goraya families in Toronto, thank you for allowing me to live in your homes and for treating me like family back in 2004. Rapinder Kaur Rakhra and family from Vancouver, I am speechless at the love you have given me all of these years. Tejwant Singh, thank you for giving me a room in your apartment for an entire season and thank you Yadwinder Kaur, Manhar, and Gurvir for making me a part of your family in those initial years of Hockey Night Punjabi in Toronto. Also, a special thank you to Harbans Singh Gill and his wife Kuldip Kaur for the incredible amount of love and support you've given me my entire life.

Blessings from spiritual figures and inspirational people from the Kirtan world have also led me to become the individual I am today. Thank you to Bhai Jiwan Singh Ji, Baba Nihal Singh Harian Vela, Giani Kulwant Singh Ludhiana, Bhai Ajit Singh UK, Bhai Chattar Singh Sindhi, Bhai Harjinder Singh Sri Nagar, Bhai Niranjan Singh Jawaddi, Bhai Harjit Singh Bittu, Bhai Gian Singh, Bhai Amrik & Bhupinder Singh Phull, Bhai Harcharan Singh Khalsa, Bhai Baldev Singh Bulandpuri, Bhai Parvinder Singh, Bhai Gagandeep Singh Sri Ganga Nagar, Bhai Satvinder Harvinder Singh Delhi, Sant

Anoop Singh, and Una Sahib for all setting such a great example, teaching me so much, and inspiring me to be the best I can be.

A bond over Kirtan holds a very special place in my heart and I've been so blessed to have met a special few souls who have become such a big part of my life. Dr. Onkar Singh from Brantford, thank you for being the older brother I never had over all these years. Thank you for the Kirtan, the guidance, and the laughs stretching all the way from Ontario to B.C. to Utah! Atamjot from Yuba City, it's as if we've known one another for many lifetimes before this one and I consider myself so lucky to be able to do Kirtan with someone so incredibly talented as yourself. Gurpreet from Surrey, your kind nature and sense of humour make me smile every day. Our collective love for Kirtan is something I cherish so much. You both are my younger brothers and I'm looking forward to the release of our first album with Amritt Saagar in 2020. Taren Kaur from the U.K., I'm lucky to call you my sister and I'm so proud of how committed you are to utilizing your amazing voice and musical talent to inspire young Sikh girls worldwide.

To all of the congregation at Guru Ram Das Darbar in Calgary, I very much appreciate all of the love you have given me for so many years. There are many friends who have helped me immensely in my life in so many different ways and it's impossible to include each and every one of you. For those who I have missed, please accept my sincerest apologies. Thank you from the bottom of my heart.

ABOUT HEROS HOCKEY

Hockey Education Reaching Out Society (HEROS) is a volunteer-driven charity that uses the game of ice hockey to teach life skills and empower Canada's marginalized youth. What drew me to volunteer and eventually join the board is the fact that vulnerable grade-four students selected by teachers are kept in the HEROS program until they graduate from high school. Just imagine the impact on a kid's life when you are nurturing their habits for so many consecutive years.

HEROS' free programs provide young people a team for life by celebrating in their first goal on the ice and assisting in their dreams off the ice. HEROS uses mentor relationships between dedicated volunteers and the participants as well as peer mentoring of older participants with their younger counterparts. I've seen firsthand how being a member of HEROS has given kids more self-esteem, a sense of belonging. By providing a safe and stable environment for young people to succeed and connect, HEROS guides its participants to become constructive citizens within their communities. For more information on how you can help, please visit, www.heroshockey.com

ABOUT THE CHEVROLET GOOD DEEDS CUP

As I've mentioned earlier in this book, a very important concept taught by our Sikh Gurus' is called seva, which means "selfless service." It's one of the reasons why I was so drawn to the project Chevrolet introduced in the 2016-17 hockey season called the Chevrolet Good Deeds Cup. The Good Deeds Cup encourages youth hockey teams to give back to their communities and rewards them for their efforts. By bonding together, these youth players learn the true value of being a good team, on and off the ice. It's been an amazing experience to go and see the impact on children and in communities such as Glace Bay, Nova Scotia, West-Carleton, Ontario, and Torbay, Newfoundland. The peewee hockey teams who win are just as excited as if they won the Stanley Cup. $100,000 goes a long way to help the team's charity of choice. For more information, please visit, www.gooddeedscup.com

HARNARAYAN SINGH is a bestselling author, renowned musician, and longtime hockey broadcaster for *Hockey Night in Canada*. In 2021, he won a Canadian Screen Award for Best Sports Play-By-Play Announcer and received the Mosaic Institute's Peace Patron Award for Dismantling Prejudice in Sport. Harnarayan Singh has received an honorary doctorate of laws degree from Mount Royal University, serves on the Board of Directors for HEROS Hockey—a charity empowering marginalized youth through mentorship—and was named the recipient of a Meritorious Service Medal by the Governor General of Canada for his contributions to Canadian society. Follow him @IceSinghHNIC.

MICHAEL HINGSTON is the author of three books, and a journalist whose work has appeared in *National Geographic*, *Wired*, and the *Washington Post*. Hingston lives in Edmonton, Alberta, with his partner and two kids.